A Century of Change in Music Education

Historical Perspectives on Contemporary Practice in British Secondary School Music

Stephanie Pitts

Ashgate

Aldershot • Brookfield USA • Singapore • Sydney

Published by

Ashgate Publishing Ltd
Gower House, Croft Road,
Aldershot, Hampshire GU11 3HR
England

Ashgate Publishing Company
Old Post Road
Brookfield, Vermont 05036–9704
USA

Ashgate website: http://www.ashgate.com

British Library Cataloguing-in-Publication Data
Pitts, Stephanie
  A Century of Change in Music Education: historical perspectives on contemporary
  practice in British secondary school music
  1. Music – Instruction and study – Great Britain – History. I. Title
  780.7'1241

US Library of Congress Cataloging-in-Publication Data
Pitts, Stephanie
  A Century of Change in Music Education: historical perspectives on contemporary
  practice in British secondary school music
  Includes bibliographic references and index.
  1. School music – Instruction and study – Great Britain – History – 20th century. I. Title.
  MT3.G7 P58 2000
  780.71'241 – dc21   99–057685

ISBN 0 7546 0097 1

Printed on acid-free paper and bound in Great Britain
by Athenaeum Press, Ltd., Gateshead, Tyne & Wear.

Contents

Contents

Preface

This book started life as a work of academic reference, charting the development of music in the secondary schools of the twentieth century, and evaluating the present state of music education in the light of recent curriculum and examination directives. It still does that, and I hope that the information contained here, particularly the access to some previously hidden archive and out-of-print material, will prove useful to those who share my interest in the origins and evolution of ideas in music teaching and learning.

As my research went through the inevitable expansions and shifts of focus, however, I became increasingly fascinated by the connections between generations, especially by those ideas that find a resonance in contemporary practice. The resulting text reflects that interest, and is intended to be questioned and considered in the light of every reader's experience of school music, in whatever capacity. We all construct our own histories, and music education is no exception, arousing as it does passionate feelings about its purpose, content and place in the curriculum. There is much to be learnt from a study of past attempts to resolve these perennial questions, and this book is only one version of the story of changing ideas and ideals in the past century of music education. There are many more stories to be told, and it is my hope that the discussion presented here will help to encourage that important task.

* * *

It is my great pleasure to thank the many people who have supported this research, notably Dr Jane Davidson for her supervision of my work and her inspiring energy in her own. I also thank the practising and retired music educators who have shared their experiences in a variety of ways, with particular acknowledgement to Professor Keith Swanwick and Professor George Pratt for their very helpful interviews. In making revisions for publication, the comments of Dr Gordon Cox and Professor Peter Hill on an earlier version of the text have been valuable, as has the assistance of Rachel Lynch and her colleagues at Ashgate Publishing. I am especially grateful to Professor John Paynter for generating my initial interest in this area of research, and for remaining a source of encouragement throughout. Finally, I offer warmest thanks to my parents, whose generous support has been unwavering and greatly appreciated, in this as in everything else.

Introduction: researching the development of music education

1 Education today: a political arena

During the course of the twentieth century the perception of music in the British secondary school curriculum has undergone tremendous change, as different aspects of music and musicianship have formed the focus for educators of different generations. Educational, musical and social goals have been continually contested and redefined, with the comments of today's politicians and educators revealing the conflicting aims that years of change have generated. In recent decades, a succession of Secretaries of State for Education have maintained a consistent political message: education is about standards, improved examination results, and the testing of teachers and pupils alike. Politics and education are now inextricably linked in Britain, with education forming the cornerstone of policies and rhetoric for all the major political parties. Educational policy offers governments the opportunity to imprint their ideas upon society, and broader social and professional resistance can seem futile, as the 'politicians charged with running an increasingly discredited system ... seek new ways to demonstrate the legitimacy of their policies' (Harland, 1988: 92). Much has been written about the political and educational implications of recent legislation (cf. Lawton & Chitty, 1988; Lawton, 1994), particularly the development and implementation of the National Curriculum. Later in this book (Chapter 6), the proposing and redrafting of the curriculum orders will be discussed in the light of the historical development of music education. It will be shown that the National Curriculum for music brought the tensions and challenges of change in music education to the forefront of teachers' minds, whilst embroiling the curriculum debate in the broader programme of reforming school organisation instigated by the government of the time.

The portrayal of teachers in the media is another essentially political factor that has contributed to educational debate in the last decades of the twentieth century. Simplistic interpretations of problems and challenges hold the teaching profession responsible for the failings of society in general, and headlines such as 'Teaching is blamed for low standards' (*The Times*, 6 February 1996) have become commonplace, the *Sunday Times* even running a feature on 'How to spot a bad teacher' (Scott-Clark & Hymas, 1996). Hostility to innovation and debate often comes from official sources such as the Office for Standards in Education (Ofsted):

> I have in mind, for example, the belief that the national curriculum militates against the teacher's responsibility to develop the unique potential of each child; the antipathy to didactic teaching, and the reluctance to *challenge* children which flows from the concept of the teacher as a facilitator. Above all else, the continuing commitment to such ideas in too many schools explains why it is proving so difficult to raise standards.
>
> (Woodhead, 1996: 18)

The perception that educational theory is inherently damaging is cultivated amongst 'back to basics' politicians, the assumption being that parents will favour the 'traditional' methods that most closely resemble their own school experience. Homework, discipline and rigorous teaching of the core curriculum are frequently cited as the priorities of parents, governors and politicians, with this 'common sense' approach giving credence to those who observe education from the outside, rather than the teachers who engage with teaching and learning every day. Launching a new National Curriculum for Initial Teacher Training in 1996, the then Secretary of State for Education, Gillian Shephard, reinforced the popular perception of teacher training institutions as the last bastion of 'progressive' theory, stating that 'the need for improvement is urgent' (DfEE, 1996: 1). The search for an educational scapegoat has led to a 'discourse of derision' (Gipps, 1993: 3) with sinister implications that go beyond the teaching profession:

> In the suppression of unwelcome research reports, the rubbishing of academics' arguments, and the marginalising of unproductive pupils and schools we see a further erosion of democracy, and furthermore will see an increase of the underclass by virtue of the type of education system we are developing.
>
> (Gipps, 1993: 9)

Music education occupies an uncomfortable position in this debate, denied the security of a 'core' curriculum subject, and often deprived of the resources for innovative teaching and effective learning. When the *Times Educational Supplement* launched a 'Music for the Millennium' campaign in April 1998, the reaction of the Secretary of State for Education and Employment highlighted a confusion of aims at government level:

> Music can underline our campaign to raise standards and provide other valuable aspects of a child's education. It can be part of a cross-curricular approach, helping with numeracy, developing the talents of those with special needs as well as the gifted. It can also draw on the tremendous history of folk music and ballad writing to reinforce understanding of the history of our culture.
>
> (Blunkett, 1998: 13)

Blunkett's views on music education show the juxtaposition of the early twentieth-century teaching goals of cultural and spiritual education, with the millennial obsession with standards and accountability. The two do not sit easily together, and there remains a danger that as literacy and numeracy are given increasing priority within the curriculum, music will be marginalised (cf. Pitts, 2000). It is evident that, far from the educational debate being over, it needs to be pursued ever more vigorously by teachers, musicians and academics who have an interest in the future of music in schools.

2 The influence of the past on contemporary practice

It is easy to accept the end-of-century media portrayal as accurate, and to assume that education is in a lamentable state. The reality, of course, is more varied and complex, and the music curriculum includes a wealth of opportunities and enthusiasms as children engage with music as composers, performers and listeners. Aldrich, who deplores the 'confrontational culture' (1996: 1) of recent educational debate, asserts the importance of an awareness of the past in understanding the present:

> Whilst a knowledge of history cannot enable us to predict the future with any certainty, it provides invaluable data for choosing between different courses of action. Historical study provides an interaction with a much wider range of human experience than is possible simply by reference to the contemporary world. Those who deliberately ignore the mistakes of the past are most likely to repeat them.
>
> (Aldrich, 1996: 3)

The current debates and challenges of music education make the historical study of twentieth-century developments a relevant undertaking, as so much of the contemporary curriculum is rooted in the ideals of past generations. Our concern that music should be a practical subject comes, not just from the introduction of improvising and composing in the 1970s (cf. Paynter & Aston, 1970), but also from the performance focus of 1950s education (cf. Long, 1959). Likewise, our respect for listening in the curriculum stems from the 'musical appreciation' movement of the early twentieth century (cf. Scholes, 1935), but accommodates the late 1970s interest in popular and world musics (cf. Vulliamy & Lee, 1976; 1982). An examination of these ideas in their original context can provide a new perspective on contemporary concerns, as the priorities and practice of previous generations are evaluated by today's teachers. In making such an evaluation, published texts must be considered alongside evidence of development at a local level, in an attempt to determine the extent to which prominent innovators influenced existing practice. The introduction of new resources, such as the gramophone, schools broadcasting, world music repertoire and music technology equipment, are also of significance in educational change, as are broader changes to school systems and management. From these diverse sources emerges a picture that recaptures the sense of opportunity and change that has characterised the critical moments in music education history.

The temptation to construct a chronology of music education that has contemporary practice as its goal is considerable, but it must always be remembered that the retrospective logic of the historian will not have been apparent to all who were involved at any given time. Holbrook, writing about developments in the teaching of English, goes so far as to suggest that those teachers who are aware of their pioneering classroom practices will keep them hidden for fear of disapproval or ridicule:

> The disturbing thing is the *down* on enjoyment amongst the old hands – raised eyebrows if they see anything unconventional going on in your classroom. Though I'm surprised how some of the young teachers do good work (and how good it is) – you have to find out about such things by stealth, as both teachers and children conspire to conceal them from 'Authority'.
>
> (Holbrook, 1961: 14)

The reality of music education, whether revolutionary or reactionary, is to be found in the experiences of former and current teachers and their pupils, but the researcher can only hope to sample these through interviews and archive research, and filter them through the existing documentary evidence. To a certain extent, the texts discussed in this book are a reflection of my own interests, and different readers will inevitably notice omissions that would form part of their own interpretation. Finding inspiration in the texts and events of the past is largely a matter of taste, but direct engagement with the ideas of past music educators, be they visionary or pragmatic, is an illuminating route to the appraisal of contemporary practice (cf. Pitts, 1998a).

Simplifying the progress of ideas is always dangerous, but the diagram below provides a framework for the discussion that follows:

National influences	*National pressures*
Published texts	Legislation
Prominent innovators	Social/political expectations
Educational theories	Status in curriculum
Perceptions of pupils	Examination syllabuses
Resources/opportunities	
Music Education	
Local influences	*Local pressures*
Teacher's own education	Examination syllabuses
Needs of pupils	Parental expectations
Resources/opportunities	Status in curriculum
Access to ideas/innovations	Timetable/accommodation
Supportive colleagues	Lack of resources/expertise
Willingness to develop	Unwillingness to change

It can be seen that at any given time in the history of music education, there are a multiplicity of factors that can work to move ideas forward, or can cause the stagnation or regression of educational thinking. Influences and pressures operate at national and local levels, with access and receptiveness to new ideas essential for the effective use of available resources. National and local pressures, which are in danger of stifling the progress of educational change, can work to positive effect, but only when combined with a willingness to develop curriculum content and teaching style at the classroom level. Throughout the century, the critical engagement with ideas, resources and curriculum innovations has been vital to the development of music education.

It is my strong belief that the history of music education is of direct relevance to teachers, and by implication to pupils, in today's classrooms. The reappraisal of early ideals in music education can help to illustrate present difficulties, with common themes often spanning the generations. So, Yorke Trotter's assertion that learning notation 'should come after, and not before, the feeling for music has been developed' (Yorke Trotter, 1914: 76), is directly comparable with Mainwaring's intention to 'proceed from sound to symbol, not from symbol to sound' (1951: 12), and with Terry's objection, some eighty years later, to the 'significant obstacle' that staff notation presents to 'creative freedom' (Terry, 1994: 109). By searching for similarities in the literature of music education, it is often possible to reconsider ideas that have apparently been rejected or forgotten, drawing the valuable points from historical texts, whilst perceiving their flaws with the benefit of hindsight. The vision of some early writings can provide an inspiring context for contemporary debate, with the work of Yorke Trotter (1914), Mainwaring (1941) and Brocklehurst (1962) offering some examples of writers who could see beyond the restrictions of the education system of their time.

Of course, it is not always easy to judge which of the texts published in a given decade were the most forward-looking, and which were providing summaries of contemporary ideas. As much can be determined from the implicit criticisms in a text as from the original ideas presented there, with the problems that the writer addresses offering an overview of the practice of the time. Education committee reports, whether regional or national, are also helpful in their descriptions of current teaching and learning, although their political agendas sometimes shape their interpretation of events. Development in music education has always been a slow process, and the overlap of ideas across the decades is still in evidence in today's classrooms. In all branches of education, the experiences of individual teachers and pupils contribute to the broader evolution of ideas and methods, and there is a limit to the generalised picture that can be drawn of any moment in educational history. What can be determined, however, is the overall mood and aspirations of a decade, as teachers of all generations responded to those ideas which were new, and those which had formed the basis of their own education. The resolution of these two influences can often be seen as a catalyst for change, with the redefining of musical and educational goals according to the changing social context providing the impetus for the development of new opportunities and ideas.

3 A note on the research methodology

Constructing a history of music education is fraught with the difficulties that attend any historical investigation. To find a continuous chronological argument amongst the fragmented accounts that are available for study is virtually impossible, and some degree of interpretation has to take place in order to achieve coherence. Imposing continuity on the narrative is necessary for an understanding of the vast and often challenging literature, but educational progress is a contested concept, and potential directions, as identified by different authors, are as important as the actual historical outcomes. There have been several previous attempts to collect the historical facts, notably Rainbow's (1989) account, which surveys developments from 800 BC onwards, and is not surprisingly somewhat limited in its coverage of the events of the twentieth century. Bentley's (1989) thesis, likewise, predates the National Curriculum for music, and does not therefore address the fusion of ideas represented by the curriculum orders. Cox's work on the late nineteenth century (1991a; 1993a) also has some bearing on the early chapters of the present volume, but I have taken care to return to original sources here, rather than following any established interpretation. Plummeridge (1991) and Metcalfe (1987) have recognised the importance of considering past ideas in any appraisal of present music education, but the task of evaluating the pace and purpose of change that constitutes music education in the twentieth century has not previously been fully addressed. The time is right for a review that places contemporary practice in its historical framework, and allows for an evaluation of past ideas and approaches from an end of century perspective.

The intention here is not to create a work of historical reference, but rather to use significant changes in the development of music education to gain insight upon its musical and social purpose for different generations. This involves a consideration of the political and philosophical ideas that have generated change, and constant reference to the way in which educators have perceived their role in fostering enjoyment and expertise amongst future listeners, performers and, more rarely, composers. As a result, the account is less complete than a conventional chronology would need to be, and focuses instead on 'snapshots' of history, using texts to reveal the priorities of the time, and archive and interview material to give a clearer picture of how practising teachers interpreted such recommendations. The division of the century into decades is, to some extent, a false device, but it is convenient to show the broad changes that took place within shorter periods of time. In a recent editorial, Paynter (1996) comments on the gradual changes in attitude that different decades have shown, and questions our position at the end of the twentieth century:

> And where are we now? The Niggling 90s? The Nervous 90s? The Not-So-Sure-After-All 90s? The prevailing philosophy seems to be, 'Don't take too much on trust; don't get carried away'. In education, that translates into breaking everything down to small, easily assessable units.
>
> (Paynter, 1996: 181)

The study of earlier writings is one way of recalling a time when music educators were not so nervous, by engaging with the innovative thinking that has contributed to the development of music in schools.

Education changes slowly when it is allowed to evolve according to the convictions and experience of individual teachers, with development only becoming aggressively rapid when government directives, such as those of the 1980s, force the pace. The effectiveness of disseminating ideas is an important strand throughout the century, with teachers bringing ideas from their own training to bear upon any available suggestions and resources. It is almost impossible to determine how influential the texts considered here were upon teachers of the time, even in the case of seminal works such as Paynter and Aston's *Sound and Silence* (1970). Published ideas often reflect a prevailing mood, and Paynter himself has spoken of the letters he received from teachers who had developed ideas concurrently with his own research and teaching (Interview: 6 June 1997). Connections between educators are often made at a local, informal level, and indeed it is often the case that an inspiring person will cause teachers to look again at their own practice more thoroughly than any written text could have done. Receptiveness to published ideas implies that the willingness to develop already existed, and hostility to innovation is not an unusual reaction from teachers whose own practice appears to be successful in its own terms. In considering published texts, therefore, it is necessary to bear in mind that the pace of change will have been varied and flexible, and also that the ideals articulated there will not always have reached fruition in the classroom. Publication dates, necessary for ease of reference, can also give a false sense of the progression of ideas, simplifying as they do the exchange and development of educational thought and practice outside the published text. Some narrative direction is necessary in order to make sense of changes over time, but the dissemination of ideas is a more complex business than the published writings reveal, and the importance of change and discovery for individual teachers and schools should not be forgotten.

Local interviews, observations and archive research from in and around Sheffield are included here, giving detailed accounts of the everyday experiences of music teaching and learning that reveal the history beyond more widely published texts. Clearly, there is much potential for further work in this area, with the study of regional developments open to comparison with the broader national picture. Informal interviews with retired and practising teachers have been an important reminder throughout the research that education profoundly affects individuals, and cannot easily be explained and documented. As Ken Robinson recently remarked, 'Mention education and eyes glaze over, but mention *their* education and they pin you to the wall'

(Neill, 1998: 26). Where possible, I have also sought the opinions of children I have taught, gathering their experiences of and ambitions for music at school. Being in the position of teacher-researcher is interesting educationally, but not ideal methodologically, and there is clearly scope for more systematic investigations of pupils' perceptions of the music curriculum. Their voices are not always clearly heard in the educational debate, but can be very helpful in reflecting on practice and imagining new possibilities (cf. Blishen, 1969; Spencer, 1993; Harland et al., 1995). Discussions with significant innovators, including John Paynter and Keith Swanwick, have provided me with valuable insight upon the developments of more recent years, with George Pratt offering an inside view of the drafting of the National Curriculum. The scope for further research in any of these diverse areas is great, as the ideas and practice of the past offer a wealth of resources for evaluating the present. This book should be taken, not solely as a work of reference, but rather as a stimulus for the unique histories which educators at every level of music teaching construct to help make sense of their practice.

4 Structure and scope

Each chapter looks at a significant period of music education history, in which the ideas and practice of a generation were established and refined. The main educational publications of the decade are considered, with links made between them where common practice or related ideas exist. It must be emphasised that this retrospective view can produce only a generalised picture of the music education of each decade, with the ideas of prominent writers not always mirroring those of the profession as a whole. Whilst archive research and oral history help to provide a context for published sources, the sense of whether an idea was innovative or reactionary is largely a matter of historical judgement. Similarly, the extent to which ideas were disseminated is hard to determine, and it must often be assumed that innovations took some time to reach the majority of secondary school classrooms. The influence of music teachers' own education, for example, is likely to have been stronger than any written sources, and the desire to reproduce a successful musical training more compelling than any need to change the course of music education in a wider sense. Nonetheless, the growing literature of music education in the twentieth century is testimony to the fact that innovatory practice often reached publication and, where the willingness to respond to new ideas existed, will have been important in moving the debate forward.

The historical development of music education is a vast subject, and it has been necessary to define boundaries for the present research. The focus, essentially, is on music in the secondary school curriculum, with innovations in other subjects and other age ranges considered only where they have a direct impact upon the secondary classroom. So, for example, primary music is given a brief discussion in Chapter 3, as having been influential on the adoption of 'creative' methods in the secondary school, and developments in art, English and drama teaching are considered where they have provided examples of relevance to music educators. By the same token, some of the more famous developments of the twentieth century, notably the work of Orff and Kodály, occupy only a small place in this study, given that their greatest impact was at the primary level. Omissions are perhaps inevitable, but the intention has been to give a sense of the priorities and perceptions of each generation, considering the work of those music educators who have addressed most clearly the preoccupations of their time.

Perhaps the most significant development over the course of the century has been the changing perception of children's engagement with music, with the 'musical appreciation' lessons of the 1920s and 1930s giving way to a performance focus in the post-war years, and gradually incorporating improvising and composing in the early 1970s. With the introduction of the General Certificate of Secondary Education (GCSE) in 1986, the 'composing–performing–listening' combination was given official credence, endorsing a curriculum that gave children access to all aspects of musical experience. The perception of children 'as musicians' is always finely balanced with their status as pupils, with music forming only one part of their total education. Whilst music in schools must have an educational purpose if it is to justify its place in the curriculum, it must also be musically authentic, with attempts to create simplified or sanitised 'music for children' only compromising the validity of the teaching and learning. Music teachers, particularly in secondary schools, are often highly trained specialists, with experience of performing or composing at a level beyond that which their pupils are likely to reach. The challenge is to relate that experience to the classroom in a way that has educational and musical coherence, providing children with the strategies to engage with music themselves. Different generations have defined 'music' in schools according to the wider expectations of society, with the amateur listening and performing of the first half of the century gradually giving way to the diverse demands of late twentieth-century music, where the musical skills of the classroom need to enable access to a wide variety of genres. The continual revision of musical and educational priorities forms an underlying thread to the practical opportunities and approaches of secondary music teaching.

Chapter 1

Music education for all:
1900s–1930s

1.1 Music education at the turn of the twentieth century

The education system of the early twentieth century was only just beginning to come to terms with the needs of the child and with the effects that education could have upon employment and social change. The 'Report of the Commission on Secondary Education' of 1895 (Curtis, 1948/67: 308) marked a new focus on secondary schooling, which had previously depended on the wealth of families, so being denied to poorer children whose parents could afford neither the costs nor the delayed arrival of another family wage. The establishment of a Board of Education in 1899, and of Local Education Authorities three years later, meant that education was given increasing political recognition, initiating a process of development and change. 'Education for all' was becoming the social and political ambition, and the task of negotiating curricula that met the various needs of pupils had begun.

The newly formed Board of Education was anxious to avoid a dictatorial role, but its co-ordinating function was quickly accepted (Lawson & Silver, 1973: 367). The curriculum suggestions offered in their handbook of 1905 demonstrated an allegiance to the independent grammar schools of the time, which were seen to be providing the most effective post-elementary education. As Curtis notes in his *History of Education in Great Britain*, secondary education was 'planned according to the needs of the minority' (1948/67: 323), and the focus on preparation for university or professional life went largely unchallenged.

Music education held a subordinate place in this educational regime, with the public school curriculum model promoting the belief that musical opportunities, where they existed, should be largely extra-curricular (Metcalfe, 1987: 98). Music was partially defined by its classroom context: with passive, silent pupils demanded for almost all other subjects, it was considered radical to have children making a noise, and singing was adventurous enough for most teachers. A tradition of instrumental teaching was already well-established, with performance examinations having been offered by the Associated Board of the Royal Schools of Music (ABRSM) and Trinity College of Music since 1876. As well as setting the precedent that serious musical skills could only be acquired from a private, expensive teacher, such a system advanced the notion that music was not for everybody, but only for the skilled or wealthy.

The general perception of music in education was apparently limited by its context, but the debate about its purpose and content was growing, nevertheless. The nineteenth-century belief that children were inherently evil, and therefore dependent on adult intervention and discipline for their moral and emotional development, was slowly being replaced by a new recognition of the importance of childhood, as being 'not merely a stage in development towards the valuable state of adulthood' (Wardle, 1976: 90). From this early advocation of 'child-centred' teaching, a rationale for different curriculum subjects could evolve, and music took its place amongst those subjects intended to foster desirable characteristics in the young:

> The concentration of purpose, the clearness of thought, the untiring energy combined with ceaseless patience, the quick and eclectic sympathy needed for and created by the earnest, persevering study of music make it a valuable means of training for the young.
>
> (Mills, 1905: 17)

In the lectures from which this extract is taken, Mills emphasises the universal benefits of music education, focusing on its extra-musical influences, rather than on the development of musical skills. Music learning was perceived as something requiring 'natural taste' or talent, but Mills asserts that music provides 'a potent and valuable means of education' even for those pupils 'more or less wanting' in ability (ibid.: 38). In his description of the ideal music curriculum, he anticipates developments that were to take several more decades to become common practice:

> It is good to read about music, better still to listen to good music, but there is nothing so powerful in promoting appreciation of good music, as working at it with either voice or instrument.
>
> (Mills, 1905: 15)

Mills, as an 'Inspector of Music in Schools for the London University', clearly took his duties to include the dissemination of good practice and innovative thinking amongst fellow music teachers. With few published texts available at the time, this sharing of ideas between music educators was a vital feature of the profession, and Mills was to be followed in this vocation by such important figures as MacPherson, Somervell and Borland (cf. Cox, 1991b). MacPherson shared the concern with children's 'whole mental development'

(MacPherson, 1922: 9), but subscribed to the 'music appreciation' model of teaching more fully than Mills had. Rhythmic and aural training were the foundations for successful music education, a view that was to prevail for almost half the century, continuing the argument that music learning was of general academic and personal benefit:

> It is an acknowledged fact that, when properly carried out, class-work in music (having for its object the training of the ear and the development of the child's appreciative powers) has most certainly the effect of stimulating the mental faculties of those who take part in it, and as a result, of improving the standard of work in other departments.
>
> (MacPherson, 1922: 13)

Defending musical appreciation, MacPherson criticises the practice of some contemporary teachers, so offering a contemporary evaluation of music education in the first decades of the century. Music teachers, he claims, were often unwilling recruits to the classroom (1922: 11), a fact which probably fostered the belief that a truly comprehensive music education was only suitable for the talented few. MacPherson saw the 'Music Appreciation' movement as a solution to the unsatisfactory state of music teaching, claiming that the acquisition of critical listening skills should replace the medley of approaches that existed in some schools:

> There are still not a few schools, usually old-fashioned and unprogressive, where the only corporate musical work is confined to a 'Singing-class', with the meagre allowance of one half-hour per week, into which there has to be crammed the singing of songs, the learning of notation, the study of breathing and voice-production, the training of the ear – and, nowadays, Musical Appreciation.
>
> (MacPherson, 1923: 17)

For teachers who remained unconvinced by MacPherson's championing of the music appreciation cause, he provides specimen lessons, intended to demonstrate the skill of making music accessible to young people, whilst avoiding the pitfalls of asking children what they 'feel' about the music or insisting that they must like an established 'masterwork'. These take the form of scripts, from which the teacher is intended to learn the style and spontaneity that should characterise successful music appreciation lessons:

> Beethoven to you may still seem a rather far-off kind of person, someone, in fact, whom you have heard older people talk of with

respect and veneration, but who doesn't somehow speak to you in *quite* the thrilling way that some other composers (less highly thought of) undoubtedly do. It may be, too, that you have struggled at the piano with a 'Beethoven Sonata' that has appeared to you somewhat of the nature of an enemy bent upon your destruction, rather than of a friend – and I think that in all this I should be inclined to sympathise more than a little with you!

(MacPherson, 1923: 118)

Following this avuncular introduction, MacPherson's classes would hear, in this case, the themes of Beethoven's first symphony, learning to sing them to help with recognition and recall. Musical examples would be played on the piano by the teacher, with the orchestral instruments mentioned only if 'gramophone records of their tone-qualities were available' (ibid.: 133). So the children would acquire a knowledge of the established repertoire, together with an understanding of music 'closer to that of the artist' (ibid.: 4). This intention was to remain the focus of music education for some years, with the tradition continued by Scholes (1935), and reinforced by the growth in radio broadcasts and recorded music.

MacPherson's ideas can be contrasted with those of Somervell, a school inspector who was responsible for many of the Board of Education documents on music that were published in the first decades of the century (Cox, 1991b: 69). Somervell's loyalties were to aural and rhythmic training, which he saw as a necessary preparation for appreciation work. His ideas are summarised in one of his later publications, *The Three R's in Music (Reading, Writing, Rhythm)* (1931), which is an amalgamation of the ideas that had been current during his career. On music appreciation, which he prefers to term 'Musical literature lessons' (ibid.: 21), he is critical of those teachers who perform the musical equivalent of handing out roses to the class and explaining the scent:

In presenting a work of art to children, be it picture, music or poem, all that the true teacher can do is to have reverence enough not to stand between the artist and the child, but to let the spirit of the artist speak to the spirit of the child; and to have faith enough not to be in the smallest degree disturbed if there is no apparent response.

(Somervell, 1931: 21)

For all the avowed spiritual intentions of Somervell's teaching, his methods were rigorous, and involved aural work, voice cultivation, sol-fa and staff notation, rhythm dictation and conducting. Like MacPherson, he offers a specimen lesson plan, which takes the 'a little of everything' approach that the earlier writer had criticised:

		mins.
(i)	Voice exercises	3
(ii)	Modulator (Sol-fa at first, Staff later)	3
	A tune Sol-faed and afterwards sung without the	
	Modulator.	
(iii)	Sight reading. Sol-fa a pattern.	7
	6 to 8 exercises, sung once each, without	
	unnecessary halts.	
(iv)	Ear training. Sol-fa a tune already learned.	1
	Rhythm dictation.	2
	Pitch dictation.	4
(v)	Songs. Learn a new tune.	3
	New song. Old songs.	17

(Somervell, 1931: 34)

This breathless use of a forty-minute session shows Somervell's determination to encourage thorough and comprehensive music teaching, and illustrates the variety of methods that were present at this early stage in class music education. The frequent references to sol-fa teaching show that the methods of Curwen and of Sarah Glover, inherited from the previous century, were an established feature of music teaching. By the 1920s, the debate over whether children should learn to sight-read from the tonic sol-fa modulator or from staff notation had not been fully resolved, but Somervell's compromise, that there should be a progression from modulator to stave, was not uncommon.

Borland's (1927) review of music teaching in the first quarter of the century takes a rather different tone, evaluating the practice and ideas witnessed during his work as a musical adviser and educational inspector in London. His survey offers a helpful summary of the ideas expressed by MacPherson, Somervell and other leading writers of the time, together with a critical appraisal of the manner in which some of those ideas were being implemented. Like many of his influential contemporaries, Borland recommends an education which is fully rounded, incorporating the best of recent practice and innovation, without becoming rigidly linked to one school of thought:

> We need voice-training up to the point of eliminating crude and harsh tones; we need ear-training up to the point of enabling the pupil to gain not only general impressions, but also appreciation of detail, without which no full love of art can exist; we need training in notation to enable the pupils to continue a self-education after passing beyond our care.
>
> (Borland, 1927: 8)

Borland describes 'a veritable revolution' (ibid.: 49) in the fifteen years prior to publication, particularly in the growth of 'music appreciation' teaching. His criticisms of this method are amongst the most perceptive of the time, his concern being that the detail of musical skills and analysis were in danger of taking second place to a consideration of the whole, often through the use of descriptive stories or the setting of words to famous tunes. Clearly deploring these extra-musical devices, Borland points out that the vague aim of teaching children to 'love music' would never stand up to scrutiny in any other subject:

> To attempt appreciation of music without sound ear-training, and at least some knowledge of notation, harmony, phrasing and form, is about as sensible as to attempt the appreciation of French literature through the mere sound of the words, without any knowledge of their meaning.
>
> (Borland, 1927: 49)

The analogy is slightly flawed, of course, in that music does not seek to convey literal meaning in the same way as a French text, but Borland's point, that music education should aim to increase listening skills beyond the surface enjoyment of the sounds, is valid nevertheless. In suggesting also that appreciation lessons could have an impact beyond the school, he is drawn by the spirit of the time into placing low value on the musical influences the child would encounter at home: as children listened to their teacher's choice of music in school, so they would discover 'that the gramophone is capable of producing good music as well as the jazz dance and the vulgar music-hall song' (ibid.: 67). Borland sees concerts for schools as an important part of this cultivation of 'the right understanding of music' (ibid.: 72), but cautions against the excessively lengthy music and, worse still, spoken introductions, that were offered at many such occasions.

In addition to his evaluation of ideas and practice, Borland's assessment of the relevance of new resources is useful to the historian, with his enthusiasm for the pianola highlighting a trend that was in fact to be relatively short-lived:

> Annotated educational rolls produced under the guidance of eminent musicians are being issued in generous numbers, and simultaneously the cost price of these instruments is being reduced by intelligent mass production, so that schools in the near future will be able to possess a pianola at a cost not much higher than that of a good ordinary pianoforte.
>
> (Borland, 1927: 62)

The recommendation of mechanical aids stemmed from Borland's gentle rebuking of those teachers whose piano playing skills were not really adequate for supporting children's singing and listening: 'It seems an ungracious act to criticise adversely the playing of those teachers who are less skilful, and yet this must be done in the interests of education' (ibid.: 61). Borland seems to have been the ideal music adviser and inspector, supporting good practice where it existed, but offering considered criticisms of those elements of music education which were not fulfilling the aim of giving 'every child ... the opportunity to enjoy music, and to enjoy it with understanding' (ibid.: 2). His summary of the first decades of the twentieth century captures the optimism for music education that characterises these years:

> Old conventions have disappeared, barriers have been broken down, and new paths have been opened. The providing of concerts for children is one of the most important of the new movements, and perhaps we may not be considered pedantic when we insist once again upon (1) early ear-training, (2) the appreciation lesson, an elevated and broadened form of ear-training.
>
> (Borland, 1927: 75)

The writings of MacPherson, Somervell and Borland illustrate the complexity of ideas that were already facing music educators in the first decades of the twentieth century. Their ideas remain reliant on the presence of trained and enthusiastic teachers, with lessons such as that proposed by Somervell needing careful presentation to remain interesting. With a shortage of specialist teachers often commented upon (cf. Board of Education, 1926: 126), it is likely that the published ideals of the time were often far removed from standard teaching practice, as some of Borland's criticisms illustrate. To supplement this picture of the classrooms of the time, it is helpful to consult the contemporary Board of Education reports, where the place of music in a broad education was gradually being recognised.

1.2 Music education in the 1920s: official perspectives

The investigation of the curriculum, particularly that of the growing secondary school population, was becoming a national concern, and in 1924 the Board of Education appointed a 'Consultative Committee on The Education of the Adolescent'. The report of this committee, known as the Hadow Report (Board of Education, 1926), was a reflection of the education system of the time, but also contained much innovative writing, concerned as it was with the new opportunities that an expansion in secondary education could bring. Hadow's committee offered 'suggestions on teaching' for each of the curriculum subjects, and although music ranks below housecraft and gardening, its place in education for all children is recognised:

> The aim of music teaching considered as part of a school curriculum should be rather the cultivation of a taste than the acquirement of a proficiency; it should lay the foundation for the intelligent study and enjoyment of music in after life.
>
> (Board of Education, 1926: 238)

The Hadow committee emphasised the importance of singing, recommending 'Dr Arthur Somervell's "Golden Treasury"' (ibid.: 239), and also support Somervell's views on music appreciation, suggesting that children should listen to gramophone or piano examples on a weekly basis:

> It cannot be too strongly emphasised, both here and through the rest of the musical curriculum, (i) that no music should be admitted which is not first-rate of its kind; and (ii) that the kind should be determined in close relation to the age and inexperience of the listeners. Children, for example, find it difficult to keep their attention fixed on a long and abstract piece of instrumental music, and it should be remembered that as soon as the attention flags the meaning evaporates.
>
> (Board of Education, 1926: 239)

In addition to singing and aural training, the committee suggested that notation and sight-reading should be taught, with 'two periods a week devoted to musical instruction' (ibid.: 240). There is support for educational broadcasting, then in its infancy, and the hope is expressed that such programmes will support the 'delight in beautiful sound' (ibid.: 242) that should form the basis of all musical education:

> If the children leave school with their memories full of fine tunes and their ambitions roused for further study and exploration, then the school will have done a great deal for their musical training. If, in addition to this, they carry away, as is quite possible, some intelligent knowledge of musical history and some apprehension of the principles of musical structure, then the place of music in a school education will be amply vindicated.
>
> (Board of Education, 1926: 242)

It is interesting that the committee defines the success of music education in terms of curriculum content, implying that a knowledge and love of music is inherently desirable. There is less direct reference to the benefits for character or concentration, which could mark a move away from Mills' (1905) and MacPherson's (1922) view, or simply reflect the more pragmatic nature of the committee's task. All are agreed on the importance of music in the curriculum, and seem to favour Somervell's multi-faceted approach, rather than placing undue emphasis on musical appreciation lessons. Elsewhere, in his contribution to the 'Home University Library' (1924), Hadow had expressed his own view that musical knowledge is essential for intelligent listening, deploring the fact that of music, alone amongst branches of study, 'a man will assert with pride that he knows nothing' (Hadow, 1924: 10). Blaming an 'intellectual snobbishness' that views music as a purely emotional undertaking and fears the loss of pleasure through detailed study, Hadow cautions that such an attitude 'puts music in its place as an occasional recreation or a kind of audible confectionery' (ibid.: 11). Perceiving such faults in adult society, it is hardly surprising that Hadow and his committee looked to schools for the remedy, seeing a broadly based curriculum as the foundation for a better informed and more astute generation of listeners.

In the year following the Hadow committee's report, the Board of Education issued a *Handbook of Suggestions for Teachers* (1927), part of an irregular series of publications to which Somervell had contributed the music sections (Cox, 1991b: 69). Not surprisingly, therefore, the suggestions are consistent with his own writings, emphasising the importance of a balanced musical education, and giving particular details on the use of vocal exercises (Board of Education, 1927: 242). Like the Hadow committee, Somervell holds teachers responsible for ensuring that children leave school with a developed musical taste, founded on the tradition of folk-songs and including the masterworks of the classical repertoire:

> A pupil whose memory is stored with these songs from his earliest school days has the best protection that education can give against the attractions of vulgar and sentimental music when school days are over.
> (Board of Education, 1927: 253)

The belief that music is essentially a practical subject was obviously becoming widespread, with Somervell recommending that teacher explanation should occupy less time than musical examples, in a ratio of 1:7. The idea of 'melody training' is encouraged, with the belief that children should 'approach Music from the other side' by writing their own tunes (ibid.: 261). This method was to gain in popularity as the radio broadcasts of Walford Davies developed in the 1920s, but its introduction in this official handbook of suggestions marks one of the earliest moves towards composing in the classroom:

> These efforts will seldom be of musical value; but the practice of expression through this medium will greatly increase musical intelligence and give a knowledge of tune structure, balance of phrase and simple modulation which can be taught in no other way.
>
> (Board of Education, 1927: 261)

Clearly, the music educators of the 1920s shared the aim of introducing children to music by allowing them to understand it from the inside. This reasoning led to different teaching practices, however, as the Board of Education's belief in elementary composition came only a few years after MacPherson's assertion that guided listening and a knowledge of the repertoire was the route to understanding music from the perspective of the 'artist' (1923: 4). The notion that musical experience was more effective than discussion was to gain prominence amongst the century's most innovative writers, with different generations drawing their own conclusions about its implications for classroom practice. In the mid-1920s, the belief that all children could benefit from an introduction to musical knowledge and skills was innovative enough, and some confusion over the best means of achieving that is understandable.

The ambitious mood of this period in music education is confirmed by a report of a few years later, carried out by the 'Consultative Committee on the Curriculum of the Senior School' in the West Riding of Yorkshire (1931). This investigation, although on a smaller scale than the Hadow report, is similarly supportive of the place of music in the curriculum, recommending daily singing and two weekly lessons for all children:

> It seems desirable that the underlying idea should be Music in its widest sense, the development not only of the voice, but also of the mind, the training of some capacity not only to perform but to listen intelligently.
>
> (County Council of the West Riding of Yorkshire, 1931: 92)

Like the Hadow committee, the West Riding group urged the appointment of a specialist music teacher in every secondary school, although in practice the recruitment of such staff was to remain difficult for some years. The idea of linking amateur musicians with school music was amongst the Council's more radical suggestions, as they proposed that local choral and orchestral societies should be asked to give short and varied concerts to children who had been prepared in school beforehand. With gramophone records only just finding their place in the classroom, this organisation of school concerts was becoming more popular with teachers, who were otherwise limited to playing musical examples on the piano.

More detailed coverage of the same period is provided by the Cambridgeshire Council of Musical Education, a distinguished group of music educators that included Sir Henry Hadow and Sir Arthur Somervell. Formed in 1924, the committee's report, *Music and the Community* (1933), focused on creating links between effective school teaching and provision for adult education and music making. Advocating the place of music in education was, they said, 'to beat at an open door' (ibid.: 1), but the development of teaching and learning methods was still a priority:

> The admitted increase of interest in music education has not been accompanied by a proportionate amount of clear thinking, and the consequent developments have resulted in a general lack of coherence.
> (Cambridgeshire Council of Musical Education, 1933: 17)

The schemes of work proposed by the Cambridgeshire committee include the systematic training of the 'voice, ear and eye' (ibid.: 21), with the intention that courses should be co-ordinated between schools to ensure progression. For 'post-primary' pupils, the study of history and harmony is recommended, with community singing and playing at the heart of school life (ibid.: 41). Even composition is mentioned, although the enlightened curriculum suggestion is moderated by the insistence that music 'should be carefully corrected by the teacher before it is performed in public, or a false standard will be created in the minds of the young hearers' (ibid.: 42).

The musical education proposed by the Council is an active one, with children singing, learning to add keyboard accompaniments to songs, beating time, and dancing. The Council's interest in community music means that a focus on amateur performance balances the still prevalent view that pupils will engage in music principally as listeners. The teacher is charged with training children to listen intelligently and to sing confidently at sight, but the dictating of musical taste is frowned upon:

> The teacher should be aware of imposing his own taste rigidly upon his pupils; varied types of music should be presented, both for practice and for listening. The child should be encouraged to form his own taste, and not to be ashamed of changing it as he grows older.
> (Cambridgeshire Council of Musical Education, 1933: 20)

The Cambridgeshire Report is an inspiring document, not so much for its ideas, which are broadly similar to those of contemporary writers, but for its enthusiasm and long-term commitment to music education. At a time when music teaching was evidently in some confusion, owing to the variety of teaching methods that were emerging, a discussion of the purpose and implications of these methods makes refreshing reading.

It is hard to determine to what extent the ideas of the 1920s were disseminated amongst teachers, but there is a clear overlap at national and local level, as teachers attempted to provide basic musical skills for all pupils. Some evidence of the success of the various methods is provided by another Board of Education report, *Recent Developments in School Music* (1933), that offers a summary of the main developments in music education during the previous decade. That such a report was commissioned is evidence of a certain degree of commitment to music in schools, and the variety of activities discussed shows that music teaching was in a healthy, if somewhat confused, state. Teachers who endeavoured to include appreciation, community singing, concerts by and for children, country dancing, competitive festivals, gramophone listening, a school orchestra and percussion band, pianoforte classes, pipe making and playing, and rhythmic work, as well as taking advantage of the new wireless broadcasts, certainly had a full curriculum to contend with. The Board of Education reports an increase in all these activities around the country, with some evidently yielding more musical results than others, as their comments on percussion band teaching demonstrate:

> Two warnings must be uttered:
> a) Worthless music must be avoided. It is a bad mistake to play down to what is considered the children's level.
> b) Inefficient pianoforte playing is fatal to a good performance and stultifies the whole work of the orchestra. There is unfortunately a great deal of harm done in this way.
> (Board of Education, 1933: 26)

The Percussion Band, with the teacher at the piano and the children adding percussion in arrangements of classical works, was to retain a level of popularity in schools despite this warning, possibly seen as a way to ensure that all children were involved as performers. Whilst the experience must have been frustrating for some children, it sounds potentially more interesting than another activity described in the Report, that of whole-class piano teaching using cardboard models of the keyboard: 'Such exercises as finding notes quickly, fingering correctly, and grouping notes into chords, tune playing and so on, can easily be done' (Board of Education, 1933: 27). With this proliferation of new and revisited methods, the purpose of music teaching was sometimes obscured, although the overriding sense that children were being initiated into a desirable aspect of adult culture remained. Expressing optimism at the developments of the 1920s, the Board of Education nevertheless gives a warning to music teachers:

> It must again be urged that no one of the newer ideas is in itself a complete musical education. That is only to be found in music itself. That so many interesting and valuable methods of approach have been evolved proves, at least, that as a race of musicians we are not educationally stagnant.
>
> (Board of Education, 1933: 32)

Such caution is to be found at any stage in the development of music education, and its statement in this Report gives a sense of how widespread the change of the 1920s had been. Disparity in practice and purpose was emerging, enabling new ideas to flourish, but also generating some confusion and the danger of unduly biased approaches resulting from strict adherence to one method. Further insight upon these important years in music education can be gained from a study of successful practice, and the published accounts of two such music teachers are considered next.

1.3 Music education in the 1920s: Individual perspectives

Finding published or archive accounts of music education practice in individual schools is essential to gain a true perspective upon developments at a given time. These documents are relatively rare, however, as the challenges of the classroom generally leave teachers with little time for written reflection. Those accounts that are available can therefore give only a partial picture, and the discussions that follow must be taken as representative of professional thinking, rather than necessarily charting typical practice.

It is not surprising that one innovative account of music education in the 1920s should come from a teacher in a public school, where traditions involving music were established to a greater extent than in state secondary schools. Wood (1925) describes ideas carried out at Tonbridge School between 1919 and 1924, studying the effect that music had upon the boys in his charge. His description of the 'musical condition' of new arrivals at the school is summarised below, and gives insight upon the perceptions of children as musicians that underpin his work. There are, Wood suggests, 'six types of new boy', summarised as follows:

1.5 % 'tone deaf' – 'music puzzles them'.
1.5 % 'actively dislike music and say so'.

23

1 % 'cranks' – precocious with decided views; may become geniuses
    with 'tact and sympathy'.
7 % 'salt of the earth' – 'natural feeling for beauty in all its aspects';
    fostered by good education and home influence.
25 % 'Balladeers' – 'These love music as a physical recreation, but
    do not possess in the least degree the power of discrimination'.
c. 60 % remaining – 'rank and file'; attitudes range from 'polite
    interest to indifference'.

(Wood, 1925: 9–10)

Having identified the musical dispositions of his pupils, Wood's greatest concern was for the 60 per cent 'rank and file', whose attitudes would be most influenced by the school music provision. He criticises those preparatory schools who fail to foster the enthusiasm of this group through 'Sing-Songs', recommending them as a 'jolly physical exercise', quite apart from the musical benefits (ibid.: 12). This fairly simplistic approach is typical of Wood, whose commitment to music education comes from experience, rather than theory. The public school ethos is evident in his love of folk-songs that 'stir the heart', and in his recommendation of inter-house musical competitions, in which everyone should take part (ibid.: 18). The wireless, he states, is mainly influential in the home, but could usefully contribute to school music:

> It is a curious fact that the fascination of machinery will reconcile its devotees to the consideration of subjects they would never even think of without its aid: people for whom 'pure' music has no interest at all will listen cheerfully to it when given by the wireless or the gramophone.
>
> (Wood, 1925: 19)

In his light-hearted acceptance of the new mechanical age, Wood shows his priorities as a teacher, rather than a musician, preferring that his boys listen to music of any kind, rather than becoming anxious about the 'low' musical influences to which they might be subjected. This is founded largely on his assumption that the 60 per cent of pupils who remain indifferent to music must be won over by some means or other, a responsibility that lies with the music teacher, whose success in his work 'can be gauged by his influence on the unmusical' (ibid.: 19).

As evidence of his belief, Wood cites the development of the 'Music Club' at Tonbridge, to which parents and friends were invited, together with as many boys as possible. This group, founded in 1920 with a five shilling subscription rate, met for chamber concerts, given by music staff and visitors. Although clearly a valuable experience for Wood's pupils, the idea of a music club reinforces the belief that musical experiences belong outside the curriculum, and indeed the majority of Wood's successes seem to have been through voluntary activities. The benefits of a school choir are applicable to state education, and indeed their existence is noted by the local and national committees of the time, but Wood apparently fails to tackle the essential question of how best to use the curriculum music allocation. His perceptions of his pupils and of the responsibilities of his music teacher are pertinent to all music education, particularly his assertion that the 'indifferent' have potentially the most to gain from school music.

Another teacher to experiment with the impact of music upon school life was Margaret Donington, a member of the Cambridgeshire Council on Musical Education, and the music mistress at Mary Datchelor School for Girls. Her account was published as *Music throughout the Secondary School* (1932), with a foreword from her headmistress, Dorothy Brock, showing support for Donington's approach:

> Music has suffered too long from nebulous theories, from the teacher who turns on the gramophone and the pupil who sits in a trance of vague 'appreciation'. An aesthetic subject needs the discipline of clear thinking.
>
> (Donington, 1932: Foreword)

Donington aimed 'to make music enthusiasts' (ibid.: 2), pursuing this end through a detailed programme of aural training, singing, and the study of musical form and history. The emphasis is on progression, with opportunities for revision as children with different musical experiences come together for secondary education. Work at sixth form level is considered, with the observation that musical appreciation classes are usually most popular with this age group (ibid.: 56). Despite her commitment to music education, Donington observed that the influence of school music would lessen as the gramophone became more widely available, urging teachers to meet this challenge by making changes where necessary:

> The problem is ever to cope with the needs of the present generation of children who necessarily are receiving different influences from those of a few years ago. Nowhere is this so apparent as in the realm of Class Music. The fundamental aims of a musical education remain stable and should be more clearly visioned by the teacher as time passes; but there must come variations in approach and emphasis.
>
> (Donington, 1932: 73)

Donington's practical suggestions are consistent with other writers of the time, and her emphasis on the importance of progression is part of the rethinking of music education that her colleagues on the Cambridgeshire Council supported (Cambridgeshire Council of Musical Education, 1933: 17). Teachers of Donington's and Wood's (1925) vision must still have been rare, with other schools struggling to find specialist teachers of music, and so failing to engage with the developing resources and ideas available. A study of some more typical schools of the time will help to determine how closely ideals and opportunities were linked.

1.4 Music education in the 1920s: A local perspective

As with the accounts of individual teachers, investigations at a local level cannot fully reflect the diversity of practice that will have existed at this time. The research reported here, conducted at the Sheffield City Archives, provides the context for later discussions with retired and practising teachers (cf. Chapter 3). Similar regional case studies, beyond the scope of the present volume, would offer an interesting point of comparison, and reveal the extent to which the local enthusiasms and resources commented upon by the Sheffield School Managers (Sheffield City Archives, 1919–22: 157) had a direct impact upon educational developments in the city.

The 1920s were evidently an important time for music education in Sheffield, with the appointment of a music adviser suggesting that the city was amongst the more forward-looking in educational terms. Educational Sub-Committee Minutes show an emphasis on developing the listening and 'appreciation' skills of pupils, with the Director of Education asserting that there is 'general moral good to the community in the cultivation and development of musical appreciation and talent' (Sheffield City Archives, 1919–22: 159). Close links between education and the broader social good come across strongly in the archive material, and music is clearly an important part of the programme of educating the respectable adults of the future. The desire of the School Managers, which they expected the teachers in their employment to share, was that children should grow up with a healthy regard for music, as an experience that fosters community spirit and a sense of cultural heritage. The need for deliberate efforts to develop music in schools is evident from the remarks of Sheffield's Director of Education, who made the following report to the Schools Staff Section on 6 July 1920:

> Almost from the outset after taking up duty in Sheffield, I have been
> impressed by the great appreciation and love of Music of Sheffield

people, and I have been no less impressed by the absence of any strong constructive influence in the musical education of the pupils and students coming within the general educational system of the city.

(Sheffield City Archives, 1919–22: 157)

The Sheffield School Managers chose to ensure the presence of a musical life in schools through the appointment of Mr G. E. Linfoot, an established teacher, as Musical Adviser to the City. Developments in Manchester, where a Musical Adviser had been appointed in 1918, were offered as a role model, and Linfoot was expected to emulate this success in training teachers and establishing musical opportunities in schools. The adviser in Manchester was Walter Carroll, now chiefly known for his piano music for beginners, but then having the status of lecturer at the University and 'Professor in Harmony, Composition and the Art of Teaching' at the Royal Manchester College of Music. The success of the Manchester Education Committee, resulting from teacher training programmes and school concerts, had generated a belief in the benefits of music that was reported to the Sheffield School Managers:

The right musical development of the child is a great educational asset. The results of such training are by no means confined to music; they are of benefit to the whole school in that they encourage mental brightness and activity, not only in the scholars but in the Teachers themselves.

(Sheffield City Archives, 1919–22: 158)

Despite Carroll's successful organisation of school concerts in Manchester, when Linfoot decided to build on Sheffield's performing tradition and organise concerts for school children he had to explain his reasons in detail, which suggests that the idea was revolutionary in the local context. Whilst access to live music would be applauded by present-day music teachers, the manner in which it was introduced reveals the priorities of the time, with the benefits to children set out by the Adviser:

1. They will have obtained a fairly good knowledge, in outline, of a representative classic in one branch of music.
2. They had an exercise in listening critically and in forming judgment in artistic matters.
3. They heard singing of a good standard of excellence which may serve as a model for their own efforts.
4. Stimulation of their own interest in music, with the probability of an improvement in their study of the subject.

(Sheffield City Archives, 1919–22: 249)

This seems an ambitious catalogue of benefits to be achieved from a performance of Gilbert and Sullivan's *Princess Ida*, given by the Teachers' Operatic Society. Clearly well meant, and innovative in its local context, the attitude of imparting cultural values to the pupils is prominent. The concert was considered a success, and throughout 1920 and 1921 further events were organised until every pupil in the city had heard a live musical performance. The educational value was not left to chance, as significant musical terms were explained before the concert, and children were taught to sing the 'chief tunes' to avoid 'vagueness of impression' (ibid.: 291a), a technique that mirrors MacPherson's music appreciation lessons (MacPherson, 1923: 118). Linfoot was able to report the success of his concert series to the School Managers:

> The keen interest shown by the children was obvious and unmistakeable [*sic*], their conduct was excellent, and their essays support the belief that the experience was to them both stimulating and enlightening.
>
> (Sheffield City Archives, 1919–22: 291a)

Whether or not the children of that generation felt they had gained significantly from their exposure to 'first-rate' music cannot be determined, but Linfoot was certainly successful in demonstrating his beliefs in the cultural purpose of music education to teachers, parents and concert promoters, with the latter starting to offer free student tickets in 1921. Music education in Sheffield was flourishing under Linfoot's guidance:

> This was a period in which 'musical appreciation' was an especially important feature of English school life, and with G. E. Linfoot as City Music Adviser full provision was made for concerts in schools, for the use of gramophones and the holding of public performances by school choirs and orchestras.
>
> (Mackerness, 1974: 130)

Although benefiting from the central guidance of the Music Adviser, Sheffield suffered from a lack of specialist music teachers, a problem that existed at a national level (Board of Education, 1926: 238) and was apparently hampering the development of music education. Linfoot attempted to solve the problem by encouraging Pupil Teachers to study 'the elementary essentials of music-reading and music-writing', reporting a generally successful programme of training and examinations, that would enhance 'their value as teachers in the schools of the future' (Sheffield City Archives, 1922: 3). Such classes had begun in the 1880s (Mackerness, 1974: 130), but it seems they were given new impetus by Linfoot and his colleagues, who were evidently aware of the importance of teacher training in the development of school music. For all their attempts to overcome the lack of specialist music teachers in Sheffield in the 1920s, a national shortage was still a serious problem in the next decade, as outlined in the *Report on Specialisation in Senior Schools* which reached the Sheffield School Managers in 1930:

> A great deal of harm can be done by teachers ill-equipped to teach subjects like Art and Music which clearly demand skill in performance and sensitiveness to beauty. But the supply of well-qualified teachers of these two subjects is inadequate to meet the demand.
>
> (Sheffield City Archives, 1930–31: 226)

If music was being taught by teachers who were relying on their own limited knowledge to survive in the classroom, it is hardly surprising that any innovations took a long time to penetrate the education system. The perpetuation of teachers' own education or musical experience was a barrier to the growth of new ideas, often seen as a threat to the teacher's own musical knowledge, rather than as a challenge to be met as a professional teacher. The ideas of musical appreciation, community singing, and aural training were becoming well established, supported by local initiatives as in Sheffield. More complex ideas were to take longer to disseminate, as the somewhat neglected writings of Yorke Trotter demonstrate.

1.5 Yorke Trotter and 'the making of musicians'

Yorke Trotter's publications span the period under discussion in this chapter, and are worthy of separate consideration because of their unique insight upon the potential direction of music education (cf. Pitts, 1998a). He is unusual in his commitment to the purpose of music education, and his reluctance to dictate desirable teaching strategies to teachers who had not considered their own position with regard to the place of music in the curriculum. Whilst his opinions often make connections with those of his contemporaries, his writing is singularly inspirational, and must have challenged those teachers who were prepared to engage with his far-reaching ideas.

The Making of Musicians was published in 1914, presenting a vision of music education that was highly imaginative in its social context. Yorke Trotter's perceptions go beyond the prevalent view of children as receivers of adult culture and values, and highlight the need to give pupils experiences of immediate, as well as longer term, interest and enjoyment. He is critical of the music education provision of his time, stating that the emphasis on musical

29

knowledge, especially the 'obsession' with notation, was often detrimental to the development of the pupil's 'natural instinct' for music:

> If, as is generally the case, the whole of this education in music has been directed to the formal side of the art, the student will have missed the one thing that is essential – that is to say, he will know a great deal about the art but will in no sense be an artist himself.
>
> (Yorke Trotter, 1914: 4)

Rainbow (1989: 278) is quick to point out that Yorke Trotter's experiences of teaching were with talented pupils at the London Academy of Music, where conditions were more favourable than in the majority of schools at that time. Whilst this may have given Yorke Trotter a practical advantage over his contemporaries, it does not detract from the persuasion of his arguments, which capture an approach to music teaching that has value independently from the actual lesson suggestions. The strength of *The Making of Musicians* is in the respect the author shows for the reasoning and commitment of the music teacher, demonstrating that underlying principles are of the greatest importance in ensuring musical and educational integrity. The finest resources cannot guarantee good teaching, and Yorke Trotter's writings illustrate the necessity of having a sense of direction and purpose in music education, whatever the circumstances.

Great emphasis is placed on music's 'natural expression in man and nature' (Yorke Trotter, 1914: 1), with that belief informing the view that music teaching 'should have as its aim the cultivation of the instinct for musical art that is found in every normal child' (Yorke Trotter, 1924: 212). An interest in aesthetic and psychological aspects of music in education is evident in *Music and Mind* (1924), where Yorke Trotter considers 'the art of music' independently of its application to education, illustrating his conviction that the purposes of music teaching were equal in importance with the practicalities that occupied contemporary teachers and writers. In all his writings he asserts the connection between music and the emotions, focusing on the experience of music for the individual child, and challenging the factual approach that dominated the curriculum of the time:

> As the feeling side of a child is by far the strongest, and as the intellectual side only grows slowly as life advances, it follows that the first teaching in music should be directed to the encouragement of the feeling for music, and the intellectual part should be built up after the feeling for music has been established.
>
> (Yorke Trotter, 1914: 11)

The arguments offered by Yorke Trotter, that 'feeling' should precede 'intellect', and the 'effect' come before the 'symbol that is used to express that effect' (ibid.: 76), remain relevant because of their musical foundation, and can be applied to styles of teaching that he would never have imagined. His assertions about the unnecessary hindering of imagination by the formal teaching of musical 'grammar', would not be out of place in a text written at the close of the century (cf. Terry, 1994; Odam, 1995).

Like MacPherson, but for different reasons, Yorke Trotter objects to the prevalence of singing in schools, and argues for a more interactive approach to learning music, with the continuous development of 'the musical instinct' as its focus (Yorke Trotter, 1914: 91). He refers to his own teaching style as the 'Rhythmic Method' and in a later book (Yorke Trotter & Chapple, 1933) is more deliberate in his attempts to pass it on to future teachers. Its main premise is that music should be taught as a coherent whole, rather than fragmented into graded skills. Melody, harmony and rhythm should be understood together, as they are when listening, so that pupils are always employing the same skills, but at a deepening level of perception. In employing this holistic approach, teachers empower their pupils to teach themselves, and so to respond to music emotionally and intellectually:

> If we consider that music is only a refined, pleasing diversion, or an elegant accomplishment, we must admit that its place in education can at best be only a very subordinate one. But if we take the view that art is the expression of what I may call the inner nature, that nature which feels, which has aspirations and ideals, which reaches out to something beyond the material needs of this world, we must claim for our art of music a very high position in the scheme of education.
>
> (Yorke Trotter, 1914: 134)

Yorke Trotter writes as though he has solved many of the perceived problems in music teaching, but the rest of the twentieth century was to prove a struggle to afford music the 'very high position' that he does. Whilst his ideas are imaginative and persuasive, his methods dated with social and educational change, and the need to rediscover ways of meeting his ideals recurred. This balance between ideals and practice is a constant difficulty for educationalists, who have to define their audience and their limitations before they can present a convincing case. Yorke Trotter's vision, however, is one that has been reiterated at significant moments in the history of music education, as later chapters in this study will show.

That these ideas were not immediately given credence is evident in the introduction of the School Certificate and Higher School Certificate which, coming only three years after the publication of *The Making of Musicians*, showed little of Yorke Trotter's regard for the place of music in education. The new examination was steeped in the traditions of the grammar school curriculum, with tests in harmony, aural training and history, so difficult that only a few candidates were entered each year. The need for a more rational debate about curriculum content was evident, and the insecure place of music in secondary education must have given impetus to the attempts of Yorke Trotter and others to establish greater recognition for their subject.

Contemporary support for Yorke Trotter's sympathetic view of the child can be found in the writings of Caldwell Cook, who also sought to change the way that pupils were subjected to an 'academic' environment, instead of being allowed the freedom to develop as individuals (Cook, 1917). Pre-dating Piagetian theories of learning development, Cook's teaching philosophy was known as the *Play Way*, and involved a rejection of the theoretical bias of much early twentieth century teaching:

> The application to our schools is this: Education nowadays is study, or at best, theoretical training. That is, the learning how things have been done or, at best, how to do them. ... But whenever we have joy in what we are doing it is then the doing that is of first importance.
>
> (Cook, 1917: 7)

Just as Yorke Trotter did not want pupils to be restricted by an undue emphasis on musical notation, so Cook referred to the 'slavery to books' (ibid.: 10) that then dominated the teaching of literature. Neither writer is advocating substantially different educational outcomes to those expected by their more conventional colleagues, as both expect that the child should master specific skills during the course of their education. It is in their preferred method that they differ from the standard teaching of the time, favouring an approach that would, in later decades, be called 'child-centred'.

What Yorke Trotter and Cook share, more than any details of classroom practice, is a sense that new vision in education is needed to foster the generation of the future. Cook claims that 'this is the age of the young men' (ibid.: 366), then held to be of greater significance than their feminine counterparts. For Yorke Trotter, the hope of the future is intertwined with effective music teaching, which will foster those qualities desirable in every individual:

> If by our manner of education we can cultivate and develop the inner nature of our citizens, we will be raising up a nation full of vitality, striving after ideals, and ever pressing on to higher and higher stages.

> Even the weariness of life, which is felt so deeply by many of us, will
> disappear with our new ideals, for the art of music will give the means
> for self expression, and will provide a new interest in life.
>
> (Yorke Trotter, 1914: 136)

It seems, then, that educational ideas are linked with aspirations for a better
society, another recurring theme throughout the century. The contrast between
this idealism and the evidence of classroom practice suggests that Yorke
Trotter's ideas found little sympathy amongst teachers who were still coming to
terms with the emerging methods and ideas of music education in the first
decades of the century. Whilst Yorke Trotter's philosophical discussions were
to have enduring value, the practical suggestions of MacPherson (1922; 1923),
Somervell (1931) and the Board of Education reports (1926; 1927; 1933) will
have had more direct impact upon his contemporaries. It was the idea of
musical appreciation that the next generation would inherit from this period of
development in music education, fuelled by the development of schools
broadcasting and the spread of the gramophone.

1.6 The wireless and the gramophone

A clear summary of the developments that had flourished in Sheffield and
elsewhere is provided by Scholes, whose book acknowledged a respect for the
classical tradition even in the title; *Music, the Child and the Masterpiece*
(1935). One priority for Scholes was to define the role of the music teacher, in
response to a contemporary debate about whether 'interpretative comment'
(ibid.: 33) should accompany class listening sessions. Scholes felt that the
teacher should be engaged in promoting children's understanding in this way,
and that through structured exercises, 'careful and deliberate listening' (ibid.:
82) could be achieved. Pupils should be able to identify with form, texture,
colour and style when listening; developing not merely a liking for music, as
'appreciation' sometimes implied, but the capacity to engage with it at a critical
level. Scholes asserts the relevance of music to all pupils, supporting the wider
social belief that listening was the most important route to musical
understanding and enjoyment:

> Surely the composer creates not for the performer but for the listener.
> The performer's intervention is necessary, of course, and, by applying
> his intelligence and musical feeling to the interpretation of the
> composer's imperfect notation he even becomes a bit of the composer
> himself. But, with all his importance, the performer is really only the

servant of the composer and the listener. *Music is composed to be heard and the performer is the means of its being heard.* Music is an ear-art, not a finger-and-voice art, though it calls for fingers and voices to give it utterance. So I see the matter!

(Scholes, 1935: 122)

With the increased opportunities provided by the gramophone during the 1920s, listening was indeed an important skill, and fostering the knowledge and discrimination needed to participate intelligently was a priority for music educators of this generation. After the novelty interest in the gramophone during the previous decade, Scholes was anxious that music should regain the focus of attention (ibid.: 173). His suspicion of the new mechanical aids to music teaching is not unusual, although it contrasts with Wood's acceptance of the interest that the gramophone and wireless might inspire (Wood, 1925: 19). The 'gramophone debate' was an important concern for music teachers, some of whom were fearful of the tendency of music to 'warp and falsify' the perception of music: 'A gramophone oboe and a concert oboe are virtually two different instruments' (Johnson, 1936: 4). Nevertheless, the gramophone could be 'a powerful ally' (ibid.: xxii) in music teaching, offering assistance to teachers, rather than threatening their professional development: 'The ambitious student and the up-to-date teacher will make use of both recorded and relayed material in conjunction, remembering, however, the distinctive value of each' (ibid.: 15). The autonomy offered to the 'ambitious student' could also have been of concern to teachers, whose control of their pupils' musical education weakened as recorded music became more widely available (cf. Donington, 1932: 73). Absorbing change in education always takes time, but the pace is forced when new technology enters the home and school, necessitating a reappraisal of methods and aims.

The contemporary development of wireless broadcasting, in which Walford Davies' music lessons were pioneering developments, also presented a challenge to teachers. The first BBC schools radio broadcast was recorded in 1924, building on the series of 'Melody Lectures' that had been issued on HMV records throughout the 1920s (Cox, 1997: 47). Davies encouraged 'tune building', with his young listeners invited to send in answering phrases to the openings played on the weekly radio broadcasts, but his main focus was on listening, and the development of 'hearty team singing, ... a decent tone, and ... the ability to sing at sight' (ibid.: 47). Davies was evidently attempting to use the opportunities offered by the new technology in order to create a more coherent programme of music education at a national level. As with today's school broadcasts, however, the need for supporting activities from teachers in schools remained, and the radio and gramophone did not revolutionise school music in the way that he might have hoped. It must be remembered that gramophones and radios were often beyond the school budget, and the use of school broadcasts was by no means universal. Johnson (1936: 7) reports that around 2000 schools were listening to schools broadcasts in 1926, with an increase to 3000 in 1935, a figure that represents only 10 per cent of the potential schools audience.

Davies' school broadcasts were one of the first means of disseminating a model of music teaching at a national level, and his gift of communication contributed to the early success of his broadcast series:

> 'There's a little girl on the back row who's not attending; I expect she's very tired,' he might suddenly remark, and all the little girls on all the back rows would be conscious-stricken [*sic*] and awe-stricken. Had this teacher with the musical voice also an all-seeing eye?
>
> (Colles, 1942: 132)

The broadcasts mirrored Somervell's (1931) music curriculum, including singing, aural training and appreciation, as well as 'melody making'. Children responded to invitations to send in their own tunes to such an extent that entries had to be limited to three from each school when the numbers reached 'menacing proportions' (Colles, 1942: 133). Music broadcasts were not, therefore, confined to appreciation lessons, and Ann Driver's *Music and Movement* broadcasts in the 1930s extended the variety of material offered to primary schools (cf. Driver, 1936).

With hindsight, it is easy to see the dangers of the technological development; namely that the equipment would begin to control the curriculum, rather than take its place in a well-reasoned course designed by a capable teacher. Scholes and his contemporaries were evidently aware of the stagnation that could occur if broadcasts were not used intelligently by music teachers, recognising the need for teachers to consider their own views of the curriculum, rather than blindly accepting those that were implied in the broadcasts. In Scholes' discussion of music appreciation lessons, the teacher retains control of the curriculum, and is urged to teach the reading of notation and the use of some musical terminology (1935: 202). When Scholes warns against the danger of talking down to children, saying that they will only develop if there is something to strive for (ibid.: 167), he is apparently addressing a fault in the music teaching of the time, indeed one for which Davies himself was criticised (Cox, 1996: 366). Connected with this is the danger of relying on programme music to stimulate interest, giving children the impression that music always tells a story. Whilst warning against these 'extra-musical restrictions' (ibid.: 168), Scholes is certain of the expressive potential of music, and concedes that description can sometimes be useful:

> The plain fact of the matter is that a phrase of music expresses an emotion, that sometimes a word or a thought can express the same emotion, and that by uttering the word or thought we may make the emotional significance of the phrase clearer to a child who, perhaps, listening half-heartedly, was going to miss it.
>
> (Scholes, 1935: 171)

Clearly convinced of the importance of teaching music to children, Scholes never resorts to the hearty 'cultural heritage' arguments that characterised the organisation of concerts for the schoolchildren of Sheffield in the 1920s. In the context of 1930s education, Scholes' views were evidently liberal, although he is recommending in effect a change of attitude rather than one of curriculum content. Equal importance should be given to 'the cultivation of the ability to *do* and the cultivation of the ability to *enjoy*' (Scholes, 1938: 318), the new concern being with the latter.

The second section of *Music, The Child and The Masterpiece* provides a more wide-ranging perspective on the music teaching of the time, as it consists of letters to Scholes, written by experienced teachers. Inevitably, the published correspondence is sympathetic to Scholes' ideals, but the teachers' elaboration of his arguments provide evidence of successful dissemination. A London school principal of thirty years' experience, Mr Kirkham Jones, reveals some of the prejudices that accompanied the teaching of musical appreciation:

> I try to make them feel and love beautiful music, not to dissect, describe, analyse, and hate it. Above all I try to get them to have their own opinions, likes and dislikes, and not to become hypocritical little prigs – to hum, whistle, and sing lovely tunes of their own accord and to persuade mother to buy a gramophone record other than a jazz tune.
>
> (Scholes, 1935: 234)

However commendable these aims, there is something inherently 'priggish' about this teacher's assured identification of 'beautiful music', which does not include the jazz of the children's home experience (cf. Borland, 1927: 67). Jones goes on to bemoan the difficulties of ensuring that children are 'truly appreciative', saying that the girls especially are either 'too polite and grateful' or 'incurable sycophants' (Scholes, 1935: 235). The term 'music appreciation' is obviously interpreted in the sense of 'gratitude' here, and the pupils at this school must have spent their music lessons attempting to express their 'own opinions' in a way that satisfied their teacher. It is unfair to criticise this approach too harshly, however, as it was part of a general perception of children's thinking, and a desire to replicate adult society in the younger generation. Although Jones has not realised the possibility of a less restrictive approach to musical learning, he has clearly thought out his teaching strategies and is acting with the best of motives. His attitude is indicative of the cultural veneration of music, and goes closer to the 'musical heritage' line of thinking than the main body of Scholes' text.

Another correspondent has a familiar name to today's musicians; Annie Warburton, immortalised by her harmony workbooks, wrote to Scholes whilst teaching at Manchester High School for Girls. Her ideals are closer to Scholes', in that she aims to 'grow the seeds of understanding' (ibid.: 251) in her pupils, focusing on effective listening skills rather than attempting to cover an extensive repertoire. Warburton was sympathetic to the attention span of adolescents, and felt that playing long symphony movements was often counter-productive:

> My present solution of this difficulty, then, is to let the girls know the main facts which will help them to listen intelligently, but to illustrate with simple music not beyond their powers of understanding, in the hope that they will apply their knowledge to more complex works as they grow older.
>
> (Scholes, 1935: 251)

Warburton expected her pupils to mature as listeners beyond the classroom, a sign that she partially rejected the traditional dependence on the teacher. Her explanation of her 'present' solution also suggests a willingness to review her educational aims when appropriate. Like Scholes, she advocated experience of live performance, saying that 'it is unwise to let the children hear an orchestra on the gramophone until they have heard the real thing' (ibid.: 252). This shows sensitivity to the children's powers of listening and imagination, but could also indicate the reservations of someone for whom the gramophone was a new idea, threatening the supremacy of concert performances.

Jessie Cruse, working at High Storrs School for Girls, in Sheffield, found that her pupils had little knowledge of composers, and saw the acquisition of these facts as a priority, encouraging home reading and the making of scrapbooks of portraits and information. This teacher clearly valued knowledge *about* music, and based her teaching on the traditional canon of 'great works'. It is interesting to remember that her school will have been affected by the Sheffield Musical Adviser's programme of concerts for schoolchildren, which will have reinforced the idea that a certain level of factual information was a prerequisite for effective listening. The High Storrs girls seem to have engaged with music outside formal lessons, but whether this reflects a lack of curriculum time or an abundance of enthusiasm is hard to detect:

> We have formed a Music Circle which holds meetings fortnightly after school; pieces are played by the girls (this week they are giving dance tunes, &c., from Bach's suites), or we have a gramophone recital, illustrating different types of music.
>
> (Scholes, 1935: 261)

There are similarities with Wood's 'Music Club' (Wood, 1925), and the performance opportunities offered to these Sheffield pupils are an enlightened addition to the school musical experience, demonstrating that such enthusiasm was not confined to the privileged public schools.

The teachers quoted by Scholes all share a pride in their work, and a desire to provide the best music education possible for their pupils. The parameters are limited by today's standards, but set within a context where the most likely adult involvement in music was in audience, the intentions are commendable. It is likely that many teachers of the 1930s shared Scholes' aim to foster an interest in music amongst their pupils, and equip them for a lasting enjoyment of the arts, replicating, in effect, their own musical pleasure:

> Throughout the whole of the musical activities in school or college the students' future musical life should be kept in view. The teacher of mathematics can hardly expect that many of his pupils will carry to a more advanced point what they have learnt under his instruction, but the teacher of literature or music whose pupils' progress stops dead on the day they leave his classroom has failed.
>
> (Scholes, 1938: 319)

The fact that the music teaching of the time was so closely linked to the priorities of the adult culture emphasises the fact that as society changes, so education must accommodate its new values. The complacency of the 1930s was to be shattered by the second world war within living memory, which inevitably caused a reappraisal of musical, social and educational values. Whilst these took some time to be assimilated into classroom practice, it is clear that the 'cultural heritage' model of music education was challenged in a way that necessitated change.

Perhaps inevitably, a somewhat confused picture emerges of the state of music education in the 1930s, with so much of its character dependent on the beliefs and interests of individual teachers, and the often isolated contexts in which they worked. The potential for development from these apparently disparate strands is clear enough with hindsight, but the writers of the time were founding their vision of music education upon their own teaching and learning experience, seeking to reproduce or improve the existing provision, rather than offering a more radical challenge. Clearly, there was scope for the instrumental training of performers to be made more accessible, and for pupils to have greater freedom in their choice of listening and their responses to music. The idea that children might engage in composition was understandably still a long way off, although the 'tune building' of Walford Davies' radio broadcasts and MacPherson's 'melody making' (1923: 57) showed some awareness that music could be understood through more creative activities. Generally, though, this potentially liberal approach was limited by the perception of music as a completed object to be received and critically appraised, and was to take decades to become more firmly established in the classroom. The challenges to the next generation of music educators were manifold; to cope with changing educational ideas on a broader curriculum level, to accommodate the new resources that were becoming available for music teaching, and to redefine the purpose of music teaching in the post-war society. The next chapter will identify some of the educators who were prepared to ask the necessary questions, and look at the ways in which their suggestions were considered and implemented.

Chapter 2

Tradition and exploration:
1940s–1950s

2.1 Musical and educational aims in the post-war years

Music education should not be considered in a vacuum, and in studying the developments of the 1940s and 1950s, it is necessary to take account of the social and cultural mood of the time. World War I was within living memory for much of the adult population, and had led to a shortage of musical facilities that the intervening years had not fully restored:

> War conditions [1914–18] affected musical activities in many subtle ways. Apart from the inevitable shortages which limited the number of new instruments that could be made (and also reduced the quantity of music printed), there was the fact that many large halls were taken over by the military authorities and were therefore not available for concerts. Although teachers of music were, on the whole, less adversely affected by war conditions than were performers, the number of entrants to the academies of music dropped, and local examinations had fewer candidates.
>
> (Mackerness, 1964: 237)

It might be expected that the start of another world war in 1939 would have had a similarly negative effect on musical life in Britain, but deliberate efforts were made to prevent this, with national and local attempts to promote a community spirit through music. Radio and gramophone had already made music more widely available, with 'musical appreciation', as advocated in the schools of the 1930s, an important pleasure for many adults. This enjoyment of music was fostered by arts organisations during the war years, with the work of the Council for the Encouragement of Music and the Arts, later renamed the Arts Council, marking a new national awareness of the importance of the arts (Metcalfe, 1987: 105). In schools, this new interest in orchestral music led to an increase in peripatetic instrumental teaching, and the establishment of the National Youth Orchestra in 1947 extended the opportunities available to young performers (ibid.: 105). As the continued focus on Sheffield later in this chapter will show, these aims were coupled with the practical difficulties that Mackerness (1964) observed after World War I. In the 1940s, however, the musical ambitions of teachers were redefined, and there was a growing determination to include performance amongst school opportunities. Amateur music making was acquiring a more socially prominent role, as sol-fa training in schools and at adult evening classes had steadily increased the number of singers wanting to perform cantatas and oratorios, accompanied by local orchestral musicians. Educational aims and adult perceptions of music were intertwined, and between them the impetus that could have been destroyed by the war was sustained.

At a governmental level, pre-war interest in education had been frustrated by the disruption of evacuation, and the raising of the school leaving age was delayed until the Education Act of 1944 (cf. Lowe, 1988). The shared horrors of war fuelled the belief that the next generation should be educated on more equal terms, and the ideas of the Hadow and Spens Reports (Board of Education, 1926; 1938) were revived, having so far had little opportunity to reach practical fruition. The Spens committee (1938) had recommended a 'three-track' secondary education system comprising grammar, secondary modern and technical schools, with reformed curricula to provide academic and vocational opportunities, and this became the goal of post-war education ministers. Barnard (1947/61) notes that 'revulsion against the folly and waste and false values of war' provided impetus for the Education Acts of 1870, 1902 and 1918, all introduced following a period of international military conflict (ibid.: 293). The legislation of 1944 continued this trend, and this time the practical effects of wartime education were also to prove far-reaching, in that teachers faced with inadequate accommodation or even voluntary schooling had, by necessity, to question many of their pre-war assumptions:

> Teachers were compelled to improvise, and to their astonishment, many of them found they could dispense with the aids which they had previously considered important. ... Handicrafts, art, and all kinds of physical activities became invested with a new importance, and the experience of these war years influenced the curriculum and teaching methods when peace followed.
>
> (Curtis, 1948/67: 375)

A comparison with the other arts in education (Section 2.2) demonstrates that music was slow to respond to this change of educational mood, remaining torn between the 'academic' side of the curriculum and the expanding opportunities of the 'practical' subjects. In the absence of any government directive on what should be taught, there was still diversity in education and consequently a need to justify the inclusion of music amongst a greater variety of subjects.

The first decades of the twentieth century had seen increased variety and purpose in music teaching, leaving the subject in a healthy state to contribute to wider educational reform. Amongst the music educators keen to put forward the case for music in a changing curriculum was Hale (1947), the instrumental music organiser for Bournemouth, who described the 'conversion' to music teaching and learning that he had witnessed during his career. Hale divides his discussion of primary, secondary and private music teaching into three periods: pre-1918, when singing was the focus of music teaching and instrumental tuition was unconnected with the school curriculum; 1918–30, when musical appreciation became prominent, with the wider use of the gramophone causing a reduction in instrumental learning; and 1930–39, when a variety of methods including percussion and recorder bands complemented the extensive teaching of appreciation, with a new confidence in music education being supported by school broadcasts (Hale, 1947: 43–6). Hale's analysis of this growth in music education is coupled with an ambition to ensure that such developments are universal, with music 'available to all according to ability and promise' (ibid.: xix):

> Education should henceforward have the following minimum aim where music is concerned: to teach the elements of which it is made up, its origin, function, and values; to teach the groundwork of intelligent listening, and afford a knowledge, if only rudimentary, of music notation; to provide such general facilities as will enable every day-school pupil to contact music as others have, say literature in the past; to locate trainable talent, particularly that which is above average; and finally, to afford opportunities for the musical development of each individual, carrying the opportunities forward throughout the student stage.
>
> (Hale, 1947: 9)

Hale's aims are laudable, but his identification of 'trainable talent' has more impact upon his policies than his 'music for all' slogan might suggest. In his 'Provisional Recommendations', Hale urges primary schools to implement a music test to gauge the potential of their pupils, so that the musical education they receive can be matched to their interests and apparent abilities. Having piloted this scheme in several schools, Hale is able to predict the results, dividing children into three groups: x (20 per cent), 'those showing promise well above average', y (70 per cent), 'those with only average ability', and z (10 per cent), 'those with no appreciable sense of music' (ibid.: 147). The test, carried out between the ages of 7 and 10, included aural and rhythmic tests, and was seen as beneficial to all the pupils involved, aiming 'just as much to prevent those totally unsuited to music from wasting their time on the subject as to enable others with natural musical talent to have their training taken in hand at a time when a good foundation can best be laid' (Hale, 1947: 148). These proposals seem less elitist when he describes his majority y group as the 'audiences of the future', outlining a course that includes singing, aural training, sight-singing and appreciation (ibid.: 151). It is in his clear identification of the most able that Hale differs from his contemporaries, enforcing his intention to make instrumental training dependent on ability rather than wealth. In that context, his ideas are more enlightened than they at first appear, with his identification of 'musicians' and 'musical persons' obviously generated in part by the frustration of dealing with over-ambitious parents:

> Musicianship itself is a *quality* – partly inborn, partly attained – that enables one to do something of a creative nature which leads, directly or indirectly, to the promotion of music, and directly to an increase of one's own appreciation of the art.
>
> (Hale, 1947: 37)

Hale's interest in musical development and selection was part of a wider interest in the psychology of music, supported by Seashore's (1938) and Buck's (1944) discussions of musical perception and understanding. The application of developmental and educational psychology to music was a relatively recent phenomenon, and had significant contributions to make to educational theory and practice:

> There is as yet no recognition, official or private, of the fact that the purpose of Education is not to make us learned, but to enable us to discriminate between good and bad, and that if we lack this discrimination in artistic things we shall miss half the joy of life. ... The real aim of those who teach any branch of Art should be, not merely to produce a select few who will paint or play better because of our teaching, but to awaken and stir the imagination of the whole body; that is our only true justification for pleading for Art in Education.
>
> (Buck, 1944: 98)

As with Hale's writings, there is an undeclared confusion of aims, as the acknowledgement that music should be for all pupils is coupled with a belief in testing children in order to select the most able for advanced tuition. The positive development of making instrumental teaching available in schools, rather than solely from private tutors, was tempered by the fact that with musical ability testing came the possibility of failure for some children. Whilst the authors of these ideas might favour the term 'measures' instead of 'tests' (Seashore, 1938: 302), the urge to classify children would have a lasting, if indirect, impact, supporting the concept of inherited musical talent rather than the more egalitarian philosophy that was emerging in educational thinking. As the scope of music education increased, the challenge of finding a curriculum that provided for all pupils was in danger of being obscured by the new interest in categorising children according to musical potential. Nevertheless, the growth of music psychology research offered a new way of looking at musical processes and understanding, giving 'scientific' credence to a subject that had always sought to reconcile its 'practical' and 'academic' roles in education. The second half of the twentieth century was, in one sense, to be a continual struggle to balance these three essential elements, bringing musical meaning, processes and practicalities together in search of new ways forward for music education.

2.2 Arts education: a broader perspective

While music educators were still putting forward justifications for their role in the curriculum, education in the other arts had made practical progress that was to take several more decades to achieve in music. Music education had been hampered by a lack of specialist staff and resources, and by the feeling that performing and composing required skills beyond those of a generalist teacher. Art and English were to catch the changing educational mood much earlier, allowing children to experiment with paint, clay, words and gesture long before the exploration of sound entered the secondary school. Developments in different arts subjects highlighted the limitations of music teaching, and were a first step in helping music educators to realise the importance of composing in the classroom. Connections between the arts were to remain problematic, with the debates begun here continued well into the 1980s (cf. Sections 4.4 and 7.6).

Art: Richardson and Read

The 1930s saw significant changes in art education, where such pioneering figures as Marion Richardson (1948), still well known for her handwriting patterns (1935), and Herbert Read (1943/56), the art critic and aesthetic theorist, had adopted the principle that the development of the child was paramount, and should take priority over the traditional focus on the expectations of school and society:

> Anyone who will give children the spiritual freedom in which to paint will find in it a thing to be esteemed for its own sake, a thing that is outside and above all would-be workaday worthwhileness. The child artist is disinterested, serene, and fulfilled.
>
> (Richardson, 1948: 85)

Richardson, whose career began as art mistress at Dudley Girls' High School, evolved her teaching style as a reaction against the limitations of School Certificate art examinations, for which children were expected to master accurate still-life drawing, rather than 'developing an art of their own' (ibid.: 17). Clearly a forward-thinking teacher, Richardson's response to London's first Post-Impressionist Exhibition is typical of her questioning of establishment views:

> Impertinent and fantastic though the idea may seem, I can only say that to me a common denominator was evident between the children's infinitely humble intimations of artistic experience and the mighty statements of these great modern masters.
>
> (Richardson, 1948: 14)

Richardson describes her exploration of the materials of art with her classes, delighting in the process of creativity that was to take many more years to become the focus of music teaching too. Her pupils were encouraged to experiment with different sizes and textures of paper, sometimes painting with beetroot juice and gravy browning in order to gain an awareness of the components of a picture (ibid.: 28). Sensing that children derived an enjoyment from scribbling and making patterns, usually discouraged in schools, she worked from doodling to writing, in the same way that a child develops speech from its earliest prattlings (ibid.: 55). An interest in developmental psychology is present, although not emphasised, in her writings, indicative of a new way of thinking that was beginning to affect all areas of the curriculum. Richardson, too, sensed the readiness for change that was evolving within schools and society at large:

> The times were ripe, the teachers' minds were ready, chiefly because of the growing respect for the individuality of the child. In art this respect is a necessity; for unless a child is expressing his own vision he is expressing nothing at all.
>
> (Richardson, 1948: 59)

With the support of the art critic and writer Roger Fry, Richardson organised public displays of her pupils' art which attracted the attention of some 26,000 visitors and were widely reviewed in the press, so contributing to the dissemination of her ideas. Her work as a school inspector also allowed her influence to spread, to the extent that her lectures, courses and workshops for teachers would attract 1500 applicants for 150 places (ibid.: 68). Discussions with teachers led Richardson to address the role of the educator in this new form of art teaching, concluding that generalists and specialists alike needed to have a 'care for the child':

> While it is impossible for any adult to teach a technique that matches childlike vision, children nevertheless need teaching if they are to feel their powers of expression keeping pace with the growth of their ideas, and so retain their interest in the subject.
>
> (Richardson, 1948: 60)

Amongst Richardson's contemporaries, Viola (1942) advocates similar methods, and acknowledges the legacy of Franz Cizek, an artist who worked with children in Vienna at the start of the twentieth century. Viola's vision is one echoed by theorists throughout the latter half of the century, as he states that art education 'should encourage and not ... suffocate the innate creative capacity of children', rather than concerning itself with training artists, a task 'beyond its possibilities'(Viola, 1942: 35). His priority was to encourage children to create rather than to copy, working from imagination in a way that parallels Richardson's dislike of School Certificate 'object drawing'. The art teacher should be like a parent, providing freedom within an encouraging 'creative atmosphere' (ibid.: 35), and teaching according to the personality of each child; 'the moment decides the method', to use Cizek's phrase (ibid.: 41). For Viola, the process of making art was more important than the completed object, the crucial outcome being the development of the child:

> Children who have done Art and Crafts from their earliest years ... become richer personalities. As a rule, such children are better in other subjects in school as well, because they are accustomed to express themselves freely; they are more sincere, and remain so.
>
> (Viola, 1942: 60)

The acceptance of 'Child Art' as a distinct category is somewhat superficial, failing to make the connection between existing art works and the creativity of children that was one of Richardson's motivations (Richardson, 1948: 14). The reasoned argument demanded by this new definition of art education was provided by Herbert Read, who published the seminal *Education Through Art* in 1943. Asserting that art should occupy a central place in the curriculum, Read sees the failure to educate beyond the 'logical subjects' as the cause of a lack of creativity that is damaging to society:

> The price we pay for this distortion of the adolescent mind is mounting up: a civilization of hideous objects and misshapen human beings, of sick minds and unhappy households, of divided societies armed with weapons of mass destruction. We feed these processes of dissolution with our knowledge and science, with our inventions and discoveries, and our education system tries to keep pace with the holocaust; but the creative activities which could heal the mind and make beautiful our environment, unite man with nature and nation with nation – these we dismiss as idle, irrelevant and inane.
>
> (Read, 1943/56: 168)

Clearly influenced by the atrocities of the recent war, Read's polemic must have made powerful reading at the time, and places tremendous faith in the power of arts education to remedy wider social evils. Read's ideas incorporated the new interest in child psychology, drawing on the notion of developing concepts of knowledge, and the belief that play was the source of artistic creativity (ibid.: 223). Primary school children, he claimed, should be viewed as different personality types, and should be given opportunities to express themselves through the all artistic media, whilst acknowledging that there was likely to be one art that most closely matched their tendencies. Musicians, it seems, are most often 'introverted intuitive' characters (ibid.: 103), a category defined by Jung as being most closely concerned with abstract, formal art. Years later, Kemp (1996) considered the implications of these personality types for music teaching, stating that 'the internal restraint and aloofness of musicians ... can so often entrap them in a pattern of communication difficulties, particularly with larger groups of pupils in the classroom setting' (Kemp, 1996: 219). The challenges to musicians in schools are therefore even more complex than Read implies, and the difficulties, particularly for those musicians who had undergone little or no training as teachers, should not be underestimated.

Read's convictions about the importance of art in education and society make his a wide-ranging and challenging book, but he returns to the practicalities of introducing primary-aged children to art in order to make his point clear. Challenging the already ambitious recommendations of the Spens Report (1938), that seven periods of the weekly school timetable should be devoted to the arts, Read proposes a more fundamental change to the curriculum, seeing 'aesthetic' concerns as vital to all aspects of learning:

47

We demand nothing less than the whole 35 [periods] into which the child's week is arbitrarily divided. We demand, that is to say, a method of education that is formally and fundamentally aesthetic, and in which knowledge and manual ability, discipline and reverence, are but so many easy and inevitable by-products of a natural childish industry.

(Read, 1943/56: 220)

Read identifies himself as a 'disinterested observer' of arts education (ibid.: 294), rather than a teacher. This position enables him to consider the education system as a whole, pointing to the fundamental flaw of separating subjects and so preventing children from achieving a creative understanding across the curriculum (ibid.: 222). Read's 'credo', published some years later as he reviewed the impact of *Education through Art*, provides an inspiring summary of his philosophy:

This is my *credo*: that the perfection of art must arise from its practice – from the discipline of tools and materials, of form and function. I believe that it is a mistake to define a world of art and set it apart from life. I believe that it is a mistake to confine the teaching of art to appreciation, for the implied attitude is too detached. I believe that art must be practised to be appreciated, and must be taught in intimate apprenticeship. I believe that the teacher must be no less active than the pupil. For art cannot be learnt by precept, by any verbal instruction. It is, properly speaking, a contagion, and passes like fire from spirit to spirit.

(Read, 1966: xiii)

At the time that Read was assessing the impact of his earlier work, music educators were just beginning to apply similar principles to classroom teaching. The idea of 'intimate apprenticeship' was nothing new to instrumental teachers, but the belief that creative activities could be pursued by a whole class took some time to replace the didactic model of music appreciation lessons. Such concepts reached English and Drama more quickly, as Holbrook (1961; 1964; 1967) and Slade (1954) explored similar ideas of shared discovery through the arts, despite the common perception of English as essentially a communication tool, rather than a means of expression. With ideas slow to disseminate between teachers of the same subject, connections across the secondary school curriculum were still some way off.

Why not Music? The case of a Birmingham primary school

Some of the difficulties with music that were felt at the time are expressed in a Ministry of Education pamphlet (1949), in which Mr A. L. Stone, the former Headmaster of a Birmingham primary school, describes his attempts to foster imagination and a 'sense of order' amongst his pupils, the inhabitants of back-to-back houses, whose education had been disrupted by air-raids:

> No taste or appreciation of beauty had been superimposed upon them from the outside world, but the amazing thing was that when they were allowed to express themselves freely in certain media of expression, they created something which was beautiful.
>
> (Ministry of Education, 1949: 7)

Stone's decision to allow experimentation in art, rather than making a knowledge-based curriculum the foundation of his school, stimulated interest and concentration in his pupils. Improvised drama, which emphasised the creative process rather than a performable product, and the telling of stories through picture sequences are described in his accounts, but it appears that he was less confident with musical exploration:

> I think perhaps why singing and reading music did not allow the children to find complete absorption was that the whole approach was too intellectual for them. How to make it less so, in order that we could keep it alive and build on that inherent interest which each child has in rhythm and pitch, so that something rich and vital could be perceived at each stage, we failed to discover, and we still did our 'tafe tates', saying them and clapping them in the usual way. ... But I never felt that the children wanted to sing with that intensity which such a strong inherent interest should bring. Is this failure due to the fact that we approach music as an interpretative art without the child having an experience of it as a creative art?
>
> (Ministry of Education, 1949: 30)

Stone provides his own answer, or at least the relevant question, identifying performance, rather than composition, as the aspect of music most comparable with painting or clay modelling. The assumption that composing was beyond the abilities of children could not be broken, even amongst teachers who embraced dance and art with enthusiasm. Fear of uncontrollable noise is one possible explanation, which lingers today to a certain extent, but whatever the reason, traditional teaching methods in music hindered its development in the primary curriculum, and were to remain unquestioned in secondary schools throughout the 1940s and 1950s. Music education did not seem to be going in the same direction as the other arts, with their belief in the importance of individual expression and creativity. The concept of music as a performance art was strongly held, and individual provision was affected by a child's apparent aptitude for learning an instrument, rather than by the need for expression that was being urged by primary school colleagues and the pioneers of art education.

2.3 Music education: the way forward

Although music education was trailing behind other arts disciplines, its internal momentum continued, with the questioning of pre-war methods beginning to emerge. Isolated voices had identified the need for all three aspects of music education to find their place in the classroom, applying musical logic to propose a new direction for education:

> [Just] as it is possible to distinguish three elements in musical experience, namely, the music, the executant interpreter and the listener, so there are three aspects of musicianship capable each of specific development, the art of composition, an executant skill, and a critical and appreciative judgment.
>
> (Mainwaring, 1941: 214)

Such perception was apparently in conflict with the practical provision of the time, with the West Riding Education Committee (1953) reporting disappointing developments in the schools of the 1940s, where singing was still the main activity in many music lessons. They attribute this failing to a 'completely inadequate supply of specialist teachers', whilst those who do have advanced musical training 'appear to be more interested in spotting and exploiting talent in their pupils than in developing to the full the possibilities that music holds for the great mass of children' (ibid.: 54).

Where success in music education was documented, it tended to focus on performance activities, with Smith (1947) describing his public school music teaching from 1925–47, which had apparently changed little within that time. Smith's achievements should not be belittled, not least because his commitment to music education had sustained the school community through five years of 'great suffering and loss' during war-time evacuation (Smith, 1947: 14). In his vision of the curriculum, Smith supports Read's (1943/56) views on the dangers of fragmented subjects:

The view which persists still in the minds of so many that a boy's day must be divided up into snippets of this and that, some essential and others unessential, is perhaps the most disastrous of all the antiquated notions about school organization that this book is designed to upset. The growth of the examination bogey is probably responsible, together with competitive games, both of them forms of pot-hunting which appeal strongly to the materialists among parents and schoolmasters.

(Smith, 1947: 15)

Smith shows an awareness of developments in art teaching, referring to Read's work and to Cizek's Child Art exhibition of 1920. His concept of music, however, is firmly linked to the performing tradition, and his quite outstanding successes in this area never prompted him to attempt any composition teaching. Appointed music master at Alleyn's School, Dulwich in 1925, Smith found the school poorly resourced with no music room, but with an established tradition of singing (ibid.: 18). His aims on arrival show his self-image as a music teacher:

The problem I had to solve seemed to be how one teacher in so large a school with this meagre outfit was to (a) make all the children artists; (b) do all to no other purpose than the glory of God as part of His creation; and (c) continue his own already highly developed musical life so that no feeling of frustration should be present.

(Smith, 1947: 18)

The last of these aims is particularly characteristic, containing as it does the assumption that the teacher's sources of musical development and satisfaction will be compatible with those of the pupils. Performances of Verdi's *Requiem* in 1926, the establishment of several school orchestras and choirs, and an annual Gilbert and Sullivan production, suggest that Smith's pupils responded well to his vision of music education, which was entirely focused on these public events:

Classes are taken by the teacher, but they are never other than rehearsals for some great work going forward and are therefore felt to be part of the creative effort to which all energies are at the moment bent.

(Smith, 1947: 22)

As with Wood's (1925) earlier account, the public school advantages are evident even in wartime, and Smith's approach would not have translated well to a state school with fewer resources and less opportunity for whole school extra-curricular music. In his own context, however, Smith was clearly an inspiring figure, and in cultivating 'the spirit of the *atelier*' (ibid.: 19) he was keen to give his pupils responsibility for their own learning:

> The teaching technique so developed is one where the teacher eliminates himself in every possible way, yet carries on with his own art, whatever it is. He is constantly consulted, and coaches principal roles in the production of large works. His advice is not necessarily followed, since there is complete honesty with one another.
>
> (Smith, 1947: 21)

Smith refers only briefly to structured classroom teaching, supporting George Bernard Shaw's definition that the easiest way to learn to sing at sight is 'to stand next to someone who can' (ibid.: 46). This method of developing musical skills by being allowed to 'flounder and recover' (ibid.: 47) is a refreshing rejection of theory teaching, relying on the fact that children 'are exceedingly curious' and will demand explanations when they are ready for them (ibid.: 47). On the subject of musical appreciation, however, Smith is not so liberal, stating that boys need guidance to influence their record buying, and that an appreciation of contemporary music should be fostered (ibid.: 94). His own commitment to music teaching leads him to propose a compulsory year of travel or research after teacher training so that only the truly dedicated will return to schools; perhaps a reaction to the hasty training of demobilised soldiers after the war (ibid.: 98).

The success of Smith's teaching was largely dependent on his own musical knowledge and enthusiasm being communicated to his pupils. Whilst this is consistent with Read's view that art is taught by contagion (Read, 1966: xiii), it makes the music teacher a central figure in the life of a school, meaning that his departure could result in the collapse of music education for those pupils. Such an approach was not uncommon in the 1940s, as the 'musical director' figure, responsible for organising school performances and ensembles, struggled to reconcile the needs of the classroom with this more public role. The determination of individual teachers meant that music teaching could achieve high levels of skill and commitment, but the post-war provision was patchy and lacked overall direction. The most successful teachers were driven by their own enjoyment and expertise in music, and as a result, tended to reproduce their own training, with an emphasis on singing, listening and, for the most talented, instrumental performance. These practical goals were apparently determined by experience, rather than theories of music in the curriculum, and whilst this could result in vibrant teaching where a willing specialist existed, other schools remained dependent on school broadcasts and communal singing.

2.4 Traditions of performance: a Sheffield case study

Smith's (1947) experiences were paralleled in Sheffield by Norman Barnes, Head of Music at King Edward VII School from 1947 to 1976. In his retirement, Barnes collected an archive of the programmes, press cuttings and school magazine reports that charted the successes of his music department (Barnes, 1983), forming a valuable localised picture of developments for the historian. Conversation with Barnes reveals a continuity with pre-war teaching, as he clearly states that the biggest influence on his teaching style was his own education:

> It seemed to me that I got all of the necessary at Oxford – I sang in the Oxford Bach Choir, I founded and trained the St Peter's Male Voice Singers and of course, St Peter's Chapel was also a parish church, so I ran a parish church choir and so on. And then when I came to practise the art, it all came back, you see. What I did then, I tried to manage here. ... I was fortunate again in that my schooling was at Magdalen College School, which was a choir school besides being an ordinary public school. ... What I learnt there, I regurgitated, as it were, in Sheffield.
>
> (Interview: 23 November 1995)

Barnes's self-confessed 'regurgitation' of his musical background highlights the difficulties of disseminating educational ideas, as teachers bring their own experiences of education to the classroom and, in the case of musicians, a high degree of training in the practicalities of their subject. His pride in those pupils who gained Oxbridge choral or organ scholarships, as he had himself, mirrors that of Smith (1947: 22). An article by Barnes in the school magazine shows his ambitions for his pupils, by outlining the career of a diligent instrumentalist, one I. A. Mottershaw:

> Having decided soon after coming to the senior school to take up an instrument (as quite a number of boys do) – and that a most difficult one, the oboe – he persevered with it (as quite a number of boys, alas, do not) to such good effect as to be able to give a fine performance of a concerto in his last year. This should be the aim of every instrumentalist: to 'improve thy talent with due care', to the great benefit of the collective orchestral effort and in the hope of attaining solo eminence. [July 1954]
>
> (Barnes, 1983: 47)

It is clear that the musical experiences of King Edward's boys were bound up with the ethos of the school and were a means to secure the approval of peers and masters alike. This is not to belittle the achievements of Norman Barnes and teachers like him, who were responding to the needs of young people perceived to have similar social and musical expectations to their own, but to emphasise the difficulties of initiating change through persuasion.

The musical activities at King Edward VII School raised the profile of music education in Sheffield, as concerts attracted large audiences and placed the performing experience at the heart of the education process. The change from pre-war ideals is dramatic, with the achievement of filling the City Hall with children 'in audience' supplanted by the pupils themselves drawing an audience to fill the same venue. The archive material collected by Barnes attests to the success of performances of the 'classical' repertoire, seen by some contemporaries as marking a new era in school music:

> These are days in which the practice of music-making in school is at least approached with intelligence. It is not so very long since music in School was centred round, say, a tonic sol-fa modulator, with possibly the added luxury of treble or two-part settings of the less imaginative folksongs. At this concert [December 1951] we heard voices well used in madrigals; we heard the orchestra both accompanying and on its own account in Haydn and in the organ concerto; and we enjoyed the fun in the beautifully played Suite for two Clarinets by Alan Frank. Indeed, times have changed.
>
> (Barnes, 1983: 25)

The descriptions contained in Barnes's archives, of the difficulties of obtaining instruments and teachers, and of organising such large-scale musical events, demonstrate his determination to bring music education to his pupils. However, his concerns with the practicalities of music teaching at King Edward's obscure the broader questions that were to initiate the changes of later decades. His definition of music education, founded on his own experiences as student, musician and teacher, resulted in an apparently successful musical life at the school, and did not demand a re-evaluation of why, or indeed whether, music had a valuable place in the curriculum. Given that teachers of every generation have been faced with concerns apparently more pressing than the long-term future of music in schools, it is understandable that changes in perspective are, if not unwelcome, not always recognised as being of relevance to the immediate needs of pupils.

As director of music, Barnes's work was part of the broader school ethos, although his methods were to change little when the school converted from a selective boys' grammar school to a mixed comprehensive in the 1970s. He attributes his success to the early recruiting of new entrants to the school, all of whom were sent a questionnaire about their musical interest and experience before arriving at King Edward's, and were auditioned for the school choir in their first week (ibid.: 251). A description of his early years at the school shows his respect for the pupils he worked with, and also offers a rare insight upon his classroom methods, as opposed to his undeniable extra-curricular successes:

> The boys were the brightest academically drawn from a wide area. They wanted to work and did so with great enthusiasm and competitiveness. They actually *liked* learning Musical Theory which formed one of the two periods a week – the other being given over to Singing, Aural work and use of the small collection of 78s on the already superannuated HMV record player.
>
> (Barnes, 1983: 2)

Music at King Edward VII School was widely respected in Sheffield, with a local journalist commenting in a review of the school's Coronation Concert that Barnes ensured 'that the boys learn the right music and perform it intelligently and to the best of their ability' (ibid.: 38). The concerts in large local venues continued to attract capacity audiences throughout Barnes's career, and old boys of the school, notably Professor Ted Wragg of Exeter University, were to recall their music education with affection:

> One of the finest teachers I had was Norman Barnes, who taught me music. His lessons were a shambles. But there were lulls in the storm. He was a complete enthusiast and gave us a lifelong love of music. [Wragg, quoted in the *Daily Express*, 1981]
>
> (Lawton et al., 1995: 144)

Barnes does not readily acknowledge the influence of published material upon his teaching, showing that whilst published works may serve as a guide to the prevailing attitudes and ideas of an era, their influence upon contemporary teachers is by no means guaranteed. In some respects, Barnes's self-assurance is mirrored by two writers representative of the 1950s, Winn (1954) and Rainbow (1956/71). Both of these authors take a relatively conservative approach to music teaching, and their desire for change relates to the specific problems of classroom practice experienced by Barnes and his contemporaries.

2.5 Constructing the music curriculum: ideals and realities

Whilst the publications of the 1950s promote music in the curriculum in a determined way, there is little sense of optimism or vision amongst the mainstream texts. Winn (1954) in *Teaching Music*, addresses the potential benefits of music education in a systematic way, before suggesting possible approaches in schools. Rainbow's (1956) book is more directly concerned with the practicalities of teaching, but includes a rationale that is sympathetic to Winn's ideals. In this post-war period of rejuvenation, both authors were keen to provide musical opportunities for pupils, and to educate pupils to be receptive to those experiences. There is some evidence of updating in the second edition of Rainbow's book (1971), and as a result Winn's is the more reliable indicator of the priorities of the age, but the general tone of all Rainbow's later writing is traditionalist (cf. Rainbow 1985; 1989) and it is clear that his ideals are firmly rooted in the classroom practice of the late 1950s.

Winn's justification for music in schools is linked to the desire to create a new and successful society following the devastation of World War II, and reflects the view that education should generate healthy and well-balanced children:

> The value of singing for reasons of health needs no defence in these days, but the study of the relations between music and the nervous system of the child, though yet in its infancy, gives cause for hope that it may play a part as a curative agency for maladjusted lives.
>
> (Winn, 1954: 1)

If Winn's reasoning stopped here, music would be placed on a level with physical education, a healthy pursuit with no aesthetic or artistic content. After recommending music as a cure for juvenile delinquency, however, Winn goes on to assert the benefits of its 'ennobling effect upon the emotions', echoing Viola's (1942: 35) view that the training of accomplished practitioners of an art is not the main aim, rather that teachers should 'restore the belief that music is as much an element in culture as a literature or science – and that it cannot be disregarded or neglected' (Winn, 1954: 3). There is some defensiveness about this statement; a stance which has recurred throughout the century as different generations have felt the need to replace outmoded justifications with new assertions of the importance of music in education. Winn's implicit definition of music is as a performance activity, marking a revival of singing and a move towards instrumental work, although the legacy of the music appreciation lessons of the 1930s is clear elsewhere in the book. Amongst the benefits listed by Winn are increased concentration, improved memory, the opportunity for self expression and the development of imagination and a sense of beauty (ibid.: 4). Despite these laudable intentions, his approach is fairly restrictive, although he seeks to involve all children and to challenge common assumptions that 'learning music' means 'learning the piano'.

Rainbow defines his aims for music education with less clarity, but urges the importance of an enthusiastic teacher who can communicate his enjoyment to pupils:

> To be a good musician yourself is not enough. Beethoven, with his short temper, dominating attitude, impatience, and scorn for the unmusical, would clearly have been a disastrous failure in the classroom. Haydn, on the other hand, judging by accounts of his geniality, sincerity, sense of humour, and the good relationships which he established with his players at Eszterháza, would almost certainly have made a fine teacher.
>
> (Rainbow, 1956/71: 2)

As Rainbow points out in a later work (1985), graduate musicians of this time were not required to undergo specialist teacher training, and so the reliance on their own musicianship and personality will have been even greater than in more recent years. The need for a clear purpose in teaching music was all the more essential, but Rainbow embodies his beliefs in practical considerations, urging teachers to counteract the passive radio listening that children might have experienced at home. He identifies the three main areas of musical experience that should be covered in a balanced curriculum, and it is interesting to compare these with the trinity of composing, performing and listening that has become firmly established in today's music education practice:

> The ideal music course will provide opportunities for three main fields of activity: singing and instrumental music – with a creative element; the consequent development of the use of notation; and 'guided' listening.
>
> (Rainbow, 1956/71: 5)

Rainbow's proposed curriculum will have appeared to offer a broad range of experience at the time, although it seems now to place undue emphasis on theoretical understanding, as opposed to practical experience. He urges that 'singing' should become 'music' through the teaching of notation and critical listening. Rainbow shares with Winn a concern that musical appreciation often relied on programme music, leading children to believe that music had to be 'about' something, rather than familiarising them with musical terminology (Rainbow, 1956/71: 9):

> One question (among many others) invariably asked by the teacher,
> after playing a record, was 'What did that piece of music remind you
> of?'. To which any honest and courageous child would have answered
> rightly, 'Music, of course': but that was not the answer desired or
> required by the teacher. 'Fairies', 'Breezes', 'Rivulets', 'Storm
> clouds', etc., was what she wanted.
>
> (Winn, 1954: 54)

Both Winn and Rainbow seek a return to traditional teaching of aural skills
and accurate performance, with the use of tonic sol-fa and rhythm names
described in detail in both books (Rainbow, 1956/71: 30; Winn, 1954: 19).
The difficulties of sustaining attention through long concerts are discussed, as
they had been a generation earlier (Borland, 1927: 72) with smaller recitals of
chamber music within school felt to be a more valuable experience than the
'novelty factor' of lengthy public concerts:

> There is such an atmosphere of the outing about the whole thing: the
> escape from school, the coach-ride, the imposing size of the hall – all
> these exciting things fill the child's mind and virtually intoxicate him.
> The music, as far as he is concerned, is eclipsed by the events and
> things surrounding it. That is, unless he is already a *musical* child.
>
> (Rainbow, 1956/71: 97)

Rainbow's last sentence above is telling: although he and Winn are both
discussing music for all pupils, in the light of expansion in compulsory
education, it is evident that they retain a preference for the musically more able.
Rainbow asserts that the music teacher's most 'effective' work often occurs
outside the timetable (ibid.: 15), presumably equating effectiveness with
satisfaction, in the same way that Smith (1947) had done. The question of
mixed ability teaching is addressed, but it seems that tolerance is the most that
can be expected from a significant proportion of pupils:

> It is surely the function of the music teacher in the Secondary School
> to make it as palatable as possible to the older boys and girls in his
> classes. For if it does not attract, it must obviously repel; there is no
> standing still in this matter.
>
> (Winn, 1954: 51)

The feeling that music education shapes the attitudes of the next generation is
clear here, but so too is evidence that the beliefs of the teachers themselves
have a significant effect upon style of teaching. Just as Norman Barnes was
proud to replicate his own musical experience for his Sheffield pupils, so the

undercurrent of Winn's and Rainbow's work is the assumption that music education involves the fashioning of pupils in the teacher's own image.

Rainbow and Winn addressed their vision of the curriculum to a specialist audience, but given the shortage of trained music teachers at the time, their contemporary Niblett was perhaps more realistic when he wrote an *Instructional Handbook* for 'enthusiastic amateurs' (Niblett, 1955: 9). Niblett retains the ideals of the music appreciation movement, calling upon teachers to encourage the development of 'taste' in their pupils:

> As the teacher endeavours to turn the child from the comic paper and the cheap novelette to the finer examples in our store of literature, so he should direct the child away from the lurid music and the banal lyrics to the better types of musical composition, simple though it may be. Let him get away from mediocrity.
>
> (Niblett, 1955: 13)

Niblett's attitude reveals the conservatism of his teaching approaches, and he deplores the tendency to condemn 'old-fashioned methods' (ibid.: 24) that he perceives in the profession as a whole. His emphasis is on singing and aural training, with the percussion band and recorder groups still seen as important:

> There is no doubt that generally the standard of sight-singing has deteriorated, and this is probably due to the fact that basic training in rhythm and pitch has not been systematically taught. ... No child will be any good at mathematics until the tables are known by heart, and no child will be able to read music with any fluency until the common rhythmic patterns, and intervals in pitch, become second nature. We must get back to the French time names and the tonic sol-fa system.
>
> (Niblett, 1955: 24)

Such ideals are unashamedly rooted in the teaching of the pre-war decades, and show a dissatisfaction with the effects of a broader, less rigorous music curriculum. Niblett cannot have been alone in this, and provides a useful reminder that, for every pioneering music educator who publishes a new framework for the curriculum, there will be plenty more who resist change or deliberately revive old methods.

Perhaps the clearest picture of the realities of post-war music education is provided by Long, a contemporary researcher whose *Music in English Education* (1959) was the result of a survey carried out between 1954 and 1956 for the Leeds Institute of Education. Long noted the wide variation in musical provision across the country, reporting a lack of specialist staff and resources, and stating that 'the enthusiasm of the headmaster or headmistress and the competence (or existence) of the music staff seem to be the determining factors' (Long, 1959: 41). Class singing, noted as being the most frequently taught aspect of music, was often the easiest option for untrained teachers faced with large groups of children in the school hall (ibid.: 19), and these practical restrictions account in some measure for the slow rate of change in the music curriculum. Long reports that 'innovative ideas' were spreading at this time, with attempts to use singing as a form of ear training and as a participatory form of musical appreciation (ibid.: 22). A very small number of pupils were taking music to examination level – 4621 in 1954 – and when Long points out that three in every four 'O' Level candidates were girls, it becomes even clearer that secondary school music, as defined by the examination syllabus, was appealing to a very select number of the school population. The legacy of the School Certificates was in part responsible, and will be discussed in the context of examination and assessment reforms in Chapter 5. Long attributes this apparent weakness not only to insufficient resources and timetable allocation, but also to a lack of purpose amongst those responsible for teaching music:

> A deeper cause of failure in the classroom arises from the fact that many teachers themselves lack any conviction of the value of their work and are not merely unable, through poor technique, to achieve their aims but are fundamentally uncertain about what their aims should be.
>
> (Long, 1959: 42)

Long's grim picture of the general trends of music education in the 1950s obscures the successful teaching that was taking place in individual schools, but clearly indicates that there was a need for a new direction for music teaching at this time. Even as Long's report was being published, new ideas were beginning to emerge in some quarters, but it is interesting to bear in mind the poor quality of provision that the 'traditionalists' of the next decade would attempt to retain. Perhaps the real priorities of the music teachers of the 1950s, like Norman Barnes, lay outside the classroom, as Long reports that school orchestras existed in more than half of grammar schools and, where they flourished, were evidence of the commitment and energy of the music teacher. Rainbow's 'musical child' (1956/71: 97) was obviously catered for in the most enlightened schools, but Long articulates the principle that would shape the 'revolution' of the late 1960s and 1970s, namely that music should be for *all* children:

> The classroom is the only place where all the members of the school receive consistent teaching; and the distinctive purpose of this

teaching – to help children fully to appreciate music – serves in different ways the needs of them all.

(Long, 1959: 48)

Like Yorke Trotter earlier in the century (1914), Long's ideals are tempered by his assumptions about what is achievable within the conventions of the existing education system. Long sees music education as providing all children with 'a love and understanding of music as literature' (1959: 47), an aim that owes much to the ideals of Scholes (1935) and the music appreciation movement. In his practical approach, therefore, Long seeks a more efficient use of traditional teaching techniques, but his beliefs, taken in isolation, mark a movement forward to the ideals of the next generation.

2.6 Moving towards change in music education

James Mainwaring, lecturer in music and psychology at Dudley Training College, had already identified performing, composing and listening as the essential elements of musical experience (1941: 241), and now went on to articulate his theory of music education at greater length (1951). Observing that music was 'lagging behind' in a time of educational improvements, Mainwaring felt that greater consistency was needed amongst music teachers:

> If music is seriously to enter school life at all it would be reasonable to
> assume that the child's musical experience should be of a continuous,
> progressive, purposive kind. ... Again, it would be difficult to discover
> any generally accepted aim for the direction of musical work in
> schools, and without such aim teaching tends to drift and to flounder.
>
> (Mainwaring, 1951: 1)

It was not the first time that a lack of coherence had been observed in music education (cf. Cambridgeshire Council of Musical Education, 1933: 17), but it seems that the intervening years had done little to resolve the absence of progression between primary and secondary music lessons. Mainwaring shares Yorke Trotter's (1914) sense of being ahead of his time in his discussion of music education, and the two educators have a common perception of the immediate benefits that children should discover at school: 'It seems vastly preferable to regard the ten or eleven years of school life as having a significance in themselves, and as providing an ideal environment for the child's development from infancy to adolescence' (Mainwaring, 1951: 2). This empathy with the child's experience of school was a logical development of the

61

new understanding of childhood creativity, and was to be more widely adopted in the following decades. At the start of the 1950s, however, Mainwaring was still speaking from a minority viewpoint, applying his ideas to music by generating five guiding principles:

(1) That the musical experiences of children in schools should be as enjoyable and as interesting to them as possible;
(2) That musical education should be based on active musical experience;
(3) That the experience should cover as wide a variety of musical activities as possible;
(4) That all such experiences should form part of a coherent and consistently pursued plan of musical development;
(5) That musical items are heard, recalled and recognised as 'wholes'.

(Mainwaring, 1951: 8)

Mainwaring's principles are well-expressed, but without specific examples they could be applied equally to the teaching of the 1920s or the 1990s. Where Mainwaring differs from some of his predecessors is in his definition of the curriculum according to inherent musical progression and personal development, rather than for 'concentration of purpose' (Mills, 1905: 17) or the 'cultivation of a taste' (Board of Education, 1926: 238). Recognising the continuing lack of specialist teachers, Mainwaring asserts that music in schools requires, not 'superlative virtuosity', but only enthusiastic music lovers, willing to undertake training 'in any unfamiliar branches of the work involved in the modern approach' (Mainwaring, 1951: 5). The ongoing training of teachers should not be seen as a weakness, but rather of a demonstration that experience is the only way to develop musicianship (ibid.: 7). This refreshing approach mirrors Richardson's (1948) willingness to allow experiment and flexibility in her art lessons, and caused Mainwaring to put practical music making at the heart of his lesson suggestions:

> Verbal descriptions and definitions are useful only when there is a fund of recallable experience to give a content of meaning to the words. Teaching should not begin with definition, it should end with it, to clinch and clarify what is known.
>
> (Mainwaring, 1951: 11)

Yorke Trotter's belief that 'the child must first have the effect in his mind before he know the symbols that should be used' (1914: 76) was now supported by musical and educational psychology, resulting in a principle of remarkable similarity; 'Proceed from sound to symbol, not from symbol to sound' (Mainwaring, 1951: 12). Mainwaring asserts that involvement in making music was the only reliable route to understanding, given that 'a very great proportion of musical recall is dependent not on having heard the music but on having reproduced it' (ibid.: 12). The previous generation of teachers had applied this idea to music appreciation teaching, with the Sheffield children's singing of the 'chief tunes' at City Hall concerts an example of common practice in the 1920s and 1930s (Sheffield City Archives, 1919—22: 291a). Mainwaring's ideas are more far-reaching, with the learning of musical instruments deemed to be more beneficial than singing. The skill of playing by ear should maintain the connection between sound and symbol, rather than notation being associated only with an action, such as depressing a piano key (Mainwaring, 1951: 13). Again, this idea was not new, as instrumental tuition had become more widespread in the secondary schools of the 1940s, but Mainwaring is unusual in his belief that such opportunities were essential to the music education of all children:

> In other words, the end-state of the process should leave the normal adolescent not only an appreciative listener, but able to take a useful part in some communal musical activity, and to have sufficient knowledge of musical notation, syntax, and idiom to read, and to write whatever imagined musical thoughts he may be capable of conceiving.
> (Mainwaring, 1951: 14)

Mainwaring acknowledges the success in practical music that some primary schools had already achieved by this time, particularly through the use of dance, rhythmic movement, and singing. Secondary education, however, was not always 'based on active and interesting musical experience' (ibid.: 48) in the same way, and needed to take account of existing musical knowledge, and of changing adolescent concerns. Where infant children enjoy movement and pattern, adolescents are developing a fascination with analysis and structure, which should be recognised by the music teacher (ibid.: 49). Secondary school music should challenge all ranges of ability and musicality, allowing the most able to engage in creative activities, and the less confident to make clear progress in musicianship (ibid.: 52). Mainwaring's suggestions still include the use of percussion band, singing, recorder playing and the learning of staff notation, but his insistence on a 'co-ordinated scheme, consistently pursued' (ibid.: 57) for all children is what makes his writing significant. He gives the teacher responsibility for directing the child's interest towards new aspects of music as appropriate; 'as when it is transferred from the playing of percussion instruments to some aspect of musical rhythm, or from interpretative dancing to music's expressive capacity, or from a musical idea to its symbol' (ibid.: 57).

Progress should be made, he suggests, from the Gestalt understanding of young children (ibid.: 15), where tunes are perceived as whole entities, to the more analytic approach to the elements of music that ought to characterise secondary music teaching (ibid.: 58). Above all, the coherence of music education should contribute to the child's developing understanding:

> In music, as in all areas of human experience, sound knowledge does not consist of the mere accumulation of oddments of learning, but, rather, in the organization of relevant experience.
>
> (Mainwaring, 1951: 58)

As well as sharing ideas with Yorke Trotter (1914), Mainwaring occupies a similar position, as a music educator who offered a new perspective on the teaching of the time, and provided the first glimpses of the next stage of its evolution. As Yorke Trotter brought his knowledge of philosophy and aesthetics to his understanding of the curriculum, so Mainwaring gives a psychological interpretation of current and imagined practice. His statements on the 'joy of creation' (ibid.: 60) herald the changes to music education that were to emerge over a decade later, but are limited in part by his acceptance of some of the resources and ideas of the 1950s. Mainwaring's most determined principle, that opportunities to compose, perform and listen should be available to all pupils, was to be defended by the next generation, with results that went beyond his already considerable vision.

Despite such isolated examples of innovative thinking, it can be seen that the 1940s and 1950s were, to a large extent, a period of consolidation in music education, with the ideas of the previous decades being assimilated by the majority of teachers. The general perception of music education was as the training of talented performers and of generalist listeners, with only 'creative' opportunities given less credence in mainstream thinking, despite their evident success in art education. The restricted supply of specialist teachers remained problematic, although the examples of Smith (1947) and of Barnes (1983) show that where committed teachers were employed, the music of a school could flourish, with benefits to the school ethos and the general education of the pupils concerned. In both these cases, the tendency to reproduce the teachers' own musical experience, noted in the 1920s and 1930s, continued, a state that is likely to have been typical, given the limited or even non-existent teacher training of many music educators at the time. The variety of performing and listening activities that had been developing during the 1930s were still in evidence, with discrepancies existing between schools according to staffing and resources (Long, 1959), and there was growing interest in developing a coherent curriculum that allowed musical development through childhood and adolescence.

The importance of classroom music was gradually to challenge the supremacy of extra-curricular music provision in the grammar schools of the day, with the priorities of Winn (1954), Rainbow (1956/71), and practising teachers such as Smith (1947) and Barnes, being questioned in the process. Where music education was flourishing in the 1950s, it was almost entirely dependent on a committed member of staff, who was able to assimilate the various methods advocated by different authorities. The exchange of good practice between schools still seems to have been limited, although an international conference in 1953 included several papers from British music inspectors and teachers, which were generally supportive of existing provision (UNESCO, 1953). Speakers on that occasion highlighted the importance of radio broadcasts and communal singing, with the value of traditional music teaching methods such as tonic sol-fa emphasised by Horton (UNESCO, 1953: 137). Clearly, British school inspectors found much to celebrate in the music teaching of the early 1950s, with the major difficulties remaining those of staffing, resources, and effective dissemination of ideas.

Further changes to music education were inevitable, as more specialists entered the profession and began to reinterpret the ideals of the pre-war years. As other arts subjects, notably English and drama, began to adopt the creative approaches pioneered in art, the impetus for music to become similarly pupil-centred became stronger. Against the established methods of music teaching, however, it would take innovative musicians and educators to bring about the necessary revolution. The next chapter will consider the developments of the 1960s and early 1970s, looking at those music educators who were prepared to ask the challenging questions that would redefine the purpose of music in the curriculum.

Chapter 3

'The use of noise to make music': 1960s–mid-1970s

3.1 The changing educational climate of the 1960s

The changing concept of music education that was beginning to emerge in the 1960s challenged the supremacy of listening and teacher-directed performance that had characterised the first half of the twentieth century. New perceptions of learning and child development were influential across the curriculum, and the success of practical activities in art, drama and English began to be applied to music. Most importantly, a reinterpretation of musical and educational aims made the connection with composition, which assumed an increasingly significant place in music teaching.

The process of change was in evidence throughout the education system, with some writers questioning the very nature of schooling in Britain. Alternative education methods, pioneered by Caldwell Cook (1917) and his contemporaries, were revived in the writings of the 'de-schoolers' (cf. Illich, 1970) who called for 'questioning behaviour' in teaching to replace the traditional belief that 'recall is the highest form of intellectual achievement' (Postman & Weingartner, 1969: 31). This freedom in education was practised by A. S. Neill at his experimental school, Summerhill, founded in 1921 but achieving greater publicity in the 1960s as the educational climate became more receptive to his ideas (Neill, 1962). The idea that children could be responsible for their own learning drew on the educational psychology of the time, and incorporated the ideals of the 'project' methods and 'integrated day' that had become popular in primary schools (Clegg, 1971). Most encouraging amongst this broadening of ideas was the belief that teachers themselves should be responsible for change and innovation in the profession:

> So-called change can be brought about by imposing it on schools, just as so-called education has in the past been brought about by imposing it on children. In either case, the effect in many instances is a lack of conviction, a lack of sincerity, and inert and sterile results.
>
> (Clegg, 1971: 41)

Even the pupils of the day contributed to the changing perceptions of education, invited by a competition in the *Observer* newspaper in 1967 to define *The school that I'd like* (Blishen, 1969). Their descriptions reveal the formality of the schooling they were currently experiencing, whilst showing a coincidence of views with many of the adult educationalists of the time:

> The fault with a lot of schools today is that teachers are not prepared to listen. ... They don't mind discussing various topics as long as it ends up with them being able to prove a point to you and not the other way.
>
> [Lynne, 15: 134]

> In secondary education today the emphasis is on passing O- and A-levels. Half-educated children emerge from school clutching their exam certificates. ... But are they better equipped to understand and live with their fellow human beings? Moreover, has their education encouraged them to think creatively and originally? Isn't this what education should be about?
>
> [Anthony, 18: 117]
> (Blishen, 1969)

As throughout the history of education, such heady idealism often translated into practice that was little different from that of previous decades, leading Blishen to observe that 'the revolution in teaching methods has barely begun to touch the secondary schools' (ibid.: 55). The 1960s are caricatured by today's politicians as a time of radical change and reckless experimentation, and it is important not to endorse the stereotype in evaluating the ideas of prominent writers. In music education, in particular, the views of Blishen's young correspondents show a traditionalist approach that had obviously been fostered by their own experience:

> Music is great fun but most schools have no music teachers or only a piano teacher. ... Schools should have (1) a baritone singer to teach boys, (2) a contralto singer to teach girls, ... [and] other instruments should be taught such as the violin.
>
> [Shivaun, 11: 102]

> No music lessons would be allowed because of the noise that might be produced by those who were inexperienced.
>
> [Jane, 15: 102]
> (Blishen, 1969)

Successful practice is often more influential than discussion, and music teachers of the 1960s were offered examples from primary schools and from secondary art, drama and English teachers of the way in which practical activities could be at the heart of arts teaching. Marshall's (1963; 1968) accounts of her 'adventures in education' give details of a project-based approach to teaching, where pupils and trainee teachers were given a theme or idea on which to base an investigation encompassing every element of the curriculum, an approach which changes the role of the teacher:

> Our aim must be to entice the children to learn, but they have to begin somewhere, and part of the teacher's function is to organise the start: it is a bit like a archaeological expedition. Someone who knows chooses the place to dig and leads the diggers to it; but from that point onwards, though he may be in overall control of the operation, the interest lies in what is brought to light.
>
> (Marshall, 1968: 57)

Music teachers, who had retained their control of the performing activities of their classes, presented a problem for Marshall, and her statements on music seem less confident:

> [Music] cannot just be pushed aside, or dealt with superficially just by the singing of a few overworn songs, or even by listening to well-chosen records. Music is not only another medium of human expression, but an active as well as a passive medium.
>
> (Marshall, 1968: 168)

Further incentives to join the 'creative' movement in education were provided by leading drama and English teachers. Slade (1954) suggested a link between dramatic and musical development, classifying the 'embryo art forms' observed in babies:

> Banging the table with meaning (e.g. 'more food') is more obviously Drama, whilst banging the table with a clear interest in the sound value and time beat only is more obviously Music. Where climax is intentionally brought in and enjoyed, Music might be said to be bordering on Drama.
>
> (Slade, 1954: 23)

Slade denies the existence of a teaching method for drama, saying that the teacher should only stimulate activities and allow 'the Child's method' to flourish (ibid.: 360). In his criticisms of the way that adult concepts of drama are imposed on the child's play instincts (ibid.: 314), direct comparisons with music are possible, as the acceptance of children's ability to compose was hampered by the belief that all music should emulate the 'masterworks' of music appreciation lessons.

Creative ideas were also flourishing in English, where educators such as Holbrook (1961; 1964; 1967) had linked ideas of child development with a new approach to teaching literature. His ardent defence of English for 'the rejected' (1964), focusing on pupils in the lower streams of secondary schools, had particular relevance for music, which had so long been selective in its provision. Challenging the tendency of secondary modern schools to mimic the grammar school model, Holbrook called upon education to 'exercise ... the whole mind and all kinds of apprehensions, not only intellectual ones' (1964: 10). Like Marshall (1968) and Slade (1954), Holbrook redefines the teacher's role as that of initiator and guide, stressing that creative decisions must be made by the children concerned:

> Creative work can't be all giving: and so children need to hear poems and stories read to them – and if it is possible, what the teacher reads should be related to current themes in their work, and current interests shown in it.
>
> (Holbrook, 1967: 15)

Holbrook's recognition that successful English teaching should involve an exchange between existing works and children's ideas offers the clearest invitation yet for music teachers to follow suit. If the false separation of reading and writing, of interpretation and expression, had been damaging to English teaching, so performing and composing were in even greater need of being reconciled in music education.

3.2 The national recognition of educational change

The educational developments of the 1960s were firmly rooted in the classroom, but evidence of changing priorities at a national level is provided by the Central Advisory Council for Education report, *Half Our Future* (1963). This enquiry, chaired by Newsom, had a remit that was very much of its time:

> To consider the education between the ages of 13 and 16 of pupils of average or less than average ability who are or will be following full-time courses either at schools or in establishments of further education. The term education shall be understood to include extra-curricular activities.
>
> (Ministry of Education, 1963: xv)

This report did not set out to glorify the achievements of the grammar schools, but to measure the success of the post-war promise that all pupils would receive secondary education according to their needs and interests. The report considers general questions of school organisation and staffing, before going on to evaluate the provision for individual subjects. As the inclusion of 'extra-curricular' activities in their definition of education shows, the committee were sympathetic to the need for a balanced and engaging curriculum, which made a careful appraisal of musical provision a likely element of their report.

Half Our Future encapsulated the ideals and realities of a generation that was responding to the effects of the post-war raising of the school leaving age, and seeking a more purposeful education for its young people. 'Liberal' education was the focus of the recommendations, the intention being that pupils should be prepared, not just for work, but for a fulfilling life that balanced leisure and employment. Amongst the committee's more radical proposals was the suggestion that the school timetable should be re-ordered, with a longer working day that included 'extra-curricular' activities, felt to deserve more recognition. This 'Newsom' day would have had direct benefit for music, allowing co-operative activities across year groups to gain greater status, but although subsequent writers have returned to the concept (cf. Kwami, 1996: 72), the idea has never been widely adopted. In the 1960s, classroom music was not sufficiently developed for this broader perspective on music education to be supported, and the belief that only the musically 'talented' could benefit from opportunities that were currently extra-curricular will have increased the resistance to their inclusion in a redesigned timetable.

The section of the report concerned with music (ibid.: 139–41) offers valuable insight upon the ideals of the time, and goes some way towards explaining why music lagged behind the other arts in its development. As in the Hadow Report (1926), music appears low down on the priority list, grouped with handicraft, rural studies and physical education in the 'practical subjects', with English and drama taking their place amongst the 'humanities'. Despite the limitations of this separation of subjects and arbitrary categorisation of the arts, the comments of the Newsom committee reveal a genuine interest in arts education, and a greater recognition of their role in a balanced curriculum.

Given the general ideals of *Half Our Future*, the detail of the music section makes chastening reading, as the vibrant musical culture of the adolescent is contrasted with a poorly-resourced and inadequate diet of school music:

> Out of school, adolescents are enthusiastically engaged in musical self-education. They crowd the record shops at weekends, listening and buying, and within the range of their preferences, they are often

knowledgeable and highly critical of performance – and the technical
performance of the music they like is frequently high.
(Ministry of Education, 1963: 139)

The Newsom committee's survey shows that the developing interest in music
amongst young people was not being met by their teachers, a point later noted
by Swanwick (1968) in his discussion of popular music in the curriculum. The
description of 'flourishing' school music departments which follows in the
Report refers exclusively to performance activities, and it is clear that the
definitions of 'music' in and out of school are not consistent. Out of school,
adolescents are seen to be 'self-educating', critical listeners; in school, they are
directed in group performance activities (ibid.: 140). Their sense of musical
identity is clearly in conflict, and it is hardly surprising that pupils behave
differently in each context, a problem also encountered in physical education
(ibid.: 138). The Newsom committee assert that the restricted content of the
lessons is to blame for pupils' rejection of 'school music', suggesting that a
variety of musical experiences would be more likely to maintain pupils' interest
in the subject:

> Apart from singing ... there is much else that can profitably be
> attempted: various forms of instrumental music, training in selective
> and critical listening with the aid of scores, a combined musical and
> scientific approach to the phenomena of sound, all can play their part
> in the scheme.
>   (Ministry of Education, 1963: 140)

Presumably, the approaches suggested here are radical for their time, implying
that class singing lessons were still the standard diet of secondary music pupils,
with more exciting performance opportunities provided outside the classroom
for those with sufficient commitment or talent. No mention is made of
composition or improvisation, which is indicative of the entrenched attitudes
that Self (1967), Schafer (1965; 1967; 1969) and Paynter and Aston (1970)
were to face when their ideas reached publication a few years later. Amongst
the report's perceptive observations, traditional values are still evident, as in
the cautious recommendation that 'pop' music should be used as a step towards
'more serious and substantial music' (Ministry of Education, ibid.: 141). The
committee's endorsement of music as a source of individual growth and
learning is laudable, but draws heavily on the community spirit arguments of
the pre-war years:

> Music can clearly be a potent force in the lives of many young people.
> It is a natural source of recreation, and one form of activity which can

be carried on from school through adult life; its contribution to both the school community and the larger community can be notable. It deserves generous encouragement.

(Ministry of Education, 1963: 141)

Half Our Future calls for better facilities and resources for music education, stating that 'music is frequently the worst equipped and accommodated subject in the curriculum' (ibid.: 141). It can have been no coincidence that music was also the subject most frequently dropped from the curriculum, with the 'unduly narrow conception of the subject' (ibid.: 140) causing boys to reject the experience of singing lessons as their voices changed. Although the practical recommendations offered as a solution are limited, the committee demonstrates some vision in supporting music education despite the lamentable evidence that had been collected. In doing so the report offered, if not a practical way forward, at least a basis of encouragement and idealism upon which the rising generation of educational and musical thinkers could build.

Other reports of the early 1960s confirm the limited role of music in the curriculum, with the West Riding Education Committee (1953; 1965) reporting an increase in peripatetic instrumental teachers, but few significant changes to classroom music. The second edition of the government report, *Music in Schools* (DES, 1956/69), also reveals a stagnation in music education practice, which was still largely dependent on singing and music history:

On the whole ... music has changed less in schools than it has done outside, partly because ideas take time to crystallise, but mainly because facilities for musical work have not kept pace with fast developing needs.

(DES, 1956/69: v)

With resources, ideas and staff training failing to keep pace with new ideas in arts education and in popular music, it is all the more remarkable that the changes to music education brought about in the decade to follow were able to flourish. The early 1960s saw innovations in composition teaching occurring in isolated pockets across the country, generated by musicians who had a new interest in fostering musical development through creative activities. Perhaps even more than for previous decades, it is difficult to determine the extent to which practice had developed before the publications of the late 1960s and 1970s brought new ideas to the forefront of the music education debate. Publication dates in themselves can be misleading, as Paynter, Self and colleagues were all active as teachers at least a decade before their ideas became public knowledge. Similarly, the slow dissemination of innovatory ideas that has been observed throughout the century will have delayed the adoption of new approaches to teaching music, creating almost a generational gap, as ideas evolve, are published and are slowly assimilated. In discussing the ideas that follow, therefore, the chronology necessary for coherent reading should not be allowed to obscure the sense of exchange and excitement that fostered new thinking in music education around this time.

3.3 A new direction for music education

The influence of the 'composer-teacher' had been developing throughout the century, with Stravinsky, Schoenberg and Hindemith amongst those who shared musical ideas and techniques with a select group of students (Lawrence, 1978: 47). In the 1960s and 1970s, this model reached mainstream schools, as a small number of young composers took up teaching posts, so bringing their musical experience to an unprecedented number of pupils. This model of education was by no means widespread, as it was entirely dependent upon the influence of individual composers, but it was part of a broader movement that was redefining the nature of music teaching:

> The teacher's task is ... to participate in enquiry, and to help his students participate also. The composer obviously welcomes such an attitude to teaching, for the nature of his own work is constantly bound up in investigation and exploration.
>
> (Lawrence, 1978: 82)

Peter Maxwell Davies' work as a 'composer-teacher' at Cirencester Grammar School provides a well-publicised example of an approach to music teaching that reflected the influences of the avant-garde within a framework of educational freedom. It must be remembered in discussing his work, however, that similar practices are likely to have co-existed elsewhere in the country, for which documentation and contemporary comment is not readily available. Davies took up his appointment at Cirencester in 1959, the same year that Long published his survey detailing the extreme variation in musical provision across the country. This further reminder that Davies' ideas and methods were unusually innovative is timely, as it is easy to exaggerate the effects of an isolated success story:

> His achievements at the school were both remarkable and praiseworthy; but his experience there was not one which he sort either to prolong or to repeat. Faced with permanency at Cirencester,

> Davies must have found himself as frustrated and restless as J. S. Bach was in his teaching post at St. Thomas's, Leipzig.
>
> (Rainbow, 1989: 333)

With Rainbow's caution in mind, it is useful to look at Davies' teaching experience, not least because its publicity will have brought it to the attention of a significant proportion of teaching contemporaries. Like the successful music educators of earlier generations (Donington, 1932; Smith, 1947), Davies' teaching style was dependent on his own musical enthusiasms and experiences, and was not easily transferable to other schools. Nevertheless, Davies and his like-minded contemporaries were exploring new opportunities for composing in the classroom which would form part of a wider redefining of music education.

Seabrook's (1994) biography of 'Max' acknowledges that the media interest in his work must have given Davies a certain additional credibility amongst his pupils, and suggests that the informal atmosphere of Davies' lessons caused the most criticism from traditionalists:

> In a system less starched, in a less rigidly conservative country, Max's methods might have been thought perhaps a trifle unconventional. In a 500-year-old grammar school in a sleepy English market town, they were regarded as quite extraordinarily iconoclastic. Yet these supposedly revolutionary methods really amounted to nothing more than the concept of getting the pupils themselves, the children and young people for whose benefit the education system existed, involved in the subject of the course – getting them right to the heart of the matter, writing and performing music of their own.
>
> (Seabrook, 1994: 51)

A refusal to talk down to his pupils apparently led to the perception of Davies as a rebel, not least because of the 'inner circle' of young friends who would visit his home for recitals and discussions about music (Seabrook, 1994: 54). Communicating with the pupils about his own work, and about their compositions, necessitated a breaking down of the traditional classroom power structures, which must have represented a threat to Davies' more conservative colleagues, and certainly to those music teachers in other schools who heard about his work without seeing its effects.

Davies' own descriptions of his teaching methods and intentions appear in the Colston Papers (Grant, 1963) and in a collection of reports on the arts in education (Britton, 1963). At the time of his speech to the Colston Research Symposium in April 1962, Davies had been at Cirencester for three years, and was able to recall the tasks of selecting and arranging music for the school choir and orchestra, and also introducing composition sessions with improvisation on primary triads:

> The very first step to composition is improvisation. Composition, after all, is much slowed-down and chewed-over improvisation.
>
> (Grant, 1963: 114)

These ideas are explained more fully in Britton's text, where Davies describes the use of his own work in the classroom and for school performances, seeing himself as a role model for his pupils: 'if one person is creating something positively, this catches on, and others do so too.' (Britton, 1963: 26). Davies taught tonal harmony as a basis for improvisation, believing that freedom would come from this secure knowledge, in a way that presumably reflected his own development as a composer. Children were encouraged to conduct the orchestra in their own compositions, allowing a real engaging with the sound, along with the opportunity of a premiere in one of Davies' concerts in Cirencester Parish Church, events that combined his own work with a showcase for school performers and composers.

Perhaps the most revealing perspective on Davies' teaching is found in the questions that delegates at the Colston Symposium put to him. The first speaker voiced the assumption that can be traced throughout the development of music education, that the teacher in question must be working with exceptionally enthusiastic and talented children. Davies' response to this might have caused wry smiles amongst his colleagues; whilst he agreed that the children were generally lively, he added 'They are rather sleepy, coming from Gloucestershire' (Grant, 1963: 116). A number of other questions focused on another perennial concern, that of classroom discipline. Unable, or unwilling, to provide the 'principles' of teaching that his audience requested, Davies asserted that his experience, developed without preconceived ideas about teaching, had shown him that a confidence in children's ability was sufficient to ensure a valuable shared musical experience.

Whilst Davies' importance as an educator can be over-emphasised, it is true to say that his years at Cirencester highlighted a number of ideas that were to be of consequence in the gradually changing approach to music education of the 1960s and 1970s. The relationship between teacher and pupil was certainly to change, as it became acknowledged that experience and learning could be shared with benefit to both parties. Similarly, the introduction of composition and improvisation to the classroom was an important step forward, although it needed further rationale before it could be adopted by teachers who were not themselves established composers. Davies' practice was important, but for the development of these ideas into a form that did not depend so much on the personality, status and expertise of the teacher, the influence of other educational and musical innovators was needed.

3.4 Cage in the classroom: the musical context

Music education up to this point had been driven by the music of the past, with pupils being trained to appreciate or perform the classical masterworks that formed the mainstream concert repertoire. Music history, notation, aural perception and sight-singing were all based on the values of the musical establishment, perpetuating the notion that engaging with sound in a creative sense was done by an élite species of musician; the composer. With the arrival of composers in the classroom from the late 1950s onwards, albeit in limited numbers, the supremacy of the performing tradition was challenged, and contemporary music began to exert an influence. Atonality, serialism and minimalism had brought a new freedom to composers, with their inherent questioning of the nature of music and composing. Music was being redefined and this exploration began to shape the direction of music teaching in schools.

> The Future of Music: Credo
> I believe that the use of noise
> to make music
> will continue and increase until we reach a
> music produced through the aid of electrical
> instruments
> which will make available for musical
> purposes any and all sounds that can
> be heard. Photoelectric, film, and
> mechanical mediums for the synthetic
> production of music
> will be explored. Whereas, in the past,
> the point of disagreement has been
> between dissonance and consonance,
> it will be, in the immediate future,
> between noise and so-called musical sounds.
>
> (Cage, 1968/78: 3)

The creed of composer John Cage, which opens his book of performance lectures and writings, *Silence* (1968/78), is interspersed with a discussion of the direction in which electronic instruments are taking the music of the twentieth century. Cage's writing, like his music, made an important contribution to thinking about music education, echoing as it did the ideas about the nature of music which supported the greater prominence of composition in the classroom. Paynter recalls the 'spirit of adventure' (personal communication, 1996) that the Americans of Cage's generation brought to Britain, and Walker, a practising teacher in the 1960s, recalls that his own teaching was influenced by the 'new possibilities in sound' (Walker, 1983: 87) that Cage's music offered. As a challenging writer and composer, Cage brought avant-garde music to the attention of those music teachers who sensed a general hostility to modern music in schools. Walker reflects on the change to his teaching methods:

> An important question is why [did we change]! There are two basic
> reasons: one is the observed effects of teaching traditional music skills
> of performance and listening in a traditional manner, and the other is
> exposure to works by contemporary composers and a growing
> puzzlement over why colleagues teaching in other subject areas like
> language or visual arts could freely use contemporary sources while
> music teachers felt a hidden pressure to ignore this obvious source of
> educational material.
>
> (Walker, 1983: 86)

Teachers with Walker's awareness of contemporary music had realised that the disparity between music and art teaching observed in the 1940s and 1950s (cf. Ministry of Education, 1949) was making school music increasingly archaic, and far removed from the developments in musical culture as a whole. Answers could not be found simply by modifying existing methods, in the manner of the slow change throughout the first half of the century, but demanded a new evaluation of the whole purpose of teaching music. This was, of course, an unwelcome challenge for many of the classically trained performers who had found a comfortable role in the music teaching profession.

Ideas resonant with Cage's exploration of musical concepts had been absorbed by composers with strong interests in music education, notably Self (1967) and Schafer (1965; 1969). *New Sounds in Class* evolved from work carried out in schools by Self in the mid-1960s, and was subtitled 'a practical approach to the understanding and performing of contemporary music in schools' (Self, 1967). Self's approach is fairly didactic, and his book includes a history of twentieth-century music for those teachers whose traditional training had neglected this study, and a collection of graphic scores to be performed by classroom percussion ensembles. Self saw the need to broaden pupils' experience of music, just as art and literature teachers were encouraging children to 'use the language of their own time':

The aim of this book is to form a link between contemporary music and instrumental work in the classroom. It is not intended to provide an alternative to existing methods of music training, but to be complementary to it. Pupils so often leave school with little knowledge of even the existence of the serious music of their own time and yet for the first time in this century it is possible to introduce avant-garde idioms into the classroom without watering down the style to such an extent that no living music remains.

(Self, 1967: 2)

Self's choice of language reveals a perception of education that is not as radical as his crusade to bring avant-garde music into classrooms would suggest (cf. Self, 1965). 'Music training' is not a phrase that suggests creativity and exploration, but rather a progression towards a fixed end. Performance activities are seen as a means of acquiring knowledge about music, and although a more active engagement with this knowledge is clearly desirable, Self is not promising the creative returns that later writers would document with enthusiasm. *New Sounds in Class* uses a form of simplified notation that encourages improvisation within certain parameters, and Self sees this as a valuable movement away from the restrictions of conventional scoring:

This is a new and valid experience ... following on well from the interesting work now being done with many infant classes, and a parallel to the freer forms of movement and painting already flourishing in our schools, which have done so much to bring out the individuality of the children. It is a sad reflection that although many children use their creative energies in painting and poetry, their musical activities are usually confined to performance and listening; with simplified notation it is possible for average children to compose music – and almost this alone would warrant its introduction.

(Self, 1967: 3)

Self's 'Contemporary Percussion Music' requires a degree of interpretation which is undoubtedly creative, but the exploration of sound is carefully controlled and the teacher retains a directing role. The sense of uncertainty that was to slow down the widespread adoption of composition in the classroom is discernible here, as the 'average' children that Self envisages are asked to work through a series of creative 'exercises'; surely a contradiction in terms. The impetus for his work is evidently the failure of music educators to acknowledge the contemporary music scene, relying instead on the peculiar genre of 'educational music':

> The rate of change of style is such that there is more difference
> between the music of 1900 and 1960 than between that of 1500 and
> 1900; – and still the presses continue to turn out music in outmoded
> styles, adding further bolts to the door barring the way of the young to
> the music of today.
>
> (Self, 1965: 126)

Self's attempt to bring new music into schools centred upon a 'simplified' notation, which he claimed would free children from the restrictions of the tonal system implicit in staff notation. His graphic scores were designed to enable classroom performances, but the improvisatory elements are carefully controlled within the score and regulated in performance by the conductor. Comparisons with the Percussion Band of the 1930s are perhaps unfair, but the lessons in *New Sounds in Class* offer a similarly predictable route through musical experience, marking a departure from tradition, but not necessarily a new creative future for music education.

A more lively approach to similar ideas was taken by Dennis (1970), who invited pupils to explore the 'new world of sound' offered by electronic distortion techniques. Drawing parallels with the music of Stockhausen, Berio and Cage (ibid.: 23), Dennis asserts that improvisation in the classroom could end the tedium of linking aural perception with the learning of notation:

> Experimenting with sound satisfies one of the most fundamental drives
> in a young person – namely curiosity or the desire to explore. ... The
> most beautiful piece of music or the most interesting piece of music
> often fails to move a child. What he discovers for himself as a
> spontaneous by-product of a practical activity more often fires his
> imagination.
>
> (Dennis, 1970: 3)

For the first time, music educators were writing from the same perspective as Richardson (1948), Slade (1954), and Marshall (1963), emphasising the effect that a children's development had on their experience of learning. More importantly, the connection with composition was being made by an increasing number of music teachers, offering colleagues a range of ideas and descriptions of practice to assimilate.

Perhaps the most challenging writings of the late 1960s are those of Schafer, a Canadian composer and music educator who published a series of books drawing on his own experience of teaching in secondary and higher education. Whilst his practical work was mostly undertaken abroad, Schafer's writings were available in Britain throughout the 1960s and 1970s, and his connection with the ideas of Paynter and Aston (1970) warrants his inclusion in the consideration of developments in this country. Schafer's commitment to an active form of music education is evident throughout his work, most clearly articulated as he embarks on his course of *Ear Cleaning*:

> It is my feeling that one learns practically nothing about the actual functioning of music by sitting in mute surrender before it. As a practising musician I have come to realize that one learns about sound only by making sound, about music only by making music.
>
> (Schafer, 1967:1)

In *The New Soundscape* (1969), Schafer expresses his concerns about the future of music in a world increasingly dominated by mechanical noise, a preoccupation that clearly links with the ideas expressed by Cage (1968/78). The creation of music, for Schafer and Cage alike, was far removed from the traditional school approaches of the 1960s and earlier, and the challenge was to bring a new understanding of music to the next generation of teachers:

> Behold the new orchestra: the sonic universe!
>
> And the new musicians: anyone and anything that sounds!
> There is a shattering corollary to this for all music educators.
>
> For music educators are the custodians of the theory and practice of music.
>
> And the whole nature of this theory and practice is now going to have to be completely reconsidered.
>
> (Schafer, 1969: 2)

As Davies had discovered at Cirencester Grammar School, a new approach to music teaching demands a fresh consideration of the teacher–pupil relationship, with perhaps the loss of some of the inherent power that the teacher's role had traditionally included. Schafer's teaching approach is demonstrated most clearly in his book, *The Composer in the Classroom* (1965), in which he initiates debate about the nature of music, dominating the initial discussion before gradually receding as the students become more confident. These are university students, but he argues that the process of questioning musical experience through practical and intellectual investigation could begin much earlier, in which case the facilitative role of the teacher would be much the same. Schafer's 'maxims for educators' (1975), summarise his views in the that 'there are no more teachers, there is just a community of learners'.

Self and Schafer's writings have a common aim in their attempts to get teachers more involved with the future, not just of education, but of music itself, given that this is directly affected by education. Rather than seeing music in schools as something isolated from the 'real' world of music, these two composer-educators want to convince teachers that their role in influencing the perceptions and experience of young musicians, using that term inclusively, is of great importance. Schafer demonstrates, through his discussions of science, psychology and philosophy, that sound and music have a pervasive influence upon society. Recommending that teachers join a 'noise abatement' society rather than a teachers' union (1969: 4), he redefines music in education, focusing on the potential for structured sound rather than the absorbing of traditional knowledge and repertoire. Schafer's challenge to teachers, echoes Cage's questioning of his listeners' assumptions, as in this extract from *45' For a Speaker*, written in 1954:

	If one feels
30"	protective about the word 'music', protect
	it and find another word for
	all the rest that enters through the
	ears. It's a waste of time to trouble
	oneself with words, noises. What it
	is is theatre and we are in it and
40"	like it, making it.

(Cage, 1968/78: 190)

Davies had already demonstrated that the teacher's total commitment to this new approach to music teaching was essential to its success, a condition that must have been hard for a good proportion of the profession to meet. Accordingly, the 1970s saw new efforts to communicate somewhat ephemeral ideas in a more constructive form, and the decade opened with perhaps the most influential of these texts, *Sound and Silence* (Paynter & Aston, 1970).

3.6 *Sound and Silence* (1970)

Readers of the *Music in Education* journal in 1967–68 would already have encountered the ideas of Paynter, Aston and Mellers, colleagues in the music department at the University of York. In a series of articles, 'Music in a liberal education', they explored the new approach to music teaching that had evolved through the music education degree at York, with Paynter focusing on the potential of creative exploration of sound (1967: 622), and Aston advancing innovative ideas on the teaching of harmony through composition (1968: 17). Mellers provided an overview of the scope and intentions of this new approach to music education:

> We don't claim that our approach to music education is the only valid one. We do believe that we ask the questions most worth asking and, in attempting to answer them, aim high, with our feet on the solid earth.
>
> (Mellers, 1968: 133)

Mellers' decision to launch a series of books on music education in 1969 provided the opportunity for Paynter and Aston to publish some of the ideas that had come from their own teaching experience. *Sound and Silence* (1970) is a series of projects, based on the workshop style of teaching that Paynter had developed in the classroom:

> Over a period of ten years I had developed these workshop techniques, based on the notion of the *atelier*, a kind of corporate endeavour: not entirely open and free, and not directed, but *led*.
>
> (Paynter: Interview, 6 June 1997)

Sound and Silence begins with descriptions of students who are encountering music at different stages of their education, implying that the relevance of the musical experience is universal. 'Alan, aged six' makes music as he acts the part of 'the Wolf creeping out of the deep, dark forest'; a group of teenage children round a camp fire improvise harmonies to a well-known song; and students in a College of Education explore sounds to create a composition for piano and drums (ibid.: 1). Although the importance of improvisation is clear from these examples, the more powerful message concerns the effect that music is having for these people. Alan is 'lost in the world of his imagination', and as such exemplifies the strong relationship between music and the individual that the authors are promoting. Also emphasised is the fact that none of these musicians have been 'instructed', but have generated music for themselves when given the opportunity. This 'ownership', to use the jargon of later decades, is particularly evident in the account of the College of Education students:

> Before this morning neither of them had ever thought of creating music. They chose to do this, decided on the sounds they wanted to explore, and have worked these sounds over and over until they have become the right sounds, the only possible sounds through which to say what has to be said. By this time tomorrow their piece will be

refined and carefully notated in a system of their own inventing. They will have thoroughly explored their own music and met on the way with the music of Cowell and Stockhausen. They will not have been *taught* anything: how can we say how much music they will have learned?

(Paynter & Aston, 1970: 1)

The creative process described here is common to all composers, as the selection and organisation of sounds is the essence of making music. The idea that pupils should be able to experience music from inside the act of creation demanded a questioning of the values held by a generation of music educators; values that were entrenched in their own education and musicianship, and therefore resistant to apparent criticism. Opposition to the work of Paynter and Aston came largely from those musicians and teachers who were unable to answer the question posed in the extract above: how to measure this new mode of knowledge?

Reaction to Paynter and Aston's ideas was inevitably mixed, but a favourable review in *Music in Education* is probably typical of those teachers who welcomed the publication of *Sound and Silence*:

> The very clarity of the language and the manner in which this excellent material is organised provides in itself a convincing argument against those whose attitudes relegate creative work to the status of meaningless 'waffle', or equally those who avoid it because of an apparent lack of ordered progress.

(Payne, 1970: 160)

Paynter recalls receiving a number of letters from teachers saying that they were working in similar ways (Interview: 6 June 1997), which suggests that where the support of headteachers and music advisers was strong, the climate was right for change. The clarification of ideas in *Sound and Silence* will have helped teachers who were experiencing differing degrees of certainty about the new style of music education, whilst providing encouragement for those already familiar with composing and improvising in the classroom. The authors' modest request, 'Perhaps we should place slightly more emphasis on creative music in schools than we have been doing' (ibid.: 3), shows a respect for developments already in place, but the need for more substantial change was becoming widely apparent.

Paynter and Aston offer practical models for teachers, but their determination to provide a clear philosophy on which to base their creative projects shows their intention that teachers, as well as pupils, should be thinking for themselves and questioning the purpose of education. *Sound and*

Silence has the appearance of a handbook for teachers, but the authors make it clear that the text is not 'a series of lesson notes' (1970: 9). The project ideas demand creativity on the teachers' part, and it is important that the approach is understood, rather than the suggestions being adopted without conviction. Whereas Read had stated 'I am not a teacher' (1943/56: 294), the authors of *Sound and Silence* express solidarity with the readers of their work:

> We who are writing this book are practising teachers and musicians who are concerned with general rather than specialist education. We believe that young people deserve a truly liberal education, alive with the excitement of discovery. This excitement is a first step: the details, disciplines and skills will follow. Without a sense of adventure true education is impossible.
>
> (Paynter & Aston, 1970: 3)

Perhaps as a result of their practising musicianship, Paynter and Aston claim a prominent place in the classroom for twentieth-century music and techniques, in the same way that contemporary art and literature had found acceptance in schools. The focus is on 'sound organisation' (ibid.: 7), engaging with the limitations and possibilities of musical materials in the same way that pupils in an art class were exploring the properties of paint and clay. The approach addresses the very nature of music; what it is that makes a musical composition. It is more ambitious and wide-ranging than the 'tune building' of earlier decades, and goes beyond Self's presentation of contemporary music as a neglected aspect of performance; the intention here being that children should be able to relate to any style of music, given their developing ability to question the processes that have gone into its creation and re-creation.

Paynter and Aston criticise the traditional emphasis on 're-creative' music in schools (ibid.: 6), resisting the common perception of music as a leisure pursuit that had underpinned music education for the first half of the century. 'Music as entertainment' had been a passive subject, with pupils effectively being trained as the next generation of concert-goers or amateur performers. Paynter and Aston were calling for something quite different; for pupils to acquire, not mere knowledge of the standard repertoire, but an understanding of why and how music exists at all. Just as their book offers practical ideas for the teacher, rather than convoluted theorising, so they intended that children should experience music as participants, rather than receivers of information. By identifying the fundamental elements of sound and silence, music becomes accessible on the grounds of imagination and commitment, rather than conventional performance ability. In claiming that music is a language, the authors propose in effect that it should be as freely available as the spoken and written word; to be discovered and explored by all pupils:

> We can begin to explore music creatively at any age; for the first and last 'rule' in making music is the ear. It is our only guide in evaluating the sounds that express things we want to say. The *true* 'rudiments' of music are to be found in an exploration of its materials – sound and silence.
>
> (Paynter & Aston, 1970: 8)

Anticipating the criticisms of their work that might come from traditionalist teachers, Paynter and Aston assert that new methods must not be allowed to supplant established, effective practice: 'Creative experiment is only one small part of music in education: but we believe it is a very important part and one that should not be neglected' (ibid.: 23). The challenges of reforming music education were far from over, with the teaching profession now caught between a traditionalist stance and a more forward-looking acceptance of modern music and its methods. Half-hearted interpretations of the 'creative approach' were to prove damaging in the following decade, as more reactionary teachers blamed the initial ideas for their own failed attempts to implement them. Nevertheless, the sense that task of teaching music could be adapted and interpreted in a multitude of ways was gaining ground, and was to prove influential in the debates over assessment and curriculum reform that began in earnest in the 1980s.

3.7 Confusion and change

Evidence exists to suggest that primary teachers were particularly receptive to the project style of composing in the classroom, adding variants of the Kodály, Orff and Curwen methods to their effective use of school broadcasts (Horton, 1972: 7). Horton's report, *British Primary Schools Today: Music*, was part of the Anglo-American Primary Education Project, and may have been an unduly positive interpretation of 1960s developments. The book comes with a record that provides examples of children's improvisations, some based on the interpretation of stories such as 'Noah's Ark' and 'David and Goliath'. The teacher's role is discussed, with Horton's conclusions in sympathy with those of Schafer (1965) and Paynter and Aston (1970):

> The role of the teacher, clearly defined as director of operations in the traditional choral singing and class-lesson situation, must obviously be

very different in relation to creative activities. ... His first task must be to provide the environment, opportunities, and materials which will make such work possible.

(Horton, 1972: 21)

Successful and inventive improvisation and composition lessons in primary schools were apparently increasing, although the Plowden Report, *Children and their Primary Schools*, had noted that teachers were slow to relinquish whole-class teaching in music in favour of small group activities (DES, 1967: 253).

Fuller accounts of the successful work referred to in Horton's report are given by Pape (1970), who documents the whole-class improvisation sessions that she initiated with her infant classes. Pape describes small groups of children making music inspired by pictures and poems, extending Marshall's project ideas (Marshall, 1963) to overcome the fear of music amongst non-specialist teachers (Pape, 1970: 63). Most of Pape's improvisation sessions were concerned with telling stories through music, with the instrumental resources selected by the children from a range offered by the teacher (ibid.: 72). Although Pape seems to have taken a fairly prominent role in organising the class performances, she is sensitive to the need for a combination of freedom and guidance:

> [Children] need an interested adult to be ready with ideas when necessary and suggestions to get over difficulties, and to help them with the technique of playing the instruments. Encouragement is certainly needed, but I find seven-year-olds can take a certain amount of criticism and act upon it. What they do not want is to have ideas imposed upon them.

(Pape, 1970: 98)

Pape's flexible approach to developing new learning opportunities in music comes across clearly in her writing, and shows the greater receptivity of the typical primary school teacher, who is not constrained by subject boundaries in the same way as a secondary specialist.

Writers who recognised the difficulties of assimilating change at secondary music level included Brocklehurst, whose early ideas (1962) were in sympathy with the innovations that were gradually coming to public notice:

> Most obvious are the opportunities music can provide as a means of self-expression, for awakening and developing the imagination and for emotional and spiritual development; the fact that the aesthetic subjects begin to make a special appeal to children during their

adolescent years makes it all the more deplorable that music should so often cease to be represented on the time-table after the second or third form.

(Brocklehurst, 1962: 6)

This commitment to music is not unusual in itself, and Brocklehurst goes on to offer a well-articulated but fairly traditional curriculum, largely based on singing and aural training. It is in the revision of his ideas for a later publication that Brocklehurst's commitment to the development of music education becomes apparent, as he demonstrates a support for innovation that is admirable in an established figure:

> Aims, like the society they serve, must be dynamic and fluid and curricular developments must keep pace with social change and be correctly oriented to social needs. Unless education mirrors and influences the quality of society and currently held social attitudes and values it will, by serving past needs and being aimed at outmoded goals, be providing an education for an obsolescent society.
>
> (Brocklehurst, 1971: 24)

Brocklehurst discusses at length the place of music in the curriculum, demanding that the teacher should believe music to be 'an indispensable constituent of a truly liberal education' (Brocklehurst, 1971: 3). Curriculum planning, he states, should be the translation of aims into method, and with his concern for pupils other than the conventionally 'musical' shaping his own method, he expresses distrust of the psychological testing that had led to selection and rejection in earlier decades:

> The function of school music should not be to separate the musical sheep from the goats, but to give each child the opportunity to acquire musical intelligence. Even if the most stimulating musical environment cannot greatly affect the likelihood of musical achievement, it can certainly exert a profound influence on musical interests, tastes, attitudes and habits.
>
> (Brocklehurst, 1971: 40)

Many writers of his generation would have gone from these high ideals to a constrained method, but Brocklehurst embraces the modern concepts of popular music in the classroom and the use of creative methods:

> Musical understanding is developed by helping children to organize their experiences in creative and linguistic work, vocal and

87

instrumental performance, movement and listening in order to create a
framework of musical concepts.

(Brocklehurst, 1971: 68)

Brocklehurst is aware of the intolerance of some of his contemporaries towards
recent innovations in music teaching. A reliance on programme music as a tool
for musical 'expression' is warned against, as is the exclusively tonal musical
experience that alienates children from the music of their own time (ibid.: 55).
Group improvisation in non-diatonic styles is suggested, and an impassioned
defence of the new methods offered:

> Experimental work ... is likely to be impatiently dismissed by many
> teachers as time-consuming gimmickry indulged in by
> composer-teachers in search of publicity. This is particularly likely to
> be so in the case of all those teachers who equate all avant-garde
> music with the indiscriminate hurling of pots of paint at canvases. In
> fact, if skilfully approached, such work can develop a highly-sensitive
> awareness of the expressive possibilities of sound and habits of
> concentrated listening and provide an added dimension to creative
> music in schools.

(Brocklehurst, 1971: 55)

As a teacher trainer, Brocklehurst had an advantage over those secondary
teachers who had been isolated in their traditional departments while these
ideas were evolving around them, and was able to apply the successes of
primary school music to the secondary level. In considering the role of the
teacher, Brocklehurst rejects the antiquated methods that still lingered in some
music classrooms:

> The once-popular action song and the percussion band, with its
> automaton-like players and its even more automaton-like child
> conductor, are relics of an age which preferred filling in to drawing
> out and ignored the importance of inventiveness and imagination.

(Brocklehurst, 1971: 74)

Brocklehurst is the archetypal music educator of his generation, conscious of
the values of traditional music teaching, but sympathetic to attempts to move
forward into a new social and educational context. Such support was essential
for his contemporaries, many of whom will have found the generous evaluation
of new developments more difficult.

A deliberate effort to foster creative approaches in secondary music was also
made by the North West Regional Curriculum Development Project (1974).
Teachers' Centres had been set up across the North West in 1968 to study the

implications of the Newsom Report (Ministry of Education, 1963), with a panel established to look at 'Creativity in the Arts' (1974: 2). The music sub-committee devised a curriculum that incorporated the growing interest in the 'creative methods' of composing and arranging, proposing a course in five stages that included 'Exploring Sound', 'Exploring Rhythm and Melody' and 'Musical Constructing' (North West Curriculum Development Project, 1974: 25). This outline curriculum was interpreted in different ways by the teachers who applied it, with 'music making', 'musical insights' and 'co-ordination skills' emphasised by those whose experiences are recounted in the report. An enthusiasm for trying new ideas is evident, and the sub-committee admits that the instruments provided for the Project will have given it extra status and impetus for the pupils involved, as one teacher confirms:

> I described briefly what we were going to try to do with these instruments. I also played a magnetic tape I had prepared using several of the instruments together, with a guitar and piano accordion. The reaction of the group to all this was extremely positive, and I stressed that their comments and ideas were vitally important to the experiment, and that what happened here might affect the whole course of music teaching in other schools in the future.
> (North West Curriculum Development Project, 1974: 44)

Despite the commitment shown by the teachers who decided to become involved in the North West project, many reported a 'mid-course plateau' (ibid.: 51), when the initial exploration was over and more extended activities needed to begin. The need for teacher guidance to prevent extensive repetition or cliché in children's compositions became apparent during the project, with some teachers finding particular difficulties with conventionally-trained instrumentalists (ibid.: 45):

> Critics of creative approaches to teaching often argue that such work is a soft option, easy to teach and lacking in either rigorous standards or sense of direction. Our experience in this project suggests that teachers approaching the work in any such spirit will encounter breakdown so complete as to render any further progress impossible.
> (North West Curriculum Development Project, 1974: 52)

Paynter (1982) was also to remark upon the damaging effects of a half-hearted approach to composing in the classroom, asserting that a lack of commitment on the teacher's part will inevitably be communicated to the children. As with all changes in music education, the adopting of a new method without an understanding of its ideals and intentions was the weakest foundation for development.

The review of the North West Project is honest in its reflections on the successes and the difficulties of the trial curriculum, acknowledging that practical constraints still presented a barrier to development in many schools:

> Many schools still have no special provision of music accommodation, and even where such is in existence it may not be suitable for creative work. ... The devastating effects of having to undertake creative activities within thirty-five-minute periods which had to include time for transportation of instruments to and from a singularly inadequate room may be left to the imagination of the reader.
>
> (North West Curriculum Development Project, 1974: 74)

Despite these problems, the majority of those involved in the Project felt that the activities they had trialled had been more successful than their conventional lessons (ibid.: 78). The curriculum, originally designed for the 'less able' in line with the Newsom project remit, was felt to be relevant to all but the most precocious pupils, challenging the existing distinction between 'O' Level students and non-examination classes (ibid.: 82). The support for the teachers involved in the project had obviously led them to a greater understanding of the new methods than would have been acquired from texts alone, showing the benefits of sharing ideas and resources amongst colleagues:

> Collectively teachers bring much wisdom, insight and skill to such work. Even more important, they can develop significantly greater measures of professional skill as the work proceeds, given scope for interacting purposefully in an accepting and supportive climate.
>
> (North West Curriculum Development Project, 1974: 87)

The North West Project had demonstrated a significant need in music education; with a wealth of ideas and resources available, teachers were in need of support to implement and evaluate innovations in music teaching. The model demonstrated here, of local teachers' centres being used for professional discussion and training, had potential benefits for music teachers across the country. Whilst the standardisation of practice was not seen as desirable, the opportunity for teachers to learn from each other offered an effective route to the dissemination of new ideas. For the majority of teachers, however, the confusion of previous decades continued, as innovatory and traditional ideas continued to be published, setting up an apparent conflict between creative methods and existing music provision in schools.

3.8 Security and tradition

Whilst Brocklehurst (1962; 1971) had shown enthusiasm for developments in music education, Rainbow (1956/71) surely spoke for a significant number of his contemporaries when he offers a more guarded evaluation:

> If this new style music-teaching is developed in isolation, it can all too easily be made to contradict the traditional aims of the music lesson. But these dangers will be avoided if the teacher sets out to integrate this new *branch* of school music into a well-balanced syllabus aimed ... towards helping the child to become musically articulate, literate and responsive.
>
> (Rainbow, 1956/71: 89)

Rainbow's retention of the 'traditional aims' of the music curriculum is unsurprising, and is likely to have been supported by teachers who had enjoyed similar success with more conventional methods. As Norman Barnes had demonstrated in Sheffield (1983), the incentive to change was weakest where established performing traditions appeared to be offering a fulfilling music education already (cf. Section 3.5).

The Schools Council Working Paper, *Music and the Young School Leaver: Problems and Opportunities* (1971), captured the ambivalent response to change in its very title. Its publication shortly after *Sound and Silence* (Paynter & Aston, 1970) demonstrated the confusion that existed, as the authors sought to define a purpose for music in secondary education:

> Some would stress [music's] purely aesthetic importance, as a mode of experience distinct from any other; some strongly advocate it as a creative medium through which the personality can be developed and enriched; others would emphasize its social function in the community; others again find in music a focus for the interrelation of subject interests and thus for breaking down barriers between disciplines.
>
> (Schools Council, 1971: 8)

Writers on music education had been investigating these problems for decades, or even centuries, but with the changing approach to the aspects of the musical experience that were to be included in the classroom, a new dilemma had emerged. Music had to be presented to young people in a way that they perceived to be relevant to their present and future needs, with the prominence of music in the teenage sub-culture paradoxically causing resentment of its presence in school teaching (ibid.: 9).

The Schools Council report includes a brief historical survey of changes to music teaching in the twentieth century, developing from the 'choral society rehearsal in miniature' (ibid.: 12) of the early decades towards the contemporary perspective on creativity and notation:

> However important it may be to make as many pupils as possible musically *literate*, it is still more important to make them musically *articulate* through engagement in playing, singing and perhaps movement; only through the growth of such active participation can the value of notation be realized.
>
> (Schools Council, 1971: 20)

That a Schools Council publication is advocating methods pioneered some years earlier, even as far back as Yorke Trotter's notion of 'the sound before the sign' (cf. Yorke Trotter, 1914: 76), is evidence of the huge delay in assimilating any educational innovation. There is little mention of composition in this report, and much reassurance is offered for teachers who are working within the 'established pattern' of classroom music (ibid.: 20). The 'Newsom' day, with its inclusion of extra-curricular activities in the timetable, is supported, and avant-garde music with its new notation is brought to the attention of readers. For some, this will have been revolutionary enough, as the range of texts on music education that emerged during this decade show that it was indeed a time of 'problems and opportunities'.

A contemporary review of the decade 1965–75 is provided by Taylor, who researched the period first as an MA thesis (1977) and then as the publication *Music Now* (1979). Her views seem to be rooted in the more traditional thinking of the time, as she states that music teaching should include the introduction to established skills and ideas, 'at the same time providing the means whereby they can develop, adapt or possibly discard that tradition as they grow in confidence and individuality' (Taylor, 1977: 128). Taylor's evaluation of the work of 'Paynter and Ashton' (a mistake she makes in both texts) shows a distrust of the new teaching ideas that cannot have been untypical at the time. Recognising the wide range of new pressures on the music curriculum, not least through the expansion of the 'commercial leisure industry' (1979: 98), she expresses a concern similar to Rainbow's (1956/71: 89) at the prevalence of so-called 'creative' methods:

> Recently the search for 'creativity' in musical activity (in the sense of both 'originality' and 'exploration') appears to have received a disproportionate amount of the timetable.
>
> (Taylor, 1979: 114)

Despite this ambivalence, Taylor refers to Davies' work at Cirencester Grammar School as 'a landmark' amongst the variable provision in existence across the country (ibid.: 17). She applauds the 'burgeoning of instrumental performance' (ibid.: 105) that resulted from the appointment of music advisers and peripatetic teachers in the 1950s, developments that in themselves show allegiance to pre-war ideals.

Taylor's ambivalent views on the value of 'creative' music education are shared by Devlin and Warnock (1977), whose proposed model for a common curriculum includes the 'aesthetic subjects', seen as essential for developing interest and imagination, as well as skills specific to each art (ibid.: 91). In the case of music, however, the arguments are almost contradictory, as the attempt to include skills and expression becomes entangled:

> Music is in a very special position ... since learning a skill may lead directly to learning about the work of composers. It is absurd to expect children to *become* composers unless they have at least some knowledge of the requirements of musical composition, and they can have the pleasures and discipline of expressing themselves by actually playing and singing the works of others. So it is a mistake to hustle them into composition, even improvisation, without a good deal of actual teaching of technique as a preliminary.
>
> (Devlin & Warnock, 1977: 91)

Some of the confusions of the time are evident here, as new teaching ideas are judged by old criteria. Nevertheless, there is some optimism in the inclusion of music amongst the subjects that should be compulsory but not examined (ibid.: 86), suggesting that the marginalisation of music was at last being challenged.

Where traditional perceptions of music in schools were retained, they were often coupled with the assumption that the training of performers was a particularly important and specialised aspect of music education. The Calouste Gulbenkian Foundation Reports, *Making Musicians* (1965) and *Training Musicians* (1978), are extreme examples of this attitude, based as they are on the assumption that those destined for careers as performers should be educated in specialist music schools. Music in the curriculum is given greater consideration in the second of these reports, but the developments in composing in the classroom are given little support:

> Some of those who gave evidence to us have seen creative music-making as a barrier to the acquisition of more traditional musical skills, such as accuracy of pitch and rhythm in singing and the ability to use musical notation. Indeed, one of the disturbing trends which was drawn to our attention is the decline in disciplined class

singing, which can often provide a solid basis for awakening young children's interest in music, as well as providing a context in which even the non-music specialist class teacher can begin to identify the early stirrings of young talent.

(Calouste Gulbenkian Foundation, 1978: 37)

Evidence of similar attitudes can be found in Bentley's (1975) view of music education, which is greatly influenced by his work on musical ability testing (1966). Bentley argues against the growing tendency to focus on 'music for all', stressing that the early identification of performing ability should not be neglected:

> Given early and reasonable experiences and facilities, children soon discover for themselves who is 'better' in musical skills than the majority; and most people would agree that the earlier any performing ability, aptitude or talent is discovered, the better for the child.

(Bentley, 1975: 16)

Singing, listening and percussion work remain central to Bentley's curriculum, with the 'nervousness and aggression' induced in orchestral players by contemporary music cited as a reason for avoiding it in the classroom (ibid.: 55). There is a sense in which the measurable elements of musical ability that Bentley had identified in his test battery provided a secure foundation for music teaching that he was reluctant to move away from. He emphasises that the 'Measures' should be carefully employed, used with 'due caution ... for the selection of children for musical activities requiring more than average abilities' and also 'to disclose hitherto unsuspected high ability' (ibid.: 103).

The conflict between the traditional instrumental training to which Bentley remains loyal and the new classroom methods that were developing is apparent, and was remarked upon by Addison, who felt that conventionally trained pupils were at a disadvantage when asked to improvise. The perceived difference between 'real' and 'creative' music felt by these children echoed the prejudice of some teachers, who remained suspicious of composing projects:

> Physical conditions, rigid time-tables, children's behaviour problems and noise are not much nearer to being solved today than they were ten years ago, and they continue to prevent teachers from working in a way that they would like. In spite of these reservations I think we can safely say that a major development in music learning has been happening during the last ten years, as children are gaining experience in handling the physical materials of music through their own creative experience.

(Addison, 1975: 60)

The belief that 'musical' children should be educated differently from the less gifted majority was apparently delaying the acceptance of classroom reforms in some quarters. Such objections were to continue into the next decade (cf. Fletcher, 1987/89), becoming increasingly vociferous as the changes in class music were more widely and successfully implemented.

It is clear that, despite the new influences in twentieth-century music and its compositional techniques, many of the ideals of the 1960s had historical precedents, representing enduring values in music education (cf. Kendall, 1989). There is a direct connection between Yorke Trotter and Paynter, for example, both in their shared concern for the importance of the individual in the musical experience, and also through shared contact with Gladys Puttick, Yorke Trotter's pupil who was later one of Paynter's teachers. As music education moved towards the psychological and sociological theorising of the 1980s, a rationalisation of new approaches began, notably in Swanwick's influential work, *A Basis for Music Education* (1979). A perceived conflict between 'traditional' and 'progressive' methods was emerging that was to shape educational thinking, and often frustrate its progress, in the coming decades. The assumption that creative methods in music teaching must necessarily supplant more structured teaching was to prove damaging, as unsuccessful attempts to encourage composing in the classroom caused concern that talented performers would be neglected.

The expansion of ideas in the ensuing decade was to lead to an increasingly complicated debate, as writers began to examine the influence of popular culture (Vulliamy & Lee, 1976/80), and to construct curriculum theories that attempted to clarify recent developments (Swanwick, 1979). Practical innovations continued to evolve (Paynter, 1982), and the place of music within the broader arts curriculum was considered as educators sought to define the aims and intentions of the new approaches (Witkin, 1974). Whereas the ideas of the 1960s and 1970s had been developed largely in the classroom, supported by national and regional reports and projects, a move towards increasing political intervention was to emerge during the following decade. The legislative fervour of the late 1980s was still some way off, but the emphasis on classroom-based discovery and evolution was to have a limited life. In the next chapter, the theories of music education that emerged from the innovations of the 1960s and 1970s will be considered in the context of the changing educational climate.

Chapter 4

Models of musical learning: late 1970s–mid-1980s

4.1 Conceptual frameworks in music education

After the practical innovations of the 1960s and early 1970s, the decade that followed can be seen as a time of reflection and of the promotion of new and often conflicting ideas. As the scope for school music expanded, so too did the awareness of popular and world musics, putting teachers under pressure to accommodate a broader musical curriculum. The continued increase in relevant publications meant that the debate on the purposes and priorities of music education widened, with a wealth of written material now available to those who chose to engage with the complex arguments and their practical implications. Several Schools Council projects were underway, showing that arts education, and music in particular, was gaining financial and political support, as Paynter's 'York Project', *Music in the Secondary School Curriculum* explored the ideas that were developing in Britain's music classrooms, and Malcolm Ross at the University of Exeter investigated connections between the arts in his *Arts and the Adolescent* research. Emerging themes began to focus the debate: how to provide a balanced and coherent music curriculum, and how to foster the aesthetic development of young people through a programme that included all the arts. There was a new tendency to theorise, as music psychology gained influence, with Swanwick (1979) providing one of the first 'models' of the music curriculum, intended to create a philosophical framework through which to rationalise the competing practical ideas.

In his introduction to *A Basis for Music Education* (1979), Swanwick observed that 'Music education is passing through an interesting, if difficult period' (ibid.: 5). His main criticism of the changes that had occurred in some secondary school music classrooms was that they lacked a 'conceptual framework' and therefore any sense of direction:

> Fundamentally we have no *rationale* that bears examination and stands
> up well against the views of different pressure groups. We have failed

to notice and publicize the central core of music education, which is
that music education is *aesthetic* education.

(Swanwick, 1979: 6)

Through his very language, Swanwick aligns himself both with teachers ('*we
have*') and academics ('aesthetic' argument). This duality of purpose pervades
his writing, making the identity of his audience sometimes unclear. Indeed,
Swanwick appears to recognise this difficulty, and encourages the teachers and
musicians amongst his readers to be receptive to their mutual interests:

> Some teachers and musicians may regard the following discussion as a
> waste of time, and indeed, for some people it may be. Yet I would
> regard an exploration of this terrain as a fundamental and recurring
> challenge to any teacher of music who is more than a mere classroom
> 'operator'.
>
> (Swanwick, 1979: 7)

It is clear that Swanwick is attempting to bring the developing academic debate
within the context of the classroom, his own immediate audience being the
student teachers he was training at the Institute of Education in London at the
time (Interview, 24 November 1997). Implicit in his remarks is a criticism of
those innovators who had put forward practical ideas without the fully
developed rationale that *A Basis for Music Education* seeks to provide. The
unsuccessful imitation of the projects in *Sound and Silence* (Paynter & Aston,
1970), for example, by teachers who may not have absorbed the reasoning that
is present in the opening chapter of that book, had created a dissatisfaction with
new ideas in education. Swanwick's determination to make the 'basis' of any
practical programme clearer establishes a new perspective on the classroom,
that of an academic observer who seeks to rationalise the processes of teaching
and learning music. Criticism of contemporary educators is implied, with a
recognition of the dangers inherent in 'creative' classroom music:

> How long can classes in schools go about 'experimenting' with
> instruments, tape-recorded sound, or tearing-up paper to make
> different sound-effects? The answer is, I think, for a little while only.
>
> (Swanwick, 1979: 10)

Whilst he does not deny the importance of enjoying the 'materials of sound',
Swanwick states that 'the processes of selection, relation and intention must
soon be brought to bear so that the making of music may begin' (ibid.: 10).
This stance is compatible with contemporary developments in music education:
the work of Schafer and Self, for example, was concerned with questioning

these very processes of musical construction and intention. Swanwick appears to be adopting a similar argument from a more obscure standpoint, but interestingly, recalls that there was little interaction between the innovatory thinkers of the time. He describes the isolation he experienced in his own years as a teacher, in terms that would be familiar to many music educators today:

> I must say that at that time there was no debate about what you should be doing, how you should be doing it; there was obviously no National Curriculum, but there was no sense of any kind of fixed position that anyone took, and there was little interaction, there was no networking with anyone else at all, you were on your own. That, I think, was common, although I wouldn't know because I wasn't in touch with anyone else.
>
> (Swanwick: Interview, 24 November 1997)

It is difficult to judge whether *A Basis for Music Education* achieved Swanwick's intention of bringing the debate to a wider audience or not, but it is likely to have been read by a significant proportion of the music teachers who trained in the 1980s, and by interested members of the profession from the date of its publication. A new intellectual challenge was reaching those teachers who had seen the work of the 1970s as being purely practical, but it was to take a great deal more discussion and exploration before the two aspects of thinking in music education could be synthesised.

Swanwick's description of the musical experience focuses on the 'meaningfulness' (ibid.: 7) and 'feelingfulness' (ibid.: 24) of the art, ideas that he references to the work of Langer and Cooke. Music, he argues, is representative of emotional schema, without being a description of meaning, thus it has formal and expressive power:

> It is the fusing together of many layers of experience that is part of the power that music has to 'move' us. It is as though feelings and emotions we know are mingled with feelings we may not have experienced, all thrown into the melting-pot, to be moulded into an object of significance, power, or beauty. The result for us is a new and distinctive feeling that has sometimes been called the 'aesthetic emotion'.
>
> (Swanwick, 1979: 28)

In explaining these complex ideas in simple terms, Swanwick is careful to avoid any common misconceptions, emphasising that music is not a representation of the composer's emotional state, and endorsing Langer's term 'sentience', rather than attempting any classification of musical 'emotions'.

Langer's own description is more vivid, and clarifies the distinction between self-expression and artistic representation:

> A work of art expresses a conception of life, emotion, inward reality.
> But it is neither a confessional nor a frozen tantrum; it is a developed
> metaphor, a non-discursive symbol that articulates what is verbally
> ineffable – the logic of consciousness itself.
>
> (Langer, 1957: 26)

Swanwick's discussion of the nature of music precedes his consideration of classroom practicalities, and can be taken as an indication that his ideal teacher would have understood their art before attempting to teach it. Like knowing a person, true engagement with music requires thought in addition to experience: 'We cannot really believe that we *know* people because they happen to be around us, or because we pass them in the street or stand crushed together in a train or bus' (Swanwick, 1979: 41). The practical application of this observation is that teachers need to provide multiple opportunities for children to engage with a variety of music, after the fashion of building a human relationship. This approach echoes the calls of earlier writers for more extensive and progressive music courses (cf. MacPherson, 1922; Scholes, 1935; Mainwaring; 1951), whilst heralding Swanwick's later work on the 'developmental spiral', which supports the principle that concepts should be revisited at a more sophisticated level as the child gains musical and emotional maturity (Swanwick & Tillman, 1986). Perhaps this proves nothing more than the fact that similar philosophical ideals can be applied to a variety of classroom approaches, a point that Swanwick guards against by providing his own practical suggestions in the second half of the book.

Swanwick constructs a model for the music curriculum that incorporates his theoretical priorities, by combining musical skills and knowledge to achieve a balanced programme, presenting this as a mnemonic:

		C (L) A (S) P
C	*Composition*	formulating a musical idea, making a musical object
(L)	*Literature studies*	the literature of and the literature about music
A	*Audition*	responsive listening as (though not necessarily in) an audience
(S)	*Skill acquisition*	aural, instrumental, notational
P	*Performance*	communicating music as a 'presence'

(Swanwick, 1979: 45)

Swanwick's reservations about the value of creativity as a focus for music teaching lead to an all-inclusive curriculum, with the traditional elements of musical knowledge, particularly listening skills, alongside more practical modes of study. This is the view that was to endure after the enthusiasm for exploratory projects had dwindled; a rationalisation of the discovery that music had relevance for all pupils. Swanwick recognises the dangers of adopting any curriculum model without a full understanding of its objectives, and warns against a return to study 'about' music, urging an awareness that the 'aesthetic response ... is central to the situation' (ibid.: 61). The decision to balance a practical approach with a structured programme of skill acquisition highlights the dilemma that was to face the music teachers of the next decade and beyond. With an increasing number of musical activities and an ever-broadening repertoire, it was no longer possible to simply add to the current provision, as had been the case in previous generations: choices had to be made about the content and direction of the musical education that schools aimed to provide. Swanwick makes his underlying position quite clear:

> I would suggest that a fundamental weakness in much teaching, and especially in general class music, lies in the failure to bring about any kind of aesthetic response or even to notice that it is central to the situation. Skill acquisition and literature studies are so easily substituted for the prime activities of composition, audition and performance.
>
> (Swanwick, 1979: 61)

This summary can be seen as a cautious response to the improvisation and composition approach that had threatened to replace all previous models of music education. The desire to ensure progression in music education, and to establish a philosophical foundation for its direction, was increasing, alongside broader discussions of the processes of making and perceiving the arts (cf. Ross, 1981; Abbs, 1987). The appropriation of aesthetic argument into educational circles raised new possibilities for thinking about teaching, whilst inviting the dangerous pursuit of amateur philosophising, a problem to which Swanwick alludes in his description of musical experience:

> The experience of music as an art helps us to *explore* feelings rather than merely encapsulate them. The meaningfulness and feelingfulness of aesthetic experience is bound up with an exploding universe of possibilities, not with an implosive attention to our own feeling states. If this is what is meant by 'the emotional development of the child' then all is well.
>
> (Swanwick, 1979: 112)

The balance between meaning and feeling also forms the basis of Swanwick's later work with Tillman, in which they construct a spiral of musical development, based on their observations of children's compositions (Swanwick & Tillman, 1986). The spiral model charts children's experience of music from the sensory manipulation of sound materials, through personal expression in imitation and imaginative play, towards the symbolic and systematic development of form, and the recognition and assertion of musical value (ibid.: 331). This development is correlated with age, and so somewhat obscures the fact that a new area of learning in music could take an experienced musician back to the beginning of the spiral, and that practical, conceptual and emotional responses to music do not necessarily develop in parallel. Swanwick was subsequently to distance himself from any undue emphasis on a 'standard timetable' of musical competence, proposing instead an 'organic' model, in which each layer of development is absorbed in the one that follows, representing an increased depth of understanding rather than a complete shift in perception (Swanwick, 1994: 90). The Swanwick and Tillman spiral has become a familiar point of discussion for music teachers who have trained since its publication, and has been tested, modified and applied to other aspects of musical learning in the later writings of both authors (Swanwick, 1988, 1994; Boyce-Tillman, 1996). As an attempt to quantify the developmental processes of musical understanding, the model served a useful purpose in the educational debate, together with work by Hargreaves (1986) and Davies (1992) which also looked closely at examples of children's musical work in order to construct sequences of development. The influence that such models have had upon music education as a whole is harder to judge, given that this strongly theoretical approach is the one most likely to be met with indifference or hostility by practising teachers, being perceived, often unfairly, to be of little relevance to everyday teaching and learning. Swanwick and Tillman state that their spiral offers a framework for curriculum development, asserting that 'it ought to be possible for a teacher to identify where a child is on the spiral at any given time' (1986: 336). What they cannot offer, however, is the scope for broader discussion, given that they are expecting pupils and teachers to fit within their model, rather than to challenge and refine it.

Whatever the criticisms of the Swanwick and Tillman spiral itself, its main drawback is one of theoretical models in general, in that it seeks to close down debate, rather than encourage new ideas to flourish. In the climate of music education in the 1970s and 1980s, this approach was one amongst many, and did not share the excitement of more practical or inspirational thoughts and opportunities that were also emerging. Significant amongst these was the expansion of the popular music culture, bringing as it did a recognition of the fact that the musical priorities of young people did not always resemble those of their teachers. Swanwick himself had addressed this in an earlier book, *Popular Music and the Teacher* (1968), and it is the continuation of this debate that will be considered next.

4.2 The expansion of 'pop' culture

The existence of two distinct genres of musical culture was nothing new, and initial teacher reaction was comparable to the antipathy to the popular music of an earlier generation, when discussions of musical 'quality' often had more to do with objective notions of taste:

> Broadcasting is giving everybody a marvellous opportunity of listening to quantities of music – good, bad and indifferent – and in listening to it they should, if they are intelligent people, not seek simply to be amused, but also to distinguish between what is good and true and beautiful on the one hand, and what is merely ear-tickling and sentiment-moving on the other.
>
> (Scholes, 1925: 178)

Just as a mechanical change – the advent of radio and gramophone – had made music of all kinds available to listeners in the 1930s, so the expansion of pirate radio broadcasts and the increasing availability of pop music records brought the music of the new generation to a wider audience. Swanwick had already commented on the implications for music teachers, expressing the belief that the interest in music aroused in children by pop music could be harnessed in the classroom, and calling on 'the educationalist to lead away from sterile attitudes and specious generalisations' (Swanwick, 1968: 127). Expressing his hope that 'we could be shaping a new and undivided community' (ibid.: 127), Swanwick captures the social evangelism of the age, but as the influence of the pop music culture grew, educational attitudes were to become more divided. Swanwick's research, carried out with groups of his own secondary school pupils in Leicester, showed that perceptions of music amongst young people were more complex than media reporting would have their parents and teachers believe:

> We can say quite firmly that about three-quarters of our adolescents in school are less willing to listen to classical music because of the existence of popular music as we know it at present. We can also say that the other quarter are able, to some degree or other, not only to resist these effects, but actually to find classical music *more* satisfying

in comparison with the particular sort of popular pieces played in this experiment.

(Swanwick, 1968: 82)

Adding the proviso that the latter quarter tended to be those of higher academic ability, Swanwick asserts that the musical characteristics of pop music need to be separated from the aggressive marketing that induced such extreme reactions as 'Beatlemania'. In conclusion, he suggests that pop music should be used in the classroom, 'not as a 'let out', but as a *way in*' (ibid.: 113).

An objection to such implicit musical hierarchies motivated the next wave of writing about pop music in education. Vulliamy, who was to become one of the most prominent authors in this field, had made it clear that the resistance of the majority of teachers to the pop music revolution was an untenable position:

> One doesn't have to enjoy the music of Stravinsky or Bartók to recognize their achievements; the same applies to the greatest jazz and rock musicians. And yet most teachers of music are completely ignorant of the type of music with which students are most familiar; as an educational principle this would seem to be very difficult to defend.
>
> (Vulliamy, 1975: 22)

The dangers of stereotyping the views of teachers and pupils are evident in Vulliamy's stance, but it is certainly true that pop music represented another challenge to the role of the music teacher. Just as the introduction of composition and improvisation had questioned the supremacy of the classical repertoire in school music, so the recognition of a new musical youth culture broadened the horizons of the most innovative teachers, whilst threatening the purpose of more traditional teaching.

Vulliamy and his colleagues extended the debate with the publication of *Pop Music in School* (Vulliamy & Lee, 1976/80), which went some way towards acknowledging the fears of teachers, and providing the background knowledge and practical suggestions that would help bring pop music into schools. The first chapter, by Rogers, gives a 'guided tour' of the varieties of pop, emphasising the sociological impact of this new musical influence:

> In the main, it was working-class youth which acted as midwife to the birth of rock 'n' roll in Britain. Perhaps it was they who felt more keenly the opportunities and freedom brought by affluence and rock 'n' roll, and who had more need to assert their own definition of their role in society. The middle classes, urged on in their beliefs by the media, tended to equate rock 'n' roll with violence, with a lower class

of person, felt vaguely to be a criminal in some undefined way, and above all of course with the Teddy Boy.

(Vulliamy & Lee, 1976/80: 8)

In a later chapter, Vulliamy points out that teachers who have trained in the European 'classical' tradition are all too likely to accept the commercial myths that pop music is homogeneous, and to perpetuate the divide between the two schools of performance (ibid.: 44). He attempts to forge links between the recent introduction of workshop teaching methods, following Paynter's ideas, and the practice of rock groups, saying that both methods encourage independent learning (ibid.: 56). The aim, it seems, is to move away from the classification of musical styles, towards a music classroom which engages with all genres through their common musical processes. Burnett, in his contribution to the *Music Education Review* (Burnett, 1977), also emphasises the incompatible 'aesthetic aims' of popular and art music:

> Pop is essentially a spontaneously created, non-literate, music with a strong, accessible, and usually straightforward emotional message. Art music, on the other hand, separates composer from performer, values literacy, and tends to value least those composers who wear their hearts too obviously on their sleeves.
>
> (Burnett, 1977: 46)

The 'collision' of the aims of pop music with a teacher's classical training is the most likely source of confusion in the classroom, according to Burnett (ibid.: 47). Teachers, he asserts, should be prepared to learn from their pupils, and he shares with Vulliamy and Lee a distrust of the 'stepping stone' approach, where pop music is used as a way in to the classical repertoire (ibid.: 56). With the aim of 'music for the majority' characterising many of the music curriculum initiatives of the time, pop culture was seen as an opportunity to avoid the alienation felt by some children when faced with more traditional teaching.

The challenges were to become more complex, and only a few years later Vulliamy and Lee expanded their argument to include so-called 'ethnic' music (Vulliamy & Lee, 1982), adding West Indian music, reggae, African drumming and Balinese music to the equation. In their introduction, they emphasise the need for more in-service and pre-service training in these new aspects of music education, as the consideration of notation, assessment and subject knowledge put increasing demands upon the teacher. Assessment, perhaps one of the most problematic aspects of music education, will be considered in the next chapter, but it is worth noting here that pop music raised many of the questions of accessibility and curriculum content that would be addressed through the CSE examination, and ultimately through GCSE.

The classroom suggestions included in *Pop, Rock and Ethnic Music in School* focus on structured listening activities, arrangement and performance, with some composition tasks. Understanding the components of the different genres is the main priority, with the focus on musical elements replacing the often sociological motivation for engaging in the music out of school. Sorrell highlights, from an ethnomusicologist's perspective, the dangers of 'applying the criteria of [our] own culture to another' (Sorrell, 1982: 107), and it is this attempt to understand the various musics on their own terms that is Vulliamy's central philosophy. In addition to providing lesson ideas and background information for teachers, the authors address many of the misconceptions that had hindered the acceptance of rock music in schools, with Fisher exposing a myth that has not been entirely eradicated today:

> It is a myth that the black child has a natural talent for rhythm which others such as whites and Indians lack. A more acceptable theory is that the black child has been exposed to a particular form of rhythm, and that he or she has been socialised into it from the surrounding culture.
>
> (Fisher, 1982: 149)

In our more globally aware age, it is difficult to imagine the social, as well as musical, challenges that faced the teachers of the late 1970s and early 1980s. Their value systems were being undermined by the need to incorporate increasingly varied styles and activities into their lessons, and the need for an underlying rationale was more urgent, given the impossibility of including everything.

Perhaps one of the first books to bring together the new concerns of musicians and teachers in a coherent argument was *Music•Society•Education* (Small, 1977/80), in which Small gives a critique of Western music, and argues that it inhibits the development of a musical education. The text is wide-ranging and accommodates many of the ideals that Cage (1968/78) and Schafer (1969) had explored some years earlier, such as the rejection of the concert hall as the only valid place to hear music, and the hope that the investigation of sound could be taken out of its professional province and made available to all. Blacking (1973) had of course paved the way for such discussions with *How Musical is Man?*, in which the links between music and society had been brought to a wider audience through discussion of the concepts of originality and creativity in different cultures (ibid.: 106). Small, though, relates his ideas more closely to education, which he recognises as a way of questioning and changing social attitudes. Beginning with a critique of the current system, Small acknowledges the influence of Illich and the 'de-schoolers' of the early 1970s, who saw institutionalised 'schooling' as being distinct from 'education' in its true sense:

> In a school, pupils are taken away from their experience of the world (which even at the age of five is considerable) and experience instead only the hermetic world of the classroom and playground. If they are successful in school, they may even learn a great deal about the world, but, successful or not, their experience of it is seriously impaired; we have produced a generation who know more about the world, and experience it less, than perhaps any other generation in human history.
>
> (Small, 1977/80: 192)

Here Small is drawing attention to the fact that changes in classroom practice imply more fundamental alterations of attitude and belief, a stance that had not emerged so clearly through the texts of the previous decade. The superiority of experience over imparted knowledge had been the driving force behind developments in music education in the 1970s and early 1980s, and Small brings this to the forefront of the debate, arguing that the educational system works against change, particularly the introduction of creative ideas. The recent change of attitude in music teaching, he suggests, had gone against the broader ideals of school teaching in general, replacing the standard preparation for adult life with something more immediate:

> Our culture's will-o'-the-wisp promise of future satisfaction in return for sacrifice of present pleasure becomes imprinted very early in children's minds, and yet another generation is conditioned to the industrial philosophy.
>
> (Small, 1977/80: 185)

Few of the music educators who had published ideas in the preceding years had drawn such overtly political inferences from their ideas, with the radical approach to education occurring most clearly as the arguments for popular and world musics became more vociferous. Small, an ethnomusicologist, calls for a broader definition of music in school and society, and champions the cause of creative music education, seeing the opportunity to explore materials and ideas as being fundamental to arts education:

> An artist (and we are all, at least potentially, artists, even if few have aspirations to making it a profession) knows what techniques he is going to need only by using them; no-one else can tell him. This is not

to say that no-one can teach him anything, but it does mean that he must be left free to decide what it is he needs (I repeat, *needs*) to learn. It is probable that most people will in fact want to learn very similar things, but the freedom to decide for oneself makes the vital difference between a living experience of learning and drudgery.

(Small, 1977/80: 202)

It should be pointed out that Small does not make any connection with the work of Paynter and Aston, Schafer, Swanwick or other educational innovators of the time. It is hard to believe that he was not aware of their work, given his interest in music teaching, but his only reference to specific arts education literature is to acknowledge a debt to Herbert Read, who also noted the importance of fostering artistic and aesthetic sensibilities in children (ibid.: 218). Small's work occupies a different role to the classroom-based writing of Paynter and Aston (1970), being concerned with the broader philosophical basis of the education system, and of music's place within it. It goes beyond Swanwick's model of the music curriculum, in that the ideals of music education are considered in their social and political context, as well as with regard to individual development. The lack of overlap is perhaps surprising, but is still indicative of a new concern with justifying change in theoretical terms, which Swanwick had begun and which the writers of the late 1980s were to continue.

Small's central thesis is in fact sympathetic to the aims of the classroom composition lessons of the early 1970s, whilst including the broader definition of musical repertoire and behaviour that had emerged in the latter half of that decade. He holds that, as creativity is vital to a healthy society, so should it be given a prominent position in the education of all children:

As the creative act is at the centre of all artistic activity, so we place creative activity firmly at the centre of musical education, from which all other, more traditional activities radiate, fed by the work of creation and in turn feeding back into it: compositional skills, notation (as and *if* needed), listening, performing, study of the work of other musicians of many periods, styles and cultures.

(Small, 1977/80: 213)

Despite Small's radical approach to schools in general, his prescription for music education seems eminently logical, and was perhaps ahead of its time in its attempt to take the best of current thinking and form a coherent programme. His reasoning is certainly rooted in its time, and his emphasis on the enjoyment of the present learning experience, rather than the pursuit of future success, is one that is rarely voiced today, as league tables of examination results give ever more credence to measurable achievement. Encouragingly, however, *Music•Society•Education* was republished in 1996, with an introduction that states 'Small's views are still news' (Walser, 1996: ix). It certainly seems true to say that Small's perceptions of musical culture and educational value systems retain their relevance, and demonstrate the process of absorbing and building upon ideas that has characterised change in music education. By providing a rational framework for the late 1970s enthusiasm for popular and 'creative' music in the classroom, Small contributed to their lasting value, ensuring that the ideas would be comprehensible to a generation that had left the heady days of early pop culture behind.

It is not the case, of course, that Small's appraisal of music and culture could solve the educational debate conclusively. This single, though significant, contribution served to highlight the complexities and challenges of music education, and emphasised the strength of feeling that was taking classroom practice in different directions. Perhaps for the first time in its history, there was no clearly dominant model of musical education, rather a plethora of apparently conflicting views, which were likely to become more entangled as new ideas were developed. For a picture of classroom thought and practice at the time, it is helpful to turn to the work of the Schools Council project, *Music in the Secondary School Curriculum* which, running from 1973 to 1980, offers an interesting perspective upon the developments of the time.

4.3 *Music in the Secondary School Curriculum* (1982)

The Schools Council project, led by John Paynter at the University of York, was established to promote discussion and dissemination of the ideas that had challenged music teachers in the 1960s and 1970s. A large number of teachers and musicians were involved in the courses and publications that the Project generated, and the emphasis was on sharing effective practice, rather than imparting ideas from the university level. In an article in the *Music in Education* journal, the editor quotes Paynter as he explains the intention of the Project:

> The aim is not to create a curriculum, though obviously our final output must give teachers help: it must give them confidence; but it must also challenge them to think for themselves and to be as inventive and creative as they can. Primarily our objective is to try to say why music should be in the curriculum at all. Music, and the arts generally, don't fit into the expected pattern of a curriculum, which is

largely information-based. We think this is a problem that people have got to face up to.

(Griffiths, 1977: 74)

Many of Paynter's characteristic aims are encapsulated in this quote: the respect for teachers coupled with a desire to help them; the belief that change in music education happens at classroom level, not through imposed ideas; and the belief that addressing the fundamental place of music in the curriculum will provide a framework for practical development. These were the guiding principles that shaped the project and that were fully explored in the book that published its investigations and findings, *Music in the Secondary School Curriculum* (Paynter, 1982).

An evaluation of the Project's methods has already been undertaken by one of the teachers who participated (Hancox, 1988), focusing on the way in which ideas can be most effectively disseminated to schools. In this, as much as in its ideas, the Schools Council Project offered a new way of thinking, establishing regional centres and recruiting pilot schools, rather than relying on a 'centre to periphery' model of diffusing ideas (ibid.: 74). Hancox comments that despite the clear intentions expressed by Paynter, that ideas should be discussed and evaluated by teachers rather than presented in their completed form without consultation, many music advisers still expected a 'York method' to emerge from the Project (ibid.: 221). Paynter recalls the hostility that the Project attracted in some quarters, fuelled by sensational media coverage that exaggerated the position that the research was taking (personal communication, June 1997). It is clear that feelings about the developments fostered by the Project ran high, illustrating the resistance to change and sense of threatened identity that the progression of music education has engendered on more than one occasion throughout the century. As practising musicians reach the classroom, the tendency to reproduce their own beliefs and training is very strong, and such a widespread challenging of the status quo inevitably led to some heated opposition. What is more significant, however, is the vast positive influence of the Project, as a network of ideas and resources grew across the country, building on established practice and addressing some of the confusion of the previous decade.

In taking an investigative approach to the Project, Paynter's work offers insight upon the challenges that were occupying teachers in the 1970s and the variety of approaches they took in developing their practice. Many examples of teachers' comments and ideas are included in *Music in the Secondary School Curriculum* (Paynter, 1982), and the lessons described were reproduced as film and audio resources for wider dissemination. In addition to this, Paynter's own influence is strong, and his discussion of the questions that had occupied the

109

Project members expands considerably on the ideas of his earlier *Sound and Silence* (Paynter & Aston, 1970). The book opens with a brief chronology of music education, emphasising the confusion and lack of resources that had developed in recent years, particularly in the potential conflict between the curricular and extra-curricular roles of the teacher. The belief that music has something of value to offer to all pupils is central to the Project's aims, and incorporates the debate on curriculum content that other writers of the 1970s had championed:

> School is a microcosm of society, and if education is to meet the needs of those for whom it is designed it cannot afford to pretend that some things do not exist. If music has something to offer to all pupils ought we not to recognise music as it is – with all its variety of style and purpose – and not take arbitrary decisions about what we can admit into the classroom and what we must, for 'academic' reasons, reject?
>
> (Paynter, 1982: 22)

The need for teachers to justify what they are teaching is also a key concern, and recognised as central to effective classroom practice. Whilst the Schools Council Project had provided opportunities for teachers to discuss ideas and develop their own thinking and practice, Paynter – in a passage that has great relevance for the teachers of today – acknowledges that this is rarely possible:

> Teachers are asked to teach too much, and serious consideration should be given to making it possible for teachers to be released for further study at reasonably frequent intervals, and to offering more opportunity for reflection, reading and discussion as a recognised part of a teacher's working time.
>
> (Paynter, 1982: 31)

Whilst recognising that conditions in many schools were less than ideal, Paynter warned against the danger of allowing inadequate resources to dictate an inadequate curriculum. Many practical suggestions are given for locating small composition groups in corners of the school and for organising projects where pupils work in rotation to maximise use of resources (Paynter, 1982: 79). The fear of noise was very real to teachers used to traditional methods, and the pressure for silent lessons was no doubt asserted by neighbouring colleagues in many cases. Discipline worries are addressed in the book, but no easy solutions are proffered, with effective class management seen to depend largely on a clearly progressive curriculum:

Poor discipline almost always arises from boredom when pupils cannot see the relevance of what they are doing and cannot feel involved. The answer lies therefore in the kind of curriculum we evolve, the relevance of the material or the ways in which it can be seen to be relevant, and the sense of progression and purpose that we are able to generate.

(Paynter, 1982: 84)

The problems Paynter chooses to confront are revealing in themselves: it is evident that lack of resources, unsupportive colleagues and poor classroom discipline had been cited by teachers as causes of 'failure' where new styles of music teaching had not generated effective results. Public criticisms of the Project had also centred on its favouring of 'creative' methods, and Paynter attributes this hostility to a fundamental misunderstanding:

For advocating the principle of music as a creative art the Project has been called 'partisan' and has been accused of promoting a restricted view. Yet the aim has been quite clearly to *enlarge* the scope of music in the classroom, to include many activities which were hitherto excluded, and to develop an all-embracing principle which can include virtually any 'method' and any content so long as pupils are actively involved with music which they have a chance to 'make their own'.

(Paynter, 1982: 93)

Extending the arguments that Swanwick's 'C(L)A(S)P' model had proposed (Swanwick, 1979), Paynter asserts that all aspects of music making are 'creative', in that they produce something that is new to the creator (Paynter, 1982: 93). The misinterpretation of creative methods as some kind of percussion-based anarchy had done much damage to the idea of composition in schools, and it is clear that the Project worked hard to overcome the resultant prejudices. The linking of musical knowledge and skills with the opportunity to explore sound is emphasised throughout, with the conclusion that the time had come to move the debate forward:

Teaching techniques have developed, and it is probably time we stopped talking about 'creative music'! All musical knowledge and skill can be put to creative use, and if it isn't it has very little value musically.

(Paynter, 1982: 137)

Music in the Secondary School Curriculum includes an appraisal of the contemporary examination system for music, and gives details of a moderation exercise that provoked hostility from some official quarters. Questions of assessment will be considered more fully in the next chapter, and at this point it is helpful to draw conclusions about the impact of the Project in other areas. Its influence appears to be twofold: in the way that the Project was carried out, the work demonstrated the wealth of ideas that were present in Britain's music classrooms; and in its ideas the Project brought together teachers' concerns and attempted to place them in a rational framework. The Project made links between research and practice that had not previously been acknowledged, whilst fuelling a debate that had evidently made a proportion of teachers and advisers very uncomfortable. It was to be one of the Schools Council's last major curriculum initiatives, as the tendency to include teachers in the formulation of curriculum suggestions was increasingly replaced by a more centralised approach to educational control. The 'deep sense of purpose' evident on curriculum committees failed to appeal to the Department of Education and Science, who disbanded the Council in 1984 (Plaskow, 1985).

It can be seen that the *Music in the Secondary School Curriculum* Project was an initiative that reflected the sense of curriculum exploration of the time, whilst addressing some of the confusions that such exploration had generated. Twenty years later, some of the ideas have dated, but the central musical principles would still support the practice of many contemporary music departments. Perhaps the most significant legacy of the Project is its recognition that educational change originates in the classroom, and that ideas need to be shared and discussed between teachers if effective practice is to develop. Sadly, such a view has little influence in today's educational climate, as will become increasingly evident in the chapters that follow. As a picture of the late 1970s, however, the Project's work provides a fascinating view of the mixture of idealism and resistance to change that had resulted from the curriculum developments of the previous decade, and emphasises the complexity of the debate that took music education into the 1980s.

4.4 The wider arts debate

It has already been noted that music lagged behind other arts in establishing itself as a creative, rather than solely interpretative, subject (cf. Section 2.3). Whilst drama, imaginative writing, art and to a lesser extent, dance, were accepted features of the curriculum, music teachers were slow to join the debate on how these different forms could be presented in a coherent or co-ordinated way. To a certain extent, music has never lost its position as the poor relation in such 'expressive arts' unions, not least because of the unique nature of musical expression, as occurring in time and free from literal meaning. By the end of the 1970s, a new tendency to see 'the arts' as a cohesive unit was emerging, with all the inherent dangers of compromise that such an approach generates. Each art has its own complexities, and whilst observing educational similarities is of value, there is a danger that pupils may experience a confused concoction in which the individual characteristics of the arts are obscured. The extent to which a performer is physically involved in drama, for example, differs from the presentation of a completed painting in visual art. The concept of whether poetry is a written or spoken medium, likewise, needs to be considered separately from the question of where, and when, music exists. Using music as an accompaniment to dramatic or visual events, whilst providing valuable performance opportunities, endangers the identity of music as an independently structured form in aural time. The early enthusiasm for combined arts projects sometimes overlooked the need for systematic skills teaching, whilst theoretical approaches (cf. Ross, 1978; 1981; 1986) tried to make music fit the mould of other arts, without adequately considering the specific nature of musical engagement.

One of the first major discussions of the arts as a generic area of education was Witkin's *The Intelligence of Feeling* (1974). Exploring psychological theories of learning and experiencing art, Witkin conducted a practical investigation of the extent to which different subject teachers addressed the emotional and expressive implications of teaching the arts. Music fares rather badly in this survey, partly because developments were more recent and therefore less consistently adopted and discussed by teachers, but also because Witkin's theory of art is centred around communication and self-expression, which are concepts that cannot be applied to music in a straightforward way. Artistic expression is, he claims, a resolution of 'sensate disturbance' (Witkin, 1974: 15), with emotion always the guiding force in creation:

> When the individual's impulse moves through the medium of sound,
> when he composes a melody, his consciousness must oscillate between
> his impulse and the sound he is making. He must be able to bring the
> two together if he is to have any hope of his impulse shaping sounds in
> ways that will recall the sensing that gave rise to it.
>
> (Witkin, 1974: 23)

The flaws in this argument are evident; even if an emotional experience is the impulse for writing a melody, this is not sufficient to sustain the construction of a complete work, which must have musical unity rather than relying on an external explanation. Witkin's insistence that art is self-expressive has considerable implications for the classroom, with the 'facilitative-inhibitive' role of the teacher (ibid.: 35) suggesting a kind of therapy that goes beyond the recognised scope of arts teaching:

> The pupil must come to respond to sensate problems that perhaps formerly could not be evoked within him and he must use his response, his feeling-impulse, to recall his sensing and thereby resolve the sensate problem. Progress is measured in terms of the complexity of sensate problems that he can handle.
>
> (Witkin, 1974: 49)

Put so clinically, Witkin's vision seems frighteningly manipulative, but his use of language is perhaps partly responsible. His assertion that art objects should have value for the pupils who make them is acceptable, and it is his insistence on the priority of 'sensate disturbances' as a means of generating art that is both aesthetically and educationally unsound. A drama teacher, interviewed in the course of Witkin's empirical study, typifies the cautious response to the intrusion into emotional realms:

> I feel in working with the emotional development of the child you're on really dangerous ground because here you're working with the non-rational aspect of the child. You're getting at the child underneath his normal natural defences which he uses in the general run of the school in English, Chemistry or whatever. He's forced to commit himself personally, wholly to reveal himself.
>
> (Witkin, 1974: 61)

This teacher apparently fears the probing of this private world, anticipating an excess of emotion with which neither pupil nor teacher would be able to cope. Witkin's belief that the 'non-rational' nature of the arts gives them a significant place in the curriculum would not be denied by many teachers, but the vision of whole class psychotherapy is perhaps too extreme a reaction to the more conventional pressures of examination success. Elsewhere, Holbrook (1967) had warned against the amateur psychology of some English lessons, where experimentation with emotional ideas had led teachers to conclude that 'a pupil is in a grim personal situation: it may be that he is merely experimenting in feeling – where children – especially adolescents – *don't* experiment, perhaps we should be worried?' (ibid.: 10). Holbrook's note of caution illustrates the range of views that accompanied the new focus on imagination and creativity in arts subjects, with his acknowledgement of the importance of emotion tempered by a respect for the pupil's privacy and independence.

Despite his collective theoretical consideration of the arts, Witkin interviews subject teachers separately in his 'praxis' section, and asserts that music occupies the weakest position in the curriculum, being 'considered by many pupils to be irrelevant to anything that really concerns them' (Witkin, 1974: 118). At the time of writing, this was not an unreasonable evaluation, and had after all been the driving force behind many recent curriculum initiatives. Witkin is sympathetic to the prejudice and poor resourcing that an innovatory music teacher must face, a problem that the Schools Council research of 1973–80 showed to be a more lasting concern (Paynter, 1982). Like Vulliamy and Lee (1976/80), Witkin suggests that the classical training of most music teachers is responsible for the conventional nature of the school curriculum, with successes in extended curriculum activities often allowed, or even expected, to deflect attention from class work:

> There is no doubt that in the establishment of choirs and orchestras many teachers find their greatest sense of achievement. One cannot help feeling that it serves as a solace for those who are disillusioned with class teaching. To be assured of a small band of dedicated musicians playing impressively at a public performance is the music teacher's moment of triumph, his hour of vindication.
> (Witkin, 1974: 127)

Witkin's research included interviews with pupils, some 78 per cent of whom would remove music from their ideal timetable (ibid.: 141). Some of the contradictory needs of pupils are revealed, and Witkin unwittingly describes the combination of skill acquisition and creative opportunity that was to characterise the next decade of music education development:

> They appear to want the opportunity to move out, to express their individuality, to participate. They also want to feel safe, to have clear guidelines and parameters to work within, to be sure of the floor beneath them, the walls around them and the way ahead. The pupil's need for security can thus conflict with his need to express himself.
> (Witkin, 1974: 147)

Witkin does not appear to see this as a contradiction of his central argument, that the arts in schools should challenge children on emotional grounds. Music, it could be argued, provides the perfect forum for this creative exploration without specific emotional exposure, but it was clearly failing to do so at the time of writing:

> It is not that [pupils] regard [music] as an academic subject but rather as one which, in their terms, is a failed art subject. They feel on the

whole that it encourages participation and self-expression strictly on
its own terms and of a kind which does not engage them.

(Witkin, 1974: 149)

The point made here, that the discipline of the school context restricts
expressive opportunities, is valid for all the arts, but becomes most apparent in
music lessons. Whilst Witkin claims to be rejecting the traditional view of
music learning as a process of skill acquisition, he fails to find a balance
between exploration and technical progress. Such a dilemma was to occur in
many classrooms where the creative compositional approach of Paynter, Self
and Schafer was implemented without full consideration of its long term aims.

Whilst *The Intelligence of Feeling* apparently offered little specific guidance
to music teachers, it was to become an established text in the new genre of arts
education theory, significantly developed by Ross through a series of Arts
Curriculum Projects based at the University of Exeter. Music was to remain,
however, a poor afterthought in the majority of the arguments, with the
differences in its practice and theory seen as failings, rather than inherent
features of the art form. Ross shared Witkin's perception of the arts as a
central process of 'image-making' which contributes to the 'imaginative life' of
the pupil who engages with them (Ross, 1978: 37). The chapter on music
teaching is disparagingly entitled 'A Note From the Back of Beyond' (ibid.:
235), an attitude that seems to have pervaded Ross's perception of music
education in his subsequent writings (cf. Ross, 1995). These 1970s ideas can
take little account of the developments that were contemporary with their
criticisms, and for a less biased overview, it is helpful to consult the Calouste
Gulbenkian Foundation research, *The Arts in Schools* (1982/89). This
publication gave official endorsement both to the significance of the arts in the
curriculum, and to the view that they should be thought of as aspects of a single
strand of education and experience.

The Gulbenkian Foundation report, whilst not a Government commission,
placed the arts firmly in the educational debate of the time, by investigating
current provision in the context of a clearly articulated rationale for arts
teaching. The timing of the report was critical, not only because of the
confusion that existed amongst arts teachers at the time, but also because the
structure of the curriculum was becoming an area of political controversy, and
the case for the arts needed to be clearly stated. Recalling the educational
climate in his introduction to the report's second edition (1989), Ken Robinson
highlights the principal concerns of the Advisory Committee that had first met
in 1978:

> The report did not set out to offer a new theory of arts education, but it did attempt a new synthesis. We were concerned that some arts practice in schools was locked into a limited conception of individual development through creative self-expression that ignored or marginalised the equal importance of developing critical and technical skills in the arts and a growing understanding of other people's work.
>
> (Calouste Gulbenkian Foundation, 1982/89: xiii)

Robinson clearly perceives the 'creative' movement to have been a significant influence on arts teaching, but it must be remembered that here he is speaking in global terms, rather than specifically about music. More detailed references to music, based on observation and interpretation, come later in the report, but the tendency to draw general conclusions can lead to a false picture of the state of early 1980s music classrooms.

With a quality rare amongst official research documents, the Gulbenkian report combines powerful educational vision with a clearly articulated sense of purpose for the arts. In considering both primary and secondary provision, the report gives an overview of the needs of pupils, and sees the arts as contributing to the present experience of pupils, in contrast with the usual focus on future success and employability:

> To see education only as a preparation for something that happens later, risks overlooking the needs and opportunities of the moment. Children do not hatch into adults after a secluded incubation at school. They are living their lives now.
>
> (Calouste Gulbenkian Foundation, 1982/89: 4)

In this belief in the immediate impact of education upon children, there is resonance with Paynter and Aston's (1970) concern with engaging the child's expressive imagination, and indeed with the Newsom Report's (Ministry of Education, 1963) focus on a balanced, liberal education that included fulfilling extended curriculum activities. Sadly, political trends were to move away from this compassionate attitude to schooling, favouring those educational ideas that demonstrated efficiency and standardisation. In the Gulbenkian report, however, there is still room for some idealism, and a respect for the needs and experiences of young people.

The Arts in Schools adopts the rather dangerous stance of arguing the benefits of arts teaching in terms of general development; of creative thought, of feeling and sensibility, of cultural understanding, and so on (ibid.: 10). All of these points are substantiated with careful reasoning, but this does not detract from the fact that if a subject is to be included in the school timetable, it must have something unique to offer in its own right. There is much talk in the report about the arts as a 'natural' mode of expression and understanding, but although their importance in education is strongly felt, the arguments, taken at face value, do not make a convincing case for the arts as the only means of achieving the ends described. To teach the arts for their 'exploration of moral values' (ibid.: 11), for instance, is not the only – or necessarily the best – way to cover this educational ground, and does not in itself constitute a reason for including the arts in the curriculum. The concept of self-expression, that had formed the basis of Ross and Witkin's theories, is also addressed somewhat ambiguously:

> The arts are not outpourings of emotion. They are disciplined forms of inquiry and expression through which to organise feelings and ideas about experience. The need for young people to do this, rather than just to give vent to emotions or to have them ignored, must be responded to in schools. The arts provide the natural means for this.
>
> (Calouste Gulbenkian Foundation, 1982/89: 11)

The philosophically dubious notion that art objects must necessarily reflect the feelings of their creator is still in evidence, but the focus on discipline and enquiry suggests a more ordered approach than some of the 1970s writings. Whilst the Gulbenkian report tackles other aesthetic ideas with confidence, such as the impossibility of 'translating' one art into another, or any art into words (ibid.: 22), there are inherent difficulties in any such brief skirmish with these complex questions. It is perhaps uncharitable to judge the report as a work of aesthetic theory, as it is a clear commitment and enthusiasm for arts teaching that is communicated by the discussion as a whole.

When *The Arts in Schools* turns to more specific considerations, it is on safer ground, and raises points that are pertinent to the educational climate of the time. The recognition of cross-cultural education in the arts, for example, was a new challenge for teachers, demanding the questioning of traditional 'high art' definitions of culture, just as popular and world musics had affected thinking about music education:

> Schools are neither islands nor cultural ghettoes. They are shot through with the values of the surrounding cultures. A very wide range of cultural traditions and expectations is likely to be represented in a large comprehensive school. For this reason schools are best seen not as transmitters of culture but as complex cultural exchanges.
>
> (Calouste Gulbenkian Foundation, 1982/89: 43)

In a passage that has particular relevance for music teachers, the committee look at the role of the teacher in the arts classroom, with the need for the relinquishing of an authoritarian position seen as vital to effective teaching and learning. Contributors to *Music in the Secondary School Curriculum* (Paynter, 1982) had expressed difficulties with the feelings of redundancy that came from a workshop style of teaching, and the Calouste Gulbenkian Foundation's answer follows similar ideals to Paynter's:

> The role of the teacher is at once vital and complicated. The task is not simply to let anything happen in the name of self-expression or creativity. Neither is it to impose rigid structures of ideas and methods upon the children. The need is for a difficult balance of freedom and authority.
>
> (Calouste Gulbenkian Foundation, 1982/89: 33)

The sense of building on the developments of the early 1970s is evident here, as it was in Paynter's report (1982), as the early days of experimentation were rationalised for more widespread dissemination.

The need for an improved level of resourcing is a familiar call, and the Gulbenkian report demands more equipment, space and time for the arts in schools. In primary schools, the priority is to enable children to explore materials and develop competence in using them (ibid.: 49), and in the secondary school, the acquisition of more sophisticated techniques and ideas requires a sympathetic timetable:

> Expressive work in all of the arts takes concentration, application – and time. Short periods often prejudice good work. Moreover, the week-long gap between lessons can mean that a large proportion of each lesson is spent picking up the threads of the work in hand – and too little in moving it forward.
>
> (Calouste Gulbenkian Foundation, 1982/89: 63)

In connection with this problem of inadequate time for creative thought, the Gulbenkian report considers the development of 'expressive arts' faculties, but sees the real need for integration as being between the arts and the rest of the curriculum. The danger of 'sacrificing depth for variety' is recognised (ibid.: 64), but the whole report is founded on the belief that common problems in arts teaching can be solved through co-operation between subject specialists. As with the generalised reasons for teaching the arts at all, the logical result of such an argument is to say that one art is as good as any other in educational terms, with an eventual reduction in provision likely to follow. Robinson's continued research as director of the Arts in Schools Project (NCC, 1990a/b), would look more closely at the difficulties involved in combined arts teaching, recognising the desire that some children will have to specialise in an art that particularly inspires or engages them (cf. Section 7.6).

The desire to secure a place for the arts in the curriculum appears to be the primary motivation of the report, with the value for individuals, schools and communities asserted in a variety of ways. Nevertheless, to speak about the arts as a collective, implicitly interchangeable, unit leads the way open for a compromise in curriculum structure, with a potential reduction in the resources and time allocated by schools. To link the arts for allegedly philosophical or educational reasons is a first step in grouping them out of economic interest. The committee could not have anticipated the more competitive political age that was beginning, and made their observations in the traditions of educational research. Whilst *The Arts in Schools* repeatedly pledges support for arts teaching, it also makes candid criticisms, that would later fuel the opposition arguments.

4.5 Dilemmas in music education

Music education moved into the 1980s in a volatile state, with curriculum developments causing controversy amongst teachers, and apparent support for arts teaching leaving music as the weak link in theories of self-expression. With an expansion in the opportunities available to music teachers, the debate inevitably became more complex, often fuelled by a misinterpretation of the term 'creativity'. Plummeridge (1980) addressed this problem directly, stating that '*people*, not activities' could be creative (ibid.: 34) and suggesting that the contemporary tendency to refer to children as composers was misplaced:

> It is often forgotten that the person who earns the title of composer
> does so as a result of what he produces and the primary feature of his
> products is their quality or, more precisely, their value.
>
> (Plummeridge, 1980: 36)

The 'creativity' advocated by practitioners of the early 1980s generally referred to the activities of experimenting with sounds and instruments (ibid.: 39), and did not always generate a complete musical product that, by Plummeridge's definition, justified the description of the child as a composer. Jones (1986) shared the assumption that 'creativity' implied a product of quality, stating that 'it is not sensible to suggest that children with a minimal music education, engaged in activities of exploration and discovery with little idea of form and structure, are working like composers' (Jones, 1986: 66). The increase in 'creative' activities across the arts curriculum had raised broader questions about 'aesthetic education' (Redfern, 1986), with some educators arguing that school timetables put unreasonable pressure on children to be creative to order:

> Both research and a mass of personal testimony show that the essential ingredient in being creative is to have time – to dream, to toy with ideas, to allow fantasies and images to come. And this kind of relaxed non-purposive atmosphere is conspicuously lacking in schools.
>
> (Claxton, 1978: 34)

At one level, the 'creativity' debate was purely semantic, with the assumption that children working with sound should produce works comparable with those of established 'composers' proving to be a diversion from the main argument. The underlying concern, however, that experimentation with sound would not always lead to greater musical understanding, was one that required practical and intellectual consideration.

The difficulties of terminology that Paynter had highlighted (1982: 137) were in danger of undermining the changes in music teaching that he and others had pioneered, as composing in the classroom was accused of following the social trend for 'instant satisfaction' (Jones, 1986: 75). Certainly, the aimless exploration of sound effects that had been observed by Paynter (1982: 81) in the course of his Schools Council research was to be vehemently discouraged, but to dismiss the entire approach to teaching music through composing and improvising on the grounds that some teachers had misinterpreted its purpose was equally illogical. Once again, music appeared to be trailing behind the other arts: the expectation that all children could be 'writers' had long been reconciled with the obvious fact that they would not all prove to be the next Shakespeare, but it seems that musicians still struggled to accept the continuum of activities included in the concept of 'composing'. Attempts to resolve the debate were made by Gamble (1984) in the first issue of the *British Journal of Music Education*, in which he asserted that 'thinking in sound' (ibid.: 16) was an important part of coming to understand music:

> Children's compositions function simultaneously as both ends and means: they have intrinsic value as unique, original, imaginative compositions which should have aesthetic value for their peers, their teacher, their parents, or anyone else who cares to listen. At the same time these compositions help children to develop musical imagination and deeper understanding of their own expressive objects as well as the work of other composers.
>
> (Gamble, 1984: 16)

Those who were hostile to the developments in music education were apparently evaluating the products of child composing in purely musical terms, rather than accepting Gamble's proposal that musical and educational value should be considered equally. There are remnants of a 1930s attitude in the implicit belief that music will be somehow damaged by contact with inexperienced children, an approach that had not been successfully eradicated by Cage's invitation to 'find another word for all the rest that enters through the ears' (Cage, 1968/78: 190). Clearly, the acceptance of so-called creative methods without a full understanding of their purpose could produce only a chaotic experimentation with sound, and was in danger of discrediting the ideas of the 1970s. To be truly 'creative', generating a musical object worthy of critical listening, required a more rigorous approach to form and structure, and a deeper commitment to the notion of learning about music by making it. As the opportunities for pupils were increased by this broader definition of music education, responsibility was placed upon the teacher to ensure that activities were purposeful and productive, taking the role of 'informed and enthusiastic' guide (Cain, 1985: 8). Whilst Plummeridge (1980) and Jones (1986) voiced the objections of teachers who felt that children could not be called composers, others were arguing the case for the processes of thinking as a composer that were at the heart of musical development in successful classroom creativity:

> After every musical idea, however simple, has been formed, the choice facing the composer is fourfold – to finish; to repeat the idea; to vary the idea; or to find a contrasting idea. By asking the right questions in the right way we can usually get our pupils to think about and experiment with developing their musical ideas in their own way.
>
> (Cain, 1985: 12)

Given that the understanding of composing in the classroom demanded a different set of musical skills from those that teachers were accustomed to using, it is hardly surprising that there was some initial hostility to the ideas of Paynter and Aston (1970) and their contemporaries. Although deliberate efforts were made to disseminate the ideas and to share evidence of successful practice, particularly through the work of the Schools Council Project, *Music in the Secondary School Curriculum* (Paynter, 1982), those teachers who had established a thriving music department based on performance activities must have found the new methods difficult to accept. Salaman (1983) reflected on the change in his teaching, focusing on the problem of balancing the 'musical director' or 'Kapellmeister' role with the new focus on more effective classroom teaching. Salaman's admission that public commendation for school concerts could not validate classroom practice must have been a difficult one for him and like-minded colleagues to make (ibid.: 10), but the realisation that music in the curriculum should be for all pupils was essential to a new understanding of music in schools:

> In the school music room, the teacher has no right to be selective. He is no more turning out professional musicians than the art teacher is turning out professional artists or the French teacher professional linguists.
>
> (Salaman, 1983: 11)

Salaman's realisation that his primary role was as an educator, rather than solely a musician, was part of a wider acceptance that music should be part of a child's whole education, rather than directed towards selecting and training proficient performers. The change of emphasis caused consternation amongst those teachers who were principally interested in their more 'gifted' pupils, and who feared that a broader approach to music in the curriculum would neglect the specific training that future professionals needed. Fletcher (1987/89) was amongst the more hostile critics of the changes in classroom music, stating that composing and improvising had only the 'limited use' of raising aural awareness:

> The common factor among all these innovations of the past twenty years has been, quite literally, their limited usefulness. They reflect, equally literally, the limited usefulness for music of the secondary classroom. The unfortunate result of these innovations, however, has been to create a belief in the unlimited usefulness of the classroom.
>
> (Fletcher, 1987/89: 36)

Fletcher's failure to perceive that music teachers and classrooms serve, not music, but children, underpins his belief that individual instrumental tuition is the only productive course for school music (ibid.: xv). His dismissal of the work of Paynter, Schafer, Self, Dennis and Ross is scathingly arrogant, with his description of the secondary music classroom showing the extent of his hostility to their various ideas:

> Few thinking musicians would ever have suggested that conscripting groups of thirty children on no other criterion than similarity of age, and placing them in a restricted space in an authoritarian institution for two prescribed periods of forty minutes every week, was an ideal or even feasible way of developing musical understanding and activity. It is only because of the fact that musicians have had to brace themselves to this seemingly inevitable task that the sorts of noises

which emanate from classrooms are seen to have anything to do with music at all.

(Fletcher, 1987/89: 39)

This attack is remarkable, given that the links between classroom music and the work of living composers was closer than it had ever been, so that Fletcher's antipathy to the idea of composing in schools seems to be founded on a misunderstanding of its purpose. Suggesting that 'composing is one of the most difficult things it is possible to undertake' (ibid.: 41), he fails to acknowledge the insight that composing can afford, bound as he is by the view that technical mastery of an instrument is the only valid goal for music teaching:

> Art experience in music can best be achieved through participation in high-level, skilled performance. It can also be achieved through attendance at live performances. I do not believe it can be achieved, initially at least, through group or individual composition.
>
> (Fletcher, 1987/89: 44)

Fletcher's association of music with performance is as strong as Scholes' conviction that it is an 'ear-art, not a finger-and-voice art' (Scholes, 1935: 122), and makes no concession to the emerging realisation that music as a creative activity could also take its place in the classroom. Opposition to composing in the classroom, together with the misunderstanding of the new ideals of music education, were hindering the development of a coherent argument that incorporated the best practice of each approach, educating children as performers, listeners and composers.

Despite an increase in published ideas and theories, the conflict between traditional and 'progressive' teaching in music, observed at the end of the 1970s, was no nearer to being resolved. The wider adoption of the ideas of Paynter, Self and Schafer had complicated the debate further, as the unsuccessful application of misunderstood methods was a hindrance to their further dissemination. Whilst confidence in composing in the classroom was apparently growing, the pressure on music teachers to add this new element to their already burdensome workload meant that the dual roles of 'musical director' and 'composition guide' could become difficult to resolve (Salaman, 1983). As in other decades, when new ideas had become additions to the curriculum, rather than causing the evaluation of existing practice, teachers were left to construct their own understanding of music in schools, often shaped by local resources and opportunities. The need for an underlying philosophy for musical education at the end of the twentieth century was growing increasingly urgent.

Perhaps surprisingly, the progress of music education was to be affected more than ever by external factors, namely the changes to examination syllabuses of the mid-1980s and the introduction of the National Curriculum in the Education Reform Act of 1988. These national changes will be examined in subsequent chapters, but it is important to remember the turbulent state of music education upon which they were imposed. For some, the arrival of the General Certificate of Secondary Education (GCSE) was a welcome resolution of the difficult balancing act that music teachers had attempted to perform throughout the 1970s and 1980s. The conflicts remained, however, and as the controversy surrounding the National Curriculum for Music was to demonstrate, the construction of a curriculum that fulfilled all the musical goals in existence in the late 1980s was no easy task.

Chapter 5

Questions of assessment: towards the GCSE

5.1 Assessing music at 16+

It is necessary to interrupt the momentum of the historical account at this point, in order to consider the effects of expansion in the examination and assessment systems. The innovative practices of the 1960s and onwards had taken little account of the way in which musical achievements could be measured and reported, and yet these practical changes had occurred simultaneously with developments in the national assessment framework. Music educators in the post-war years had rejected the notion that music should be taught as a pseudo-academic subject, gradually accepting that whilst notation, sight singing and aural training might yield quantifiable results, the relative ease of assessing these achievements should not be allowed to drive the curriculum. Composition and performance were proving more difficult to evaluate, but the impetus to include these in examination syllabuses meant that the problem had to be confronted.

The position of music in the curriculum has always been affected, not only by its perceived value and relevance to pupils, but also by its ambiguous status with regard to public examinations. The pressures upon schools to train pupils in literacy and numeracy have meant that the pursuit of music as an examination subject has often been reserved for a minority, either through the external instrumental examinations of the colleges of music, or by opting to study music in the final years of compulsory education. The debate over the desirability of assessment in the arts appeared to reach its peak with the development of the General Certificate of Secondary Education (GCSE) in the mid-1980s, which was intended to bring the previous systems of 16+ examinations together across the curriculum. To consider the significance of this development, and its impact upon music teaching, it is necessary to look at the background to the GCSE and the associated questions of assessment in the arts.

The history of assessment in music education charts a long struggle to question traditional approaches to testing, working towards a system that measured essentially *musical* skills and understanding, rather than dictating what could be taught by first defining what could be tested. Examinations had originally been established as a way of selecting candidates for university places, and the School Certificate, introduced in 1917, followed the broadly academic model of the matriculation tests it was designed to replace. Candidates were required to pass in a group of subjects, rather than acquiring qualifications in individual disciplines, and music was given only optional status within the structure, and did not count towards the final assessment. This restriction was modified in 1929 to allow two subjects to be chosen from the optional Group IV – which included music, handicraft and art – in order to 'emphasise the importance' of these subjects (SSEC, 1932: 25). The problems were compounded, however, by the music syllabus itself, which was judged to be far too difficult for the majority of candidates, and did not 'commend itself to the schools':

> There is no doubt that teachers regard the examination as being beyond the abilities of the average pupil at sixteen. The result is that only the specially gifted pupils at a small proportion of schools are presented for examination in Music. Those who had hoped that the examination would be a means of broadening and improving the musical education in the schools are disappointed at this unexpected result.
>
> (SSEC, 1932: 138)

The syllabuses offered by the various University Examining Boards were 'vaguely worded' (ibid.: 138), and made demands that were unreasonable within the usual time allocation afforded to music in the curriculum. There were broad similarities between them, with all including aural, harmony and history, and some asking for sight singing. Vocal or instrumental performance was not compulsory under any of the Examination Boards, and composing was an option only for candidates predicted to gain a credit or distinction. The Secondary School Examinations Council report also criticises the questions set for the examination, saying that the coverage of music history was too broad and ought to be limited to one text book, and that the very nature of some of the questions was dubious:

> 'Do you prefer Mozart to Beethoven, or the reverse? Give your reasons.' This, according to the syllabus, is a question testing musical taste; a proceeding of very doubtful value.
>
> (SSEC, 1932: 140)

It seems that music suffered under the School Certificate in all directions, being hindered by its peripheral status in the examination structure, and also by the unreasonable demands made of those candidates who opted to pursue it. With the influence of examinations inevitably growing as increasing numbers of school leavers were encouraged to 'secure the magic parchment' of a qualification (Petch, 1953: 80), there was a real danger that music's position in the curriculum would be undermined.

With the culture of examinable achievement taking hold in schools, the need for a review of the system became apparent. The Education Act of 1944, which included the raising of the school leaving age and the advent of compulsory free secondary education for all, brought a new urgency to the debate. Shortly before the war, the Spens Report (Board of Education, 1938) had recommended a move to subject based examinations, rather than the 'group' arrangement then in existence. Such a change was likely to benefit music, but the outbreak of war halted the investigation of new alternatives. The next significant contribution was made by the Norwood Report (1943) which, whilst it was careful to give the arguments for and against examinations, was particularly critical of the restrictions that the School Certificate placed upon the curriculum and its undue focus on achieving paper qualifications:

> At present the examination dictates the curriculum and cannot do otherwise; it confines experiment, limits free choice of subject, hampers treatment of subjects, encourages wrong values in the class-room. ... [Pupils] absorb what it will pay them to absorb, and reproduce it as second-hand knowledge which is of value only for the moment.
>
> (Board of Education, 1943: 31)

This enlightened attitude to the potential longer-term benefits of education, which the School Certificate had allegedly suppressed, has much in common with contemporary views of music education as something to be fostered in school, and continued throughout adult life. The Norwood Committee acknowledge the value of the 'aesthetic subjects' (ibid.: 123), but the assumption that they ought to be compulsory at examination level is refuted on the grounds that not all pupils can be expected to 'appreciate' them equally. Music in the early secondary years, it is suggested, ought to follow on from the work covered in primary schools, and should be appropriate for all ability levels, with due allowances made 'for failure owing to physical defect or sheer lack of taste or ability':

128

Children who after tuition are incapable of singing or playing an instrument (probably fewer in number than is commonly supposed) ... derive great enjoyment and value from being shown how to listen to music. It is part of the teachers' work to cater for both; admittedly the 'teaching' of appreciation is a matter which calls for exceptional skill, if harm is not to be done by the forcing of the teacher's judgement upon the pupil.

(Board of Education, 1943: 126)

Perceptions of musical ability and 'giftedness' shaped the views of the committee, with the misplaced assumption that not everyone can be taught music forming a barrier against its wider development in the curriculum. Lack of resources and specialist teachers, recognised in this report and in others, had restricted the potential of music teaching in schools, leaving the subject in a weak position from which to demonstrate its relevance to a general education. Nevertheless, with the transition to the subject-based General Certificate of Education (GCE) in 1951 came a revised music syllabus, with the opportunity to remedy the faults of the School Certificate, not least the discouraging effect of its unduly high standards.

5.2 The GCE: a model of musical assessment

If the GCE reforms were intended to resolve the problems of music examinations, it appears that they were largely unsuccessful, retaining as they did the misconception that music at examination level was appropriate only for selected candidates. Designed as a continuum, GCE 'Ordinary' and 'Advanced' Levels preserved the syllabus content of the School Certificate, namely harmony, aural, and historical knowledge, with performing and composing now included, but not seen to be readily examinable. Contemporary writers on music education make little mention of the GCE (cf. Winn, 1954), which implies that developments in the lower school curriculum were of greater significance at the time. Long (1959), in his survey on English music education, confirms that music remained a minority subject amongst examination candidates, even in comparison with art, which had also been hampered by Group IV status under the School Certificate:

	1954 'O' Level	1954 'A' Level
English Language	135,682 candidates	12, 167 candidates
English Literature	92, 133 candidates	('English')
Art	38, 588 candidates	1, 875 candidates
Music	**4, 261 candidates**	**698 candidates**

(Long, 1959: 37)

Whilst music educators were writing about the need for music to have relevance for the majority of pupils, it appears that the elitism of examination courses in music had not been challenged, with the standards and syllabus content retaining the exclusivity criticised in the School Certificate.

The introduction of the GCE by no means concluded the debate about the place of external examinations in education, with some teachers and educationalists continuing to voice their objections to the influence of examinations upon the curriculum:

> Like the School Certificate examination which it replaced, the G.C.E. soon acquired great prestige in the eyes of pupils, parents, teachers and employers; and the Council's hope that the needs of children following non-selective courses would be met by arrangements akin to those suggested in the Norwood Report, namely systematic internal examinations, perhaps with a measure of external assessment, together with an extended use of school reports, was not fulfilled.
>
> (SSEC, 1963: 98)

As with the School Certificate, the expectations of employers, parents and pupils increased the prestige of the examination, reinforcing the unsatisfactory position of music in the educational hierarchy. The association of GCE with the grammar schools, representing the cream of English secondary education, was perhaps partly responsible for a reluctance to make further changes, and the style of music 'O' Level was to remain largely unaltered over several decades:

June 1973 (University of London):
- Describe any three passages which you think might support the statement that 'Interest in orchestration as an art may be said to begin in Weber's time'.

June 1977 (Oxford Local Examinations):
- What do you consider to be the main characteristics of the songs by Schubert that you have studied?

June 1987 (Oxford Local Examinations):

- Elgar dedicated the Enigma Variations to his 'friends pictured within'. What impressions do you get from Elgar's music of the people depicted in the variations you have studied?

Of themselves, these questions offer scope for interesting musical discussion, but as part of an examination syllabus for 16-year-olds, they are more likely to have constrained the teaching of the course, emphasising as they do the ability to write about music and to recall facts and opinions about a limited repertoire. Taken in the context of the whole examination, it is not unreasonable that the history paper should test specific skills in this way, but this is only one example of the study *about* music rather than *through* music that had characterised public examinations in the subject so far. Music was struggling for an identity, and by adopting the 'academic' stance felt to be appropriate for examination status, was in danger of losing sight of its musical essence. The impact on the curriculum at all levels of secondary music education was inevitably felt:

The stress on paper-work in G.C.E. syllabuses (paper examinations are easier to administer than practical) not infrequently conspire[s] to pervert the music curriculum even to the point where forms of eleven-year-olds, who should be singing their heads off and their hearts out, sometimes spend forty minutes at a stretch inserting bar lines in melodies which are largely incomprehensible to them, and in making arithmetical computations far below their proper mathematical standard. They may enjoy it, but it is not music.

(Simpson, 1964/68: 33)

Dissatisfaction with GCE was spreading across the curriculum, putting music teachers in a stronger position to argue their case in the next wave of examination reforms. Concern that the 'O' Level was failing to provide for the majority of pupils was in part caused by the expansion of secondary education that had originally led to its implementation. With the influence and credibility of examinations increasing all the time, it was apparent that a qualification appropriate for only the top 20 per cent of grammar school students was no longer serving the needs of schools and school leavers (cf. Ministry of Education, 1960: 9).

The committee appointed by the Secondary School Examinations Council to investigate examinations 'other than the GCE' (Ministry of Education, 1960) reported that whilst significant numbers of secondary modern school pupils were being entered for three or four 'O' Levels, there was a proliferation of regional and national examination boards offering independent qualifications as an alternative. Fearing that the influence of these examining bodies would grow, along with the uneven marking and inadequate moderation that the committee observed, the Minister for Education was urged to intervene by giving official approval to those examinations held to be beneficial, or by initiating the provision of a new system (ibid.: 27). The committee recommended an examination that, rather than reproducing the 'O' Level at a lower ability level, adopted an altogether 'different character and aims' (ibid.: 30). GCE was to be retained as the grammar school examination, but a system for recognising the educational achievements of the ability band below that was seen to be desirable. Whilst not specifically mentioning music, the committee's discussion of new methods of assessment offered hope for curriculum reform:

> We think it important that, wherever the subject allows, the examinations should provide for practical work. We hope that in all subjects they would encourage candidates to show a genuine interest, or what might be called 'involvement' in their subjects, and would give credit for freshness of approach, intelligence and ability to write good English, as well as for remembered facts and textbook learning.
>
> (Ministry of Education, 1960: 34)

With GCE music clearly displaying the faults that the committee implies, the time was ready for reform, and this was to come in 1965 with the introduction of the Certificate of Secondary Education (CSE). For the first time, the changes to music education that non-examination courses had been able to explore were to be recognised as part of an externally assessed programme. The new examination was not intended to replace the GCE 'O' Level, and could therefore be seen as an alternative, rather than a threat. It is possible that the dual system helped to encourage experimentation because of this safeguard, broadening the opportunities for assessment in music education, rather than completely redefining the examinable potential of the subject. At its inception, the CSE was an optimistic development, although the overall status of the examination in relation to GCE syllabuses was to prove more of a hindrance than could have been anticipated.

5.3 The CSE: a new definition of music assessment

The election of a Labour government in 1964 encouraged the demise of the 'academic' superiority of the grammar schools, supporting the interest in the average and less able pupil that had been shown by the Newsom Report (Ministry of Education, 1963). The gradual move towards comprehensive schooling that followed, far from eliminating the differences between the former grammar school and secondary modern pupils, highlighted the fact that reform was needed at a curriculum and assessment level, not merely in the realm of school organisation. In 1965, the examination intended to meet the needs of the lower than average ability band was introduced by the Secondary Schools Examinations Council:

> The C.S.E. [Certificate of Secondary Education] examinations are not to be regarded as watered down versions of the examinations at the ordinary level of the G.C.E., nor is it intended that they should be used as selection tests for G.C.E. courses. The two examinations systems must be free to develop in their own ways, according to the needs of the majority of the pupils for whom they are designed. And in many subjects, though not necessarily in all, this will mean that the two systems ought properly to adopt different syllabuses, and to assume different approaches to teaching.
>
> (SSEC, 1963: 8)

The *Suggestions for Teachers and Examiners* from which this advice is taken emphasises the flexibility of the new system throughout, stating that the examinations should have 'freshness and vitality' (SSEC, 1963: 3). The major change was that teachers were to be involved in the examination process to an unprecedented extent, both in devising the syllabus content and in acting as internal examiners. The CSE was to be administered by regional examining boards, with variations according to local expertise and resources monitored by the Secondary Schools Examinations Council to ensure equality of assessment across the country.

In the general guide to the new examination, each subject is considered separately, and the need for changes in assessment approaches are discussed throughout the curriculum. In the section on music, the difficulties of assessing skills that are truly musical, rather than measuring associated knowledge, are foremost in the debate:

> Music ... presents unique problems to the examiner, mainly because one of its most valuable, educational aspects, namely corporate music making, does not lend itself to individual testing. Since practical music making throughout the secondary school must at all costs be encouraged, not least when the pressures of examinations begin to assert themselves most powerfully, it will be necessary to devise forms of examination in music that will take account not only of the candidate's full knowledge and skill, but also of his contribution to corporate musical activities of various kinds.
>
> (SSEC, 1963: 66)

The emphasis on 'corporate music making' reflects the priorities of early 1960s music education: the idea of composing in the classroom was not yet established, and the days of whole-class singing lessons were a very recent memory. There is no rationale as to why ensemble playing is preferable to solo performance; this is presumably an organisational concession, reflecting the contemporary practice of class percussion and singing ensembles.

The CSE in music was intended to demonstrate competence in music reading and aural perception, as well as providing evidence that candidates had participated in corporate music making throughout the course. The tests were to involve a minimum of writing, a feature that showed insight upon educational psychology, acknowledging that the abilities of pupils could differ between subjects. Aural perception was to be based on real musical examples, encouraging the application of musical thinking, rather than training for specific tests. Similarly, musical knowledge was to move away from the study of set works, towards a more general acquisition of musical understanding:

> The unorthodox features of the suggested examination are (a) the inclusion of ensemble work as a requirement, though not strictly speaking examinable, (b) the method of testing analytical listening, and (c) the method of testing general musical knowledge. The remainder of the examination, although it does not closely follow current practice, is based upon well tried methods about which a good deal is already known.
>
> (SSEC, 1963: 69)

Details of the thinking behind the music examinations can also be found in the report of the experimental CSE courses that ran in 1964 (Schools Council, 1966). The inspectorate, asked for their views on music testing at an early stage in the discussions, had expressed a reluctance to impose examination requirements upon teachers, but moderated this view with a realisation that to be excluded from the new system would be potentially damaging for music. The aims of the new syllabuses for music were therefore articulated as follows:

a) to stimulate corporate music making as an essential part of the examination;
b) to suggest some new ways of testing musical literacy, based largely upon the kind of aural perception required in actual performance;
c) to encourage a wide knowledge of musical literature rather than an analytical knowledge of two or three set works;
d) to provide an incentive for candidates to pursue some individual musical interest.

(Schools Council, 1966: 1)

Trial music examinations were held in 32 schools in June 1964, with comments from teachers invited at all stages. The first aural perception test was based on a simple tune from the *Beggar's Opera*; a 16-bar melody with an AABA structure. Pupils were given a skeleton score, to which they had to add a time signature, copy in given notes, and carry out melodic and rhythmic dictation:

> The purpose of the test was to see how much candidates could perceive and record of the form of the piece, its instrumentation, phrasing, dynamics, indications of tempo and other marks of expression, as well as its rhythm and melody. ... As there seemed no point in making the exercise a race against the clock, no time limit was set and the recording was played seven times, as candidates required.
>
> (Schools Council, 1966: 2)

Although the performance of candidates indicated that some of the questions were too difficult, pupils and teachers alike indicated that the new style of test was an improvement on more traditional methods. In the trial tests of musical knowledge, there was greater dissent, as the wide-ranging questions were not felt to demonstrate candidates' true ability. The test included references to jazz, dance styles and classical works, some questions relying on general knowledge, but others showing the expectation that certain masterworks would still hold a place in every teacher's curriculum:

- Here is a song by Schubert sung in German. What is the title usually given to it in English?
  The Trout – 'Die Forelle', Schubert
  What is the name of that song?

- This music is not by Bach but it is in a form that Bach often used. What is this form?
  Fugue – from Toccata and Fugue in F major, Buxtehude
  What form was that?

- If you were asked to invite a famous soloist to play in this concerto whom would you choose?
  The name of any famous violinist – Violin Concerto, Beethoven
  Which famous player would you ask to play that solo part?

  (Schools Council, 1966: 19)

The fifteen questions on the musical knowledge paper may have required only single-word answers, but they drew on a vast repertoire, and assumed a variety of knowledge for which these trial candidates had not been prepared. Teachers proposed that a certain area of music should be specified for study, to enable a broad approach within reasonable limits, echoing criticisms of the old School Certificate (SSEC, 1932: 139).

Initial difficulties with CSE music centred upon resources; with many homes possessing better audio equipment than could be found in schools, it was recognised that the new examinations would require investments of time and money in order to be a success (Schools Council, 1966: 7). The Schools Council concluded that the proposed examination was generally welcomed by teachers, who were keen to explore the new assessment techniques, and their implications for music in the curriculum:

> The framework of C.S.E. offers opportunities for new developments which schools are keen to seize, and one of the most valuable things the examination has done so far is to bring groups of teachers together to discuss not only problems of examining but the whole question of music in secondary schools. All this augurs well for the future and gives confidence that lively progress will be made.
>
> (Schools Council, 1966: 10)

With hindsight, it is easy to see that the dual system of examinations, although not intended to be hierarchical, would inevitably result in the CSE being perceived as a low status examination. However necessary the reform to the academic dominance of the GCE, the traditional model was likely to retain its supremacy, just as the 'A' Level would later overshadow attempts to create vocational qualifications at 18+. In the short term, however, it seems that CSE music generated a new interest in music teaching and assessment, and led to the development of courses that varied from the knowledge-based traditions of 'O' Level teaching. The dual existence of GCE and CSE was to be the motivation for further reform in the 1980s, and further study of both examinations in practice provides an illuminating background to the development of the GCSE.

5.4 The dual system: implications for music teaching

The CSE in music did not, of itself, suggest that a different approach to the content of music lessons was desirable, except in its recognition that performance should be at the heart of the curriculum. In practice, however, the control that teachers had over the syllabus content led to the development of new courses that emphasised particular musical interests, such as electronic music, improvisation or popular music. While the GCE 'O' Level retained its identity as potentially the first step on the route towards a university music degree, the CSE became disparate, determined at a local level by the interests of teachers and the needs of pupils. As the debate on the place of popular music in the classroom became more vociferous, the CSE was often cited as a means of recognising pupils' achievements in this new branch of music learning. A detailed account of developments of this genre is provided by Farmer, whose *Music in the Comprehensive School* (1979) brings together the wider reforms of the 1970s with the new direction of musical thinking.

Following the outline of the CSE, Farmer proposes three main areas that should feature in a balanced music programme: 'practical work', which consists of playing instruments and singing, 'listening', including appreciation and aural, and 'non-practical work', incorporating theory and musical knowledge (Farmer, 1979: 13). He articulates the aims of music teaching, which should be achieved through a balance and flexibility in the three areas:

1. To encourage and enable pupils to make music;
2. To expose pupils to a wide range of music, and to encourage them to listen to it and exercise judgement;
3. To equip pupils with the necessary non-practical skills for playing and listening, and to involve pupils in other non-practical activities where desirable for their own sake.

(Farmer, 1979: 14)

It should be noted that Farmer's goals lack the idealism of earlier writers, and focus instead upon the practicalities of classroom music teaching. His book is intended to be of real assistance to music teachers, and there is little attempt to provide a rationale for engaging with the arts. Perhaps this is the first sign of the examination dominance that Her Majesty's Inspectors had warned against (Schools Council, 1966: 1), with the assumption that the framework for music teaching had already been determined, and simply needed transferring to classroom practice. Farmer acknowledges the influence of the CSE upon his thinking, seeing it as a solution to the faults of 'O' Level teaching:

> Music is a subject which is perhaps particularly prone to all that is worst in examinations, mainly because of the way exams in music have been largely concerned with propositional knowledge. Just as it has been easiest to teach facts about music to classes, rather than teach them how to play, say, the guitar, so testing of factual information has also become easier than assessing performance or practical ability.
>
> (Farmer, 1979: 16)

Farmer's ideas centre around the Mode 3 CSE, in which the teacher could propose a syllabus that was specifically written for the needs and interests of a group of pupils. At the time of the CSE's introduction, attempts had been made to accommodate many of the views expressed during the consultation period by constructing a threefold system across the whole curriculum:

'Mode 1' was essentially an examination marked by external examiners on a syllabus prepared by the subject panel of the regional board. 'Mode 2' was an external examination on a syllabus submitted by a school or group of schools and approved by the board. 'Mode 3' was a type of examination set and marked internally in the school or group of schools, being approved and moderated by the regional board.

(Montgomery, 1978: 51)

Farmer reports that at the time of writing, the West Yorkshire and Lindsey Examining Board were running seventy Mode 3 music courses, with biases that included popular, electronic and medieval music. This flexibility was to generate its own problems, as each syllabus had to be approved or moderated, and was then sometimes discarded by the school after one year, leading to high costs for the examining board (Montgomery, 1978: 51). Whatever its educational validity, which would certainly not be tolerated in today's age of standardisation, Farmer's view is that these customised examinations make music widely available in the school community, a more satisfactory approach than limiting music to an option chosen by only a few:

While music is left as a subject *to be chosen*, in competition with many other subjects, its nature will inevitably be dictated, at least to some extent, by the *type* of pupil who chooses it. Yet exactly who ends up taking this subject may simply depend on the relative position of subjects in a school's option list.

(Farmer, 1979: 50)

Despite his confidence in the role of CSE in music education, the sample syllabuses provided by Farmer often show a tendency to include 'O' Level and CSE approaches in the same examination; a huge undertaking both for pupils and teachers, and not one that really addresses the different views of music education that the two systems represent. Pupils could be expected to produce a folio of compositions, a performance, a substantial essay and even a musical instrument, in addition to taking written history and aural papers. The attempt to include all aspects of music making in a single examination is understandable, but the lack of focus could generate the confusion and alienation that it had been designed to avoid.

Much of Farmer's thinking is influenced by this multifaceted view of music education, which is representative of attempts to absorb both the traditional and the innovatory models of music teaching that had developed over the century. Instead of moving entirely towards CSE, he seems to advocate an approach that includes the best elements of 'O' Level teaching, whilst selecting from the range of musical activities and skills to which CSE had given recognition. This transition is typical of the gradual absorption of new ideas in music education, with teachers attempting to extend their work through the inclusion of new ideas, rather than completely changing direction in response to innovation. For many teachers, themselves trained in the traditional style of music learning, the CSE will have seemed a strange addition to the curriculum, with 'O' Level retaining its status in the education of conventionally 'musical' pupils:

> In addition to examination needs, it is no bad thing if one or two periods a week can also be given to fourth and fifth year pupils not taking the subject to 'O' level to sustain the earlier course, to extend discrimination in listening and to round off the training of boys' voices. The new Certificate of Secondary Education offers interesting possibilities for those not on an 'O' level course, and might well form a good means of continuing earlier training to a definable end.
>
> (Gilbey, 1964/68: 93)

Gilbey, a grammar school headmaster, makes it apparent that his priorities lie with those on the 'O' Level music course, but appears to recognise the CSE as a means of focusing musical education for those who would otherwise cease to study it. These varied uses of the CSE were predicted in the initial consultation documents but, in practice, must have done little to increase the understanding of the qualification amongst parents and employers.

Concern over the dual assessment system had begun to surface in other subjects, and was the focus of policy reviews throughout the 1970s and early 1980s. Even before the CSE was fully established, the authors of *Half Our Future* (Ministry of Education, 1963) had cautioned that the two systems would still not cater for low ability children, for whom the continuous assessment of 'coursework' would form a more appropriate strategy:

> No pupil, however, ought to be occupied exclusively with examination work, or to feel that time and energies spent on anything else are wasted. ... A pupil's programme will be justified only if it makes educational sense as a whole, whether it is subject to external examinations or not.
>
> (Ministry of Education, 1963: 83)

Whilst a minority of educational writers continued to urge against the dominance of examinations, the dual pressures of GCE and CSE on the curriculum were to lead to a demand for further reform. For every writer who shared the Newsom Committee's respect for non-examination courses, there was someone ready to urge the importance of a focus for the work of school leavers:

> An examination marvellously focuses the mind. It can be replaced by alternative forms of assessment, by 'continuous assessment', or the marking of 'course' or 'project' work, for example; there are many forms other than a two-and-a-half- hour written paper. Without assessment, however, a pupil may lack guidance and lose his sense of purpose; without structure and tension life can become aimless.
>
> (Montgomery, 1978: 19)

Combined with the increasing political interest in education, the tendency to direct all education towards recognised qualifications was growing stronger, and a system was needed that would resolve the confusions of the existing assessment structures. Support was growing for a single system of examinations to replace the GCE and CSE, which would address the needs of all pupils, in every kind of secondary school. Whilst the potential benefits of ending the unspoken competition between existing qualifications were evident, the proposals met with a certain amount of resistance:

> Many of the concepts of CSE examining were strange to those with only GCE experience, who regarded teachers' assessments, continuous assessment, course work and project work with sentiments ranging from mild distrust to those of outraged morality.
>
> (Montgomery, 1978: 61)

The momentum for change was underway, however, and a study of developments in music as the preparations for the first General Certificate of Secondary Education (GCSE) examinations began, reveals some of the difficulties and challenges that were peculiar to music education.

5.5 GCSE music: compose, listen, perform

The evolution of a single system of assessment at 16+ can be logically traced through questions of school and curriculum organisation, but the implications of the reform for music teaching raised more complex dilemmas for the authors of the new syllabuses. In the previous decades, music teaching in schools had expanded to an unprecedented extent, with wide regional variation in the amount, quality and nature of provision. To encapsulate the best of this practice within the proposed reforms was an enormous challenge, and one which had the potential either to move music teaching forwards, or to stultify the innovation that existed. A recognition of this challenge was made in the HMI report, *Music from 5 to 16*, which summarised the important features of the new national criteria:

> The national criteria for music in the GCSE examination emphasise the central importance of performing, composing and listening. Although performance has figure[d] in most CSE and some O-level syllabuses for some time, the appearance in the new examination of composition (disregarding the elementary pastiche in earlier harmony papers) is something of an innovation. Assessment of the listening component is likely to be concerned more than hitherto with the actual sound and structure of music than with information about when and how it came to be written.
>
> (DES, 1985a: 16)

The decision to give composition such a prominent place in the new examination was a bold one, welcomed by teachers who had embraced the developments of the 1970s and 1980s, but necessitating professional support for those who had remained loyal to the more traditional models of their own training. For the first time, the idea that there are three essential, integrated musical experiences – composing, performing and listening – was given official credence, in an examination that paid tribute to both of its predecessors, without being constrained by their structures. Training at a local level was needed to ensure teachers were familiar with the new ideas, and written guidance was produced by regional examining boards to supplement a programme of in-service training that was not always adequate. One such guide was issued by the Southern Examining Group (SEG), with an explanation of the new criteria that echoed the optimism of the HMI description:

> The GCSE sets out to rationalise the existing 'O' level and CSE, while drawing on the best aspects of both. In GCSE Music the opportunity has also been grasped to correct previous imbalances: in particular to make the central focus of both courses and assessment procedures essentially musical; rather than in any way limiting them to a concern with things only about music. This new opportunity should offer flexibility to teachers and promote interest amongst learners.
>
> (SEG, 1987a: 7)

The sense of opportunity that the GCSE generated was reminiscent of the inception of CSE music, but with the new system designed to replace, rather than supplement, what had gone before, the need to ensure that all teachers were familiar with the new assessment techniques was more important. Ideas that had been regarded as revolutionary little more than a decade earlier now had official status, and for those teachers still working within the history and appreciation style of 'O' Level teaching, the new prominence afforded to composing and performing must have appeared threatening. The Southern Examining Group's *Teachers' Guide* (SEG, 1987a) acknowledged the changes to classroom practice that the new examination required:

> A predominantly less didactic, more pupil-focused teaching style will need to be extended over a much wider spectrum of music making. Teaching and learning, especially in practical subjects like music, are more about the contexts and processes applied to lesson content than just content alone; learning and skill acquisition are to be undertaken in the context of musical activities.
>
> (SEG, 1987a: 16)

Teachers in all areas of the country were issued with guides similar to the SEG publication, with explanations of the new criteria and sample moderation exercises, to be discussed with colleagues and music advisers. To a greater extent even than CSE, teachers were to be involved in the internal assessment of coursework, with pupils submitting a folio of compositions and preparing performances for continuous and summative assessment. This dual role of teacher and examiner led to concern over difficulties of distinguishing between legitimate assistance during the process of composition, for example, and undue intervention that would affect the grade awarded to the candidate. The signing of 'authentication statements' to confirm the level of help given to pupils was an acknowledgement of teachers' professionalism, although there would soon be objections to examinations consisting only of coursework, particularly some of the first English Literature syllabuses.

With composition given such prominence in the new examination, methods of assessing the work of candidates had to be devised, and this was to prove a contentious area. Criteria were published, both for performing and for composing, that attempted to quantify the processes of analysis and criticism that any listener would bring to a piece of music, but the terminology was not always carefully chosen. In assessing composing, credit was awarded for the process of redrafting ideas, with candidates at the highest level showing 'outstanding powers of self-criticism' (SEG, 1987b: 13). Simplicity was assumed to be an indication of lower ability, with the weakest candidates showing only 'some grasp of rhythmic and melodic construction'. Clearly, with little prior knowledge of the compositions that 16-year-olds were likely to produce, the criteria needed to allow for huge variations in style and competence. With performing, the examiners seem to have felt on more certain ground, but the specifications are still questionable, displaying a particular view of music that should perhaps have been given more careful consideration:

Excellent The performance is fluent and expressive, leading to a totally convincing interpretation.

Very good The performance is fluent, with some sense of conviction in interpretation.

Good The performance is adequate to the technical demands of the piece but does not convey its meaning completely.

Fair The performance does not convey completely the intentions of the composer due to technical inadequacies.

Poor A performance which barely communicates the intentions of the composer.

(SEG, 1987b: 5)

Whilst the distinction between interpretation and technique is a logical one, such phrases as 'the intentions of the composer' discredit this approach, calling upon candidates and teachers to achieve understanding that cannot be determined from the printed score. Similarly, talk of musical 'meaning' may infiltrate casual conversation, but its use here seems dubious. Such criticisms will have emerged as teachers implemented the new criteria, with the result that the language of the later criteria was reconsidered, as demonstrated in the 'excellent' and 'poor' criteria for 1998 performance examinations:

Excellent The performance is excellent in every respect and leads to a totally convincing interpretation. The performance will be accurate and musical, demonstrating a high level of technical skill, expression and imagination as the particular piece demands.

Poor The performance conveys, at a minimal level, the intentions of the piece although errors of pitch and rhythm are evident. Fluency, accuracy and interpretative qualities appear only occasionally.

(SEG, 1996: 16)

The criteria for composing underwent more significant changes in the same period, with the 1998 syllabus including the category 'Communication of process and purpose of composition' and emphasising the assessment of the 'intended effect' (SEG, 1996: 30). This is evidently an attempt to resolve the dilemmas of coursework by giving due recognition to the creation of the music, as well as the final composition. However, such well-intentioned ideas can often have the side-effect of creating a burden of paperwork as candidates and teachers try to rationalise their work in order to satisfy a moderator, with the result that the assessment process begins to dominate teaching and learning.

It may seem futile to quibble over the wording of the assessment criteria, but given their influence upon the work of teachers and the success of candidates, their implicit values need to be carefully appraised. More fundamental criticisms have been offered by Swanwick (1988), who objects to the attempt to disguise subjective judgements within an apparently objective system of grading candidates' work. He proposes alternative categories, based on his 'spiral' of musical development (cf. Swanwick & Tillman, 1986), which demonstrate the progression from sensory exploration and manipulative skills towards systematic reflection upon musical processes (Swanwick, 1988: 77). Candidates achieving the highest grades would therefore be engaging in 'symbolic' musical processes, in which 'technical mastery serves musical communication', whilst the average candidate, at Grade C, would be operating at the 'speculative' level, where 'limited musical materials are generally well handled' (ibid.: 152). Swanwick's view of musical development has itself attracted criticism, and his search for 'formal relationships and expressive power' seems no less subjective than the SEG criteria of 'originality, skill and craftsmanship of a high order' (SEG, 1987b: 13). Experienced music listeners will no doubt hold opinions on Western composers to whom they would award a Grade C under either system. What Swanwick acknowledges, more readily than the examination board, is that the process of musical appraisal is an ongoing part of music education for both teacher and pupil:

> To teach *is* to assess, to weigh up, to appraise; in order more adequately to plan for and facilitate richer response, to accept that arts teaching is arts criticism.
>
> (Swanwick, 1988: 149)

The GCSE went a long way towards ensuring that self-evaluation and continuous assessment were a key part of an essentially practical music course. The system inevitably had its critics, and was susceptible to varying degrees of interpretation, meaning that teachers could retain the 'O' Level ideology and resist the innovations of GCSE if they were sufficiently determined. Inevitable concerns over falling examination standards generated some anxiety about the fairness of coursework, with the result that listening examinations were afforded slightly greater weight in the syllabus. These changes could not detract from the overall effect of GCSE, which was to secure the place of composing and performing in the curriculum. According to research carried out in 1983, when the proposed criteria were circulated to schools and colleges, the initial response from teachers was generally supportive of change:

> 86% of the teachers in the 1717 schools and colleges which responded, considered that the statement of Assessment Objectives drawn up by the Working Party for all the syllabuses in Music was appropriate; over 73% said that the statement matched the way in which they would like to teach the subject. If there were teachers who would have preferred to stick to the well-beaten, if arid, tracks of traditional syllabuses, they must have been relatively few in number and not very vocal in their opposition.
>
> (Vickerman, 1986: 194)

At a broader curriculum level it could be argued that, as with CSE, the optimism that greeted the new examination was misplaced, and the structural changes to the assessment process failed to resolve the problems that had led to their implementation. GCSE was intended to end the hierarchy of examinations that existed before, but the phrase 'GCSE at grades A–C' soon came to be the equivalent of an 'O' Level pass, with grades of D or less taken as indicators of CSE level ability. Changing the language of assessment tools does not change the essential problems, and whilst GCSE had many beneficial effects upon music education, disparities in provision remained.

Much of the objection to GCSE came from the 'right wing' stance; traditionalists who were later to cause similar difficulties over the development of the National Curriculum, particularly in music. North's compendium, *The GCSE: An Examination* (1987) is hostile to the 'child-centred' approach that is implicit in the introduction of coursework and investigative learning. In the chapter on music, Wyatt criticises the apparent lack of emphasis on 'the masterpieces of Western music' (1987: 98), and claims that the attempt to cover the music of other cultures will result in 'superficial' coverage:

> The wisdom of such a wide exposure for all is to be doubted, especially when it will operate at the expense of that music which is part of the foundation of our cultural heritage. Even a university or college course which aims to study a history of music from the Renaissance to the present day barely surveys the period; much less a secondary school course which includes Eastern, African,

Afro-Caribbean and Asian music alongside Western European music of the baroque, classical and romantic periods.

(Wyatt, 1987: 99)

Wyatt's criticisms, and those of his fellow reactionaries, fail to take account of the GCSE's emphasis on musical skills, as opposed to musical knowledge. A child who is exposed to the music of other cultures, as well as of other eras, will construct a wider definition of music than one who studies a narrow range of set works, with successful candidates able to apply their broad knowledge and listening techniques to whatever they hear. The question of access and elitism inevitably follows, with Wyatt barely able to conceal his concern that conventionally 'musical' pupils will suffer under the new system:

> Presenting such a wide variety of music to such a wide range of ability makes it impossible to cater adequately for everybody. The difficulties in asking the 'right' questions will mean that the most able will have to answer questions which they will find ludicrously simple, and other candidates will have been trained by teachers to avoid those they cannot do. The true aural ability of all candidates will not have been fathomed.
>
> (Wyatt, 1987: 103)

Throughout his criticisms, Wyatt makes it apparent that his priority is the training of future musicians, rather than the reflection of achievement in music education for a wider group of pupils. With regard to performing, he objects to the notion of continuous assessment, saying that to take a candidate's best performance is to provide a cushion from 'the disciplines and realities of performing' (Wyatt, 1987: 104). In a ruthless way, he has a valid argument, but overlooks the fact that an examination at 16+ should assess the achievements of pupils over a two-year course, during which time they will hopefully have shown development, but may have suffered set-backs for which they should not be penalised. The examination boards had indeed recognised the musically untenable scenario that Wyatt predicts, trusting teachers to avoid training candidates in the performance of a selected piece:

> In relation to prepared pieces, only one assessment occasion may be admitted for the purposes of final assessment. This prevents the unreasonable possibility that a piece assessed on one occasion may then be subjected to further improvement and re-assessed, probably at a higher level, and that later assessment admitted for the purposes of an award.
>
> (SEG, 1987a: 68)

In purely practical terms, then, Wyatt has got his facts wrong, but his objections illustrate a deeper disquiet with the notion that GCSE music should be available to pupils beyond the select group typical of 'O' Level candidates. The belief that music education should be for the majority, articulated by prominent innovators of the late 1970s and early 1980s, had been afforded recognition by the examination system, rendering these outdated criticisms increasingly ineffectual. Drawing his conclusions, Wyatt admits that he has focused upon the worst possible teaching that the GCSE criteria would permit, struggling with the greater flexibility that is afforded to teachers:

> The Criteria and the syllabuses are on the whole sufficiently broad to allow teachers to teach and to maintain the standards in which they believe. Our children *need* not suffer. However, in the wrong hands there could be abuse, and it is the serious possibility of this that I am determined to expose.
>
> (Wyatt, 1987: 112)

Wyatt's commentary, published before the first candidates had taken the new examination, is indicative of the levels of resistance with which changes in music education were received amongst some members of the teaching profession. That an educational debate was active at the time of GCSE's inception is important, as the opportunities for public discussion of new ideas were becoming rarer, and the futility of doing so was to become increasingly apparent as new legislation proceeded with little genuine recognition of professional opinion.

5.6 Theories of assessment in music education

The changes to the examination systems described in this chapter have been largely motivated by influences beyond the curriculum; school organisation, the need to provide for the less able pupil, or the desire to create a recognised qualification appropriate for all school leavers. What has resulted from the various developments, however, is a change in the teaching and learning of music, and more particularly in its assessment. Whereas the traditional GCE syllabus demanded that candidates should be knowledgeable *about* music, more recent assessment schemes have encouraged children to be actively engaged *with* music, with knowledge seen as a by-product of performing, composing and listening. In defining how music is to be assessed, the creators of examination syllabuses are also concerned with what is assessed, and the development of GCSE did much to question the accepted dominance of musical facts and to replace them with musical activities.

The problem of how to assess music has wider implications for the curriculum, and has been considered by many authors who did not have the task of devising an examination to guide their thoughts. Resistance to the very concept of examining the arts was not entirely forgotten, with the Calouste Gulbenkian Foundation report 'seeing only a limited case for examinations in the arts, because examinations ... can measure only limited aspects of the arts – not necessarily the most important aspects' (1982/89: 90). The committee favoured instead the more time-consuming but very flexible process of 'profiling', where a child's achievement is recorded on an individual basis and assessed by the teacher. Such objections are valid only when the examination begins to dominate the curriculum: if assessment is not allowed to inhibit children's musical development, it surely matters little that the final examination fails to quantify every aspect. What is important, however, is that teachers are engaged in formative assessment at all levels of the curriculum, regardless of whether or not an external examination will follow. Children need to be aware of the criteria by which their work will be judged, in order that they can develop self-criticism and be conscious of their own stages of development.

Paynter devotes a full chapter to examinations and assessment in his *Music in the Secondary School Curriculum* (1982), remarking that many of the teachers consulted during the York Project expressed doubts about the relevance of assessment to the new style of music teaching. An exercise in moderating pupils' compositions was part of the Project, but reaction from examination boards was generally hostile, one respondent writing that he was 'depressed and sickened' by the whole experience (Paynter, 1982: 179). Even those examiners who admitted interest were sceptical about how such a system could work, making its implementation as part of GCSE a few years later even more remarkable. Paynter advises caution over making judgements about candidates' work; the task requires more than a cursory first hearing if it is to be educationally constructive:

> Obviously there is much to be said for approaching an aural art aurally! ... But in the case of these young composers we need to know more about their work leading up to the pieces submitted. For we are not critics making a judgement about a single work but educators with an overall responsibility for the development of musical understanding in those we teach.
>
> (Paynter, 1982: 185)

This approach is reflected in the SEG criteria, with their emphasis on a candidate's ability to develop and refine musical ideas; an acknowledgement that composition and education are both processes that evolve gradually, requiring constant commitment from pupils and teachers alike.

Further thoughts on assessment can be found in the series of publications edited by Ross, *Curriculum Issues in Arts Education* (Ross, 1981; 1986). Strongly influenced by the work on self-expression in art that Ross carried out with Witkin in the early 1970s (cf. Witkin, 1974), the notion of assessing and examining in arts education is discussed under the subtitle *A Necessary Discipline or a Loss of Happiness?* (Ross, 1986). Ross's own chapter is less ambiguously entitled 'Against Assessment', his argument being that to assess a child's art work is to invade their process of self-expression:

> In artistic composition it is we ourselves who become composed; in artistic creativity it is, ultimately, ourselves we create. So, at the heart of any form of evaluation in this sacred domain will be self-evaluation. We must learn to know, and hence to judge, ourselves.
>
> (Ross, 1986: 92)

Lest Ross's ideas be dismissed as the legacy of 1970s idealism, it is important to note that his more recent views on assessment (Ross et al., 1993) are similarly dismissive of conventional summative techniques. He proposes instead a system of negotiated assessment through interviews between teachers and pupils, given the name PACT; Pupil Assessment Conversations with Teachers (Ross et al., 1993: 34). In these conversations, art teachers are required to discuss the meaning of pupils' creations with them in a kind of post-creative therapy. Typically, Ross makes little mention of music, in which there is no concrete object around which this conversation can take place, and as a result he fails to engage with the difficulties of translating any art into the spoken medium for evaluation. As an ongoing process in arts classrooms, the opportunity to discuss ideas with pupils is undoubtedly valuable, but hardly offers a solution to the problems of final assessment, given that it tests children's levels of critical articulation more than their artistic achievements and perceptions.

The policy changes and associated theorising of the last forty years demonstrate the complexity of assessment in the arts, and can offer no easy answers for teachers keen to ensure creative development within a broader educational context. The criterion referenced system that now operates at GCSE offers a focus for assessing composing and performing, and allows for the differences in skill and maturity that candidates will demonstrate. The process of moderation can never be completely objective, as there are no right answers in the creation and interpretation of music, but even a fallible method of assessing essential musical experiences must be preferable to restricting the syllabus to that which is more readily examinable. At GCE 'A' Level, where development has been much less dramatic, the legacy of both approaches can be seen, as candidates are required to demonstrate musical skills under examination conditions, including historical knowledge and aural perception, and also to engage with music throughout their course by performing and composing to a high level. Originally designed as an extension of School Certificate work, and then intended to build on GCE 'O' Level in a similar way, sixth form music education has always been a specialist subject. With political reluctance to interfere with the 'gold standard' examination affecting all 'A' Levels during the years of Conservative government, the legacy of the Higher School Certificate can still be seen in the disciplined approach to musical study. Given that today's candidates are usually building upon their GCSE experience, however, the emphasis is slowly changing, as practical music making assumes greater importance for the candidates, if not always for the examiners. A move towards the modular re-structuring of 'A' Level courses for examinations in 2000 may also increase the pace of change, as the international model of a broader sixth form curriculum becomes more politically fashionable. With young musicians moving through higher education, changes can be seen there that also mirror the practical approaches of GCSE and take account of the wider, if possibly less rigorous, experience of music that today's students bring from their school education. As the next generation of music teachers are trained, the cycle continues, with new ideas fed back into the school curriculum to ensure continued development, as Swanwick, at the Institute of Education in London, has observed:

> I'm really delighted because I think that we are now seeing graduate musicians who are much wider than they were. ... More and more of them, of course, have had experience at their own school now; they will have done performance in small groups and they will have composed.
>
> (Swanwick: Interview, 24 November 1997)

Spencer's (1993) survey of undergraduate opinion of GCSE music suggests that this cycle is not always as beneficial as it could be, with some of his respondents feeling that the examination was insufficiently demanding and did not serve as adequate preparation for 'A' Level (Spencer, 1993: 74). These students, presumably some of the most able taking the course, were disdainful of the popular set works included by some examining boards, and had tended to perform classical repertoire, often taken from the Associated Board of the

Royal Schools of Music (ABRSM) instrumental examination syllabuses. Conservatism in education is not, it seems, solely the province of teachers and examiners.

Music education is, of course, one of the few subjects in which children participate in examinations outside school, through the instrumental syllabuses of the Associated Board of the Royal Schools of Music and other London music colleges. Whilst the history of these systems is not strictly relevant to changes in classroom music, the fact that the alternative system existed may have slowed down the development of public examinations in music (cf. Metcalfe, 1987: 99). The assumption that performances can be judged and graded has apparently caused less controversy amongst instrumental examiners than it did at the inception of GCSE, and certainly the debate about considering the process, rather than solely the final product, does not form part of the ABRSM philosophy. Recent reforms to aural tests, for example, have attempted to make that examination more satisfactory, but have not questioned the fundamental validity of requiring a child to play to an audience of one and to receive detailed criticism and a mark out of 150:

> Examinations are designed to offer a framework for a progressive
> musical training providing periodic, impartial assessment. Marking is
> as objective as possible, in accordance with long-established criteria.
> (Harvey, 1982/94: 16)

Reforms to instrumental and vocal performance examinations have taken place on a much smaller scale than the GCSE and 'A' Level developments, working from the premise that assessment is a valuable motivating force, rather than questioning its validity as a tool in musical development. Teachers in the classroom have had to make more significant changes to their practice, with CSE and GCSE both serving to force the pace of change by giving credence to relatively innovative ideas. A certain pressure on teachers, to adapt to the new requirements of coursework and teacher assessment, provided a definite impetus for development, reinforcing the ideas published in the previous decades, whilst retaining the focus on externally awarded qualifications. This resolution of apparent contradictions had an important function in disseminating and rationalising the variety of good practice that had emerged in the preceding years.

It is clear that the goals of increased accessibility and greater practical involvement that have generated change in music education across the generations, have also driven changes in examinations, securing a place for creative music teaching amongst the pressures of the more 'academic' curriculum. Recent years have seen an increase in those pupils who take GCSE music on the strength of their lower school music teaching, rather than because they have had private instrumental tuition. Further reforms are necessary to the schools' instrumental services, which have suffered under the budget pressures of recent years, before the ideal of equal opportunities can be fully realised in music examinations. There is much encouragement to be gained, however, from the priorities encapsulated in the GCSE criteria, and the far-reaching effects that these have had on music teaching throughout the secondary school.

The debate over assessment in music education is brought up to date by looking at discussions associated with the National Curriculum and its implementation. Perhaps surprisingly, given that new forms of examination had been one of the most significant changes in the 1980s, the Music Working Group who drafted the curriculum made little explicit reference to assessment, and it is only now that due consideration is being given to this vital aspect of music teaching. The complex process of legislation that resulted from the 1988 Education Reform Act will be discussed in the next chapter, before a return to the broader concerns of music education that have formed the philosophical and practical context for the national directives.

Chapter 6

Music in the National Curriculum: policy and practice

6.1 Designing the curriculum: Interim Report (1991)

The changes brought about by the Education Reform Act (ERA) of 1988 went beyond the immediate practicalities of the legislation, marking a turning point in the way that educational ideas were negotiated and implemented. With a National Curriculum in place for the first time in the history of compulsory secondary education, the framework for debate was defined by Government policy, and the culture of schooling changed to meet the competitive demands of the new political agenda. Music teachers, it can be argued, were left relatively unscathed by the ERA, provided as they were with a minimalist curriculum document, accompanied by the news that music was no longer to be a compulsory subject in the later years of secondary schooling. If the Government had hoped for an easy ride as a result, they were to be disappointed, as the music curriculum caused public controversy at the drafting stages, and remained a source of contention in the first decade of its existence. An examination of the processes and problems of designing and implementing the curriculum can help to shed light on the political dimensions of music education at the end of the twentieth century.[†]

The brief pamphlet that comprises the music curriculum today disguises the lengthy process of investigation and consultation that went into its design. Music, inevitably a low priority for a Government interested in raising standards of literacy and numeracy, was one of the last curriculum orders to be drafted, with the Interim Report completed in December 1990 (DES, 1991a). The Music Working Group, a committee appointed by the then Secretary of State for Education, Kenneth Baker, had been debating the curriculum content for several months, visiting schools and consulting with teachers, academics

---

[†] The National Curriculum, as a political animal, has inevitably brought new jargon into the teaching profession, and this, together with the membership of the Music Working Group and the changing personnel at the Department of Education, is outlined in an Appendix (p. 217).

and musicians before submitting their first proposals for public consultation. Their Interim Report was a substantial document, containing much of the reasoning that was to be omitted from later versions, and making it plain that the Working Group intended to build upon the developments that had generated the healthy state of music education at the time:

> The main aim of music education in schools is to foster pupils'
> sensitivity to, and their understanding and enjoyment of music,
> through an active involvement in listening, composing and performing.
>
> (DES, 1991a: 3)

In this statement the Working Group encapsulated the aims of music teaching in the 1990s; not so different from those of previous generations, except for the insistence on 'active involvement' in all aspects of musical experience. Alarmingly, it was to be this principle that musicians and educators would have to defend most strongly against the more financially-motivated perceptions of the politicians.

By 1990, when the Music Working Group was formed, the National Curriculum had already grown to cumbersome proportions, with the core subjects of mathematics, science and English leaving little room in the timetable for anything else. The authors of the final consultation documents – for art, physical education and music – were instructed to keep their recommendations to a minimum, as Graham, then chairman of the National Curriculum Council (NCC), recalls:

> It had been agreed that the attainment targets in art, music and PE
> would not be so detailed as those of the other subjects. The working
> groups could be seen as being lucky in not being so circumscribed,
> with the freedom that would bring, or as downgraded without the full
> influence of the earlier groups.
>
> (Graham & Tytler, 1993: 76)

This debate over status was to be revived on publication of the Interim Report (DES, 1991a), but it is evident that the main concern of the Working Group was to provide a music curriculum that was supported by its own rationale, and that its relatively low status position in the National Curriculum was not allowed to obscure musical and educational priorities. Professor George Pratt, a member of the Working Group, recalls an initial decision to make the curriculum a document that would ensure the future development of music education:

> We were very conscious on the Working Group ... of the question 'Do we create a curriculum, or propose a curriculum, which will fit into the present level of resourcing, funding, space, equipment, understanding of teachers – particularly of teachers' knowledge and understanding?'. Or, do we take the bull by the horns and say 'Now is our opportunity to say what we would really like, and if it doesn't come into being for five years or twenty years, at least we've demonstrated what really perhaps should be there'?   And we took the latter view, of course.
>
> (Pratt: Interview, 6 February 1996)

Perhaps as a result of this decision, the Music Working Group began their Interim Report with a statement of the 'Aims and Nature of Music in Schools' (DES, 1991a: 3).   Such philosophical discussion is conspicuously absent in other National Curriculum documents and, indeed, was not communicated to teachers in the final presentation of the music curriculum.   In their introduction, the Music Working Group identify the personal and social development that can be fostered through musical activity:

> Music derives from and contributes to culture and society.   It is an important mode of communication and understanding, which has its own conventions and rules, and may thus be described as a non-verbal language.   Traditions in the creation and performance of music develop within communities; but people also respond to music as individuals, deriving from it varying degrees of emotional, intellectual and spiritual satisfaction.
>
> (DES, 1991a: 3)

The idea of 'music as language' is a familiar one, but the argument presented above is so general as to be lacking in conviction.   Out of fairness to the Working Group, it must be remembered that the audience of this report was to include professional musicians, teachers and politicians, and there is a sense in which the Group are attempting to please all their readers, and therefore risk communicating little to any of them.   In the next paragraph, these differences in musical response and experience are drawn into the classroom, with the intention that music can be seen to have relevance to *all* pupils (even future politicians):

> Music education aims to cultivate the aesthetic sensitivity and the artistic ability of all pupils.   For those who show high levels of motivation, commitment and skill, it can provide a preparation for employment in the music profession, the music industries and teaching.   For many others, who choose different career paths, it can

supply instead the foundation for greatly enriched leisure pursuits, both as listeners and as participants in amateur music making.

(DES, 1991a: 3)

This reasoning, although probably what political thinkers would want to hear, is disappointing in terms of defining a role for music in schools. Teaching children music so that they can become music teachers is a somewhat circular argument, and the idea that music is a pleasant leisure activity is also inconsistent with the power of the 'non-verbal language' that the Working Group were defending in the earlier extract. Perhaps unwittingly, the Music Working Group are entering the debate concerning the whole purpose of compulsory education, and seem to side with the political stance that dominated the National Curriculum, expressing the belief that education is for future employment and leisure, not for the present benefit of the children concerned. Whilst the curriculum proposals also emphasise the importance of musical experiences and sensitivity, this apparent conflict of purpose highlights the difficulties of producing a report that is to be politically analysed, and must conform to the established view of schooling.

The next section of the report considers the contribution that music can make to the whole curriculum, developing imagination, analytical skills and communication ability in pupils. Following the political controversy over whether the arts should be taught separately or combined to take up less of the timetable (cf. Graham & Tytler, 1993: 76), the Working Group also address the question of relationships between the arts:

> The making and understanding of music share certain processes with the other arts, and with dance and drama in particular. ... It is possible, therefore, that some of the attainment targets for music may be capable of being met through courses in performing or expressive arts, including music theatre and opera. The success of such combined courses, however, will depend on there being a clear rationale for the combinations concerned, and on the teachers and pupils having first established a secure foundation of skills, knowledge and under-standing in each of the subjects to be combined.

(DES, 1991a: 9)

Whilst emphasising the flexibility that the Working Group wanted to build into the music curriculum, this statement is once again open to varied and conflicting interpretation. The political drive towards an economy of time and resources for the arts can use this argument to link the arts together, ignoring the warning that a secure foundation in the individual arts is needed before pupils can make the links between them. There is a danger, when music education is argued for in terms of 'aesthetic appreciation ... study skills ... self-motivation' and all its other attendant benefits (ibid.: 8), that it has no unique qualities to offer, and can therefore be subsumed in a hybrid course of 'combined arts'. Read more cautiously, the Music Working Group appear to favour the combination of arts as a development from the separate subjects, not a replacement for them. In the context of the National Curriculum, perhaps the ideal is to see a combined arts course beginning in Key Stage 4, as a creative antidote to the pressures of examination courses (cf. NCC Arts in Schools Project, 1990a). It had already been confirmed by the Secretary of State, however, that music and art were to be optional subjects in the last two years of secondary schooling. This decision effectively weakens any argument in favour of the arts: if they are acknowledged to be of importance to lower school pupils, how can they be so readily abandoned when the more 'serious' business of gaining qualifications arises?

The Working Group had been asked to supply 'Attainment Targets' for music, but because prescription was to be kept to a minimum, were not required to specify the ten 'Levels of Attainment' that had formed the basis of the core subject curricula. Inevitably, the Working Group wanted to include everything they felt to be important, despite the danger of overcrowding the curriculum that had occurred with many of the groups of 'experts' appointed to consider different subjects (Graham & Tytler, 1993: 75). They chose, therefore, to produce non-statutory guidelines for teachers that included the ten levels, and grouped the attainment targets (ATs) in two 'Profile Components', *Making Music* and *Understanding Music*. Amidst all the National Curriculum jargon, the debate about curriculum content which followed the publication of the report was sometimes lost, but the Working Group helped to clarify their chosen terms by providing a rationale for each of their attainment targets; *AT1 Performing, AT2 Composing, AT3 Listening,* and *AT4 Knowing*. In describing Performing and Composing, the Working Group acknowledged the work that had been established in schools since the 1970s, stressing the importance of a creative approach to music education. They placed a particular emphasis on singing as a performing experience, whilst encouraging the exploration of instruments in the context of composition. In the *Understanding Music* component ('Listening and Knowing'), there is some foreshadowing of the debate that was to follow the publication of the report, as the Working Group attempted to balance active music education with the traditionally more passive approach to listening:

> *Listening* should include being aware of sounds and silences, and
> listening actively to music so as to identify its structural and
> expressive elements (dynamics, pulse, speed and so on), to respond to

musical cues in groups and individually, to identify structures and styles, and to enjoy music aesthetically.

(DES, 1991a: 14)

The intention of this rather enigmatic passage is explained in a later paragraph, when the Music Working Group assert the need for children to be educated as listeners whilst performing and composing, as well as when 'in audience' (cf. Swanwick, 1979: 45). This seems to make musical sense, and the idea itself was widely accepted, the contention apparently being with how it was expressed in the document. Even more controversial was the fourth attainment target, the strangely-titled 'Knowing':

> *Knowing* should include naming and talking about the characteristics of music and musical instruments, knowing about musical symbols and contexts (historical, geographical, social), and being able to read music and to analyse and evaluate performances and compositions.
>
> (DES, 1991a: 14)

Those who had embraced the reform of music education since the 1960s, would be justified in feeling some hostility to this reinstating of musical 'knowledge', redolent of the 'passive' learning of earlier decades. Swanwick, for example, points out a general movement away from teaching Western staff notation, resulting from 'the awareness that some music is notated in other ways and some not at all' (Swanwick, 1992a: 7), an awareness that does not appear to be addressed in the 'Knowing' attainment target. However, the Working Group go some way towards pre-empting these objections, with a paragraph of further explanation:

> Knowledge about music should be taught in the context of practical musical activities: that is, the needs of a particular task in listening, composing and performing should determine the facts to be taught.
>
> (DES, 1991a: 15)

This statement seems more palatable, but the overall impression left by the structure of the proposed curriculum is one of fragmentation. It is easy to imagine teachers, having recently adapted to planning their lessons around the prescriptive documents for the core subjects, choosing to do a lesson in which they tackle the 'Knowing' target, and in which, therefore, the children make no music. The Working Group devote a section to explaining their 'holistic approach' to the curriculum, stating that every lesson should include all aspects of musical experience. This is reasonable enough, but the taking apart and rebuilding of that experience through the proposed attainment targets was a potentially damaging process, especially given that the political readership would have more power of interpretation than the professional one.

6.2 Negotiating the curriculum: Final Report (August 1991)

The decision to change the attainment targets proposed in the Working Group's Interim Report was, in the end, a political one, rather than one motivated by an educational or musical rationale. In a letter to Sir John Manduell, the Group's chairman, which was published as part of the Report, Kenneth Clarke, Secretary of State for Education, called for a 'simpler' structure, by which he meant fewer attainment targets (DES, 1991b). Clarke wanted the reporting structure of music to be the same as that for art and PE, the subjects that shared music's low status position in the final phase of the National Curriculum. He also raised an objection that was to become a notorious example of his failure to understand the nature of music education:

> I am ... concerned about those pupils – of whom I think there may be many – with a real appreciation of music but perhaps a limited aptitude for its practice. I find it difficult to see how the framework you are proposing, based on your view of music as essentially a practical study, will encourage and allow such pupils to develop their knowledge and understanding of the repertoire, history and traditions of music.
>
> (DES, 1991b: 70)

In some ways, the Music Working Group had suffered from the changes of Education Secretary: appointed by Kenneth Baker, they had served briefly under John MacGregor, before submitting their proposals to Kenneth Clarke. Changes in political focus had occurred during this period, with Baker's 'entitlement' curriculum being considerably reduced. After MacGregor's rather ineffectual period in office, Clarke was keen to wield his own influence on the curriculum:

> More than any other Education Secretary hitherto, Clarke was willing to intervene personally on matters concerning teaching method and the content of the curriculum: there was a prolonged row between politicians and experts on both art and music where Clarke wanted to give priority to 'knowledge' over 'performance'. ... It was also Clarke who ruled that history ended twenty years ago.
>
> (Lawton, 1994: 79)

Clarke's apparent ignorance of developments in music education over the previous decades made clear the futility of arguing, on educational grounds, what had become an essentially political matter. Despite this, the Working Group were able to comment in their Final Report (DES, 1991b: 3) that they had received some 700 responses to their original proposals, and had attempted to address those in compiling their final recommendations. This consultation process was a well-established feature in National Curriculum writing, and was to prove effective until the National Curriculum Council (NCC) began the final revision of the music curriculum.

The professional response to the attainment targets suggested in the Interim Report was also in favour of a reduction, and the Working Group supported the consensus that 'Knowing' should be incorporated with the three main musical activities, performing, composing and listening or 'appraising'. The majority of comments reported by the Working Group were concerned with the structure and language of the Interim Report, and these were also taken into consideration, an expanded glossary of musical terms being provided for non-specialist teachers. This problem over the technical language of music exposed another difficulty faced by the Group, as they were attempting to write for self-confessed 'non-musicians' in primary schools, as well as teachers with a high degree of specialist musical knowledge. Their efforts to overcome this are well-meant, but possibly led to the criticisms of both reports by those who picked out the examples rather than the rationale (cf. O'Hear, 1991).

Other changes in the Final Report are clearly politically, or more specifically, economically, motivated. In the Interim Report, the Group had included the development of instrumental skills in the higher level performing targets, envisaging the support of instrumental teachers for classroom work. The Final Report still argues the case for proficiency in performing, but can only offer a plea to schools to consider the importance of providing tuition and of integrating individual lessons with class music:

> Instrumental teachers should be fully aware of the point their pupils have reached in following the general music curriculum, of the detailed scheme of work involved, and of the tasks and materials used in the classroom. The instrumental music lessons should be regarded as an alternative form of delivery, not as an adjunct or optional extra.
>
> (DES, 1991b: 58)

The decline of the instrumental service in the years since that was written has illustrated the hopelessness of arguing without financial backing. As power has been taken away from Local Education Authorities, so they have lost the ability to provide a central music service, and the goals expressed above by the Working Group have become increasingly distant.

It was in the Working Group's Final Report that the controversial term 'appraising' first appeared, replacing 'listening' as an attainment target. The intention of this term, although not clearly articulated in the document, was that children should listen *and respond* to music, making listening an active musical experience. Pratt describes the difficulties of finding appropriate terminology to communicate this idea:

> What we wanted was a word that would ensure that the listening we are talking about is *active* listening: it is really hearing something and then responding in some way to it, either by the way you think, the way you feel, or by what you do.
>
> (Pratt: Interview, 6 February 1996)

By this definition, a listening reaction in performance, such as adjusting tuning, is as important a part of appraising as the task of being an 'audience listener' (DES, 1991b: 21). This is a concept not fully articulated in the Working Group's final document, and Pratt acknowledges that work done since the publication of the report has taken the concept further than the original understanding. Flynn and Pratt (1995) have conducted extensive research into the idea; investigating teachers' perceptions of appraising, identifying different ways of expressing musical understanding, and separating the concept from 'appraisal', the assessment of teachers that unfortunately adopted a similar word around the same time. 'Appraising', in the Working Group's Final Report, was a more complex term for 'listening', that attracted some criticism as being unnecessarily confusing, but its preservation has perhaps contributed to the ongoing development of effective listening strategies in the classroom.

6.3 Politicising the curriculum: NCC Report (1992)

The music curriculum documents had already attracted an unprecedented level of professional comment in their consultation stages, but it was the revised document by the National Curriculum Council (NCC) that was to provoke the most heated debate. David Pascall, the newly-appointed Chairman of the NCC, congratulated the Working Group and expressed his desire to build on their 'sound proposals' (NCC, 1992a: introduction), but went on to demonstrate the somewhat different intentions of the Council:

> Council has strengthened the content of the curriculum in the areas of the history of music, our diverse musical heritage and the appreciation of a variety of musical traditions. Although this concept is included in the Working Group's rationale, the choice of repertoire and periods to be studied has been very largely left to teachers. We consider that National Curriculum music should ensure that children have studied major periods of music history and are aware of the major music figures although we do not consider that the statutory Order should define particular musicians by name.
>
> (NCC, 1992a: introduction)

This clear shift towards the defence of 'musical heritage' shows a blatant disregard for the consultation that had occurred between Working Group documents, when professional musicians and teachers had expressed concern at an undue emphasis on musical knowledge. The decision of the NCC brought the music curriculum into line with the rest of the curriculum, in which a right-wing traditionalist view of desirable cultural knowledge was presented. There are clear resonances too with the proposals of the Music Curriculum Association (1991), led by O'Hear and Scruton, who submitted their own curriculum to ministers, asserting that the 'western classical tradition' should be at the heart of music in schools, and that composition should be closely linked to the teaching of notation (Music Curriculum Association, 1991: 8). The NCC recommended further change to the attainment targets, combining them as *AT1 Performing and composing* and *AT2 Knowledge and understanding*. The Council seemed satisfied that it had solved the problems that had surrounded the language of the music curriculum, but with a high level of professional interest already aroused, it was unlikely that this change would go undisputed. An Appendix to the report acknowledged that only 6 per cent of the 1707 responses received supported a reduction to two attainment targets (NCC, 1992a: 34), but these statistics were interpreted very liberally by the NCC:

> Council recognises that [their] arguments for a two AT model run counter to the views expressed by the majority of respondents in consultation. However, Council believes that much of the support for the original three AT model was based on the erroneous assumption that an approach through two ATs would inevitably weaken the music curriculum and reduce, in particular, the emphasis on composition. ... Council believes that its proposal for two ATs meets the underlying fears of many respondents, and ... strengthens the coherence and manageability of the music curriculum as a whole.
>
> (NCC, 1992a: 14)

The separation of making and understanding music was indeed one that had been rejected by the Music Working Group and their respondents at an early stage, due to concerns that the holistic approach to the curriculum that they envisaged was not effectively communicated in two attainment targets:

> We wanted to make sure that everybody did perform, to the best of their ability, and compose to the best of their ability, and when you wrap the two up in one attainment target, you get the opportunity to say 'Well we did composing a year last Pancake Tuesday, and we haven't done any more, but we've done composing, so we've fulfilled the target'. ... There was also a strong feeling among us that really we wanted one attainment target – we wanted 'Music'. We used the word 'holistic' so many times: we were very concerned that it should be integrated and inter-related and holistic.
>
> (Pratt: Interview, 6 February 1996)

In recalling the battles with words that were an ongoing feature of the consultation process, Pratt highlights the difficulty of making music fit into the curriculum model that had been established for the core subjects. The Working Group had begun by assimilating and interpreting ideas and good practice in music education, but by the time the NCC document was published, the argument was more about the place of music in the overall National Curriculum. As a result, the final drafts of the curriculum were dominated by political drives towards economy of all kinds, with words and resources equally limited.

The dispute over the music curriculum moved more prominently into the public domain at this point, with Simon Rattle, then conductor of the City of Birmingham Symphony Orchestra, leading a media campaign against the proposed emphasis on musical heritage and knowledge. Rattle's television broadcast (1992) included film footage of performing and composing in a variety of schools, and argued that music teachers were providing valuable opportunities for children, and needed supporting in their role. This was a welcome retaliation against the Government's portrayal of falling standards and incompetent teachers that had led to the conception of the National Curriculum and was being perpetuated by the popular press.

The response from educators and academics was also defensive of teachers and of the Working Group's ideas, and it is likely that this dual onslaught made the Government take a less provocative position on the curriculum than the NCC had. Swanwick (1992a) claims the credit for reinstating 'appraising' in the attainment targets, suggesting that 'the advice of a "professional" appears to have been of value in a confused situation of do-it-yourself curriculum writers intruding into an area without experience or expertise' (Swanwick, 1992a: 31).

Wherever the responsibility lies, the compromise reached and published in the first statutory Orders for music (DES, 1992) was that there should be two attainment targets; *AT1 Performing and composing* and *AT2 Listening and appraising*. In discussions before the publication of this document, it had been proposed that the practical aspects of music (AT1) should be more heavily weighted in terms of time and assessment, but this 2:1 ratio was never put into effect in the document:

> Somewhere or other we were promised that although there would be two attainment targets, one would be twice the size of the other; the 'Performing and Composing' would be twice as big as 'Listening', and it was going to be just 'Listening'. And that, I'm quite certain, was promised us, and it was only after the Order had gone through Parliament that it dawned on some of us that this hadn't happened, they just hadn't done it, so we had two equal ones, 'Performing and Composing' and 'Listening and Appraising'.
>
> (Pratt: Interview, 6 February 1996)

Regardless of the feelings of the Working Group, and of all the other musicians and teachers who had expressed opinions, the consultation process was over, and the Government's final version of the curriculum had become law. Non-statutory guidance was also published (NCC, 1992b), a more colourful presentation of the national requirements, but still lacking the rationale that had been an important part of the Working Group reports. There can have been few practising music teachers at that time who were unaware of the controversy that had surrounded the writing process, and the published curriculum must have been a carefully read document as a result.

6.4 Revising the curriculum: the Dearing review

By the time that the first phase of the music curriculum was implemented in 1992, other National Curriculum subjects that had been operating for several years were already running into difficulties, owing to the complexities of the over-prescriptive Orders. It was decided that a review of the entire curriculum was needed, with the aim of reducing the statutory content of each subject and the cumbersome amount of published material that primary school teachers, in particular, were expected to work with. Sir Ron Dearing, as Chairman of the Schools Curriculum and Assessment Authority, led an investigation into each subject, including, in 1994, music. Dearing's criteria reflected the difficulties that teachers of all subjects had encountered:

> The review of individual subjects should be guided by the need to:
> - simplify and clarify the programmes of study
> - reduce the volume of material to be taught
> - reduce overall prescription so as to give more scope for professional judgement
> - ensure that the Orders are written in a way which offers maximum support to the classroom teacher.
>
> (SCAA, 1994: introduction)

These goals are clearly sympathetic to classroom practice, and resulted in the removal of the ten levels of achievement in all subjects, and of the examples that had cluttered the earlier documents. For the first time, the National Curriculum was considered as a whole, and unnecessary discrepancies between the structure and assessment of subjects were reduced. Few substantive changes were made to the content of the music curriculum, possibly because it was already one of the less prescriptive documents. A new statutory Order, incorporating Dearing's recommendations, was issued to schools in January 1995 (DfE, 1995), along with a Government announcement that there would be no further curriculum revisions for another five years. It seems that the continual debate over the curriculum had wearied even its initiators.

Music teachers were faced with two new publications in 1995: in addition to the revised curriculum, a book *Teaching Music in the National Curriculum* (Pratt & Stephens, 1995) was published by the Music Working Group, who were anxious to preserve the rich debate that had informed the construction of their reports. Retitled, the 'Music Forum' expressed their admiration for Dearing's work, and set out to fulfil their new role of supporting practising teachers. In doing so, they identify the future problems of the National Curriculum, and the need for continuing training and resources for teachers:

> We want to articulate, as precisely as possible, what is necessary for a rich musical education for young people; the development of potential through skills, knowledge and understanding, an enjoyment and above all a love of music.
>
> (Pratt & Stephens, 1995: xii)

This desire to refocus the discussion towards musical and educational goals and away from politics, is echoed by those teachers who have absorbed the National Curriculum into their classroom activities. The wrangling over terminology and structure completed, teachers and musicians can return to the task of teaching music, as these secondary school heads of music explain:

> I think it's actually made us think, but I don't think we've changed anything dramatically because of it. I suppose it just reinforces what you're doing and makes you think of things you're not doing that you could do better.
>
> (JW: Interview, 13 December 1995)

> I've found the most useful thing has been the final National Curriculum. It's incredibly flexible for music and the reassuring thing is that we found that most of what we can do we can fit into it, you know, without having to change dramatically.
>
> (HC: Interview, 25 March 1996)

Both these teachers identified other factors as having had a greater influence on their teaching, citing the introduction of GCSE and the thought of imminent Ofsted inspection as prime examples. For them, at least, the curriculum debate has been a small part of changes to the educational environment, and one which has not had a profound effect on their work.

A group of sixty Year 7 pupils in a Derbyshire comprehensive school who were asked (by the author, also their teacher) to plan their ideal music lesson seemed to perceive a similar sense of balance in current music provision, with all of the children giving their imagined lesson a practical focus, and the majority choosing to include listening, performing and composing, in the holistic manner favoured by the National Curriculum Working Group. The children's responses reflected their existing experiences through the inclusion of singing, keyboard work and composing, and perhaps reflected their disappointed expectations too, in suggesting that music lessons should feature playing the drums, learning any instrument that they wanted to, or singing to a karaoke machine. The children's reasons for learning music at all centred around skill acquisition and potential employment, with only one child stating that music should not be taught in schools, and two giving the more ambitious reasons of 'to give us wider expectations' and 'so we can be inspired and express feelings'. Essentially, the children sought fun, enjoyment and recognisable progress from their music lessons, and many of the more experienced instrumentalists referred to 'letting people have a chance to learn something, which is very enjoyable and which some people would never have a chance to do'. Music was seen as something 'you might need to know about when you're older', but the children were largely agreed that present participation and satisfaction in lessons was the most important goal. For the most part oblivious to the wranglings of the National Curriculum committees, these children seem to have defined similar purposes and activities for music education, showing that it is the everyday encounters between children and music that really matter:

> However we argue about the terms and conditions of the National Curriculum, in the end its usefulness is dependent entirely upon what teachers of skill and imagination can make of whatever kind of framework it offers.
>
> (Paynter, in Swanwick, 1992b: 176)

Political intervention is now an established part of the educational scene, but Paynter's contribution to Swanwick's symposium marks the slow restoration of confidence in professional ability and the value of educational debate. The initial motivation for the National Curriculum had been a questioning of the competence of teachers, and reclaiming their rightful place at the heart of educational discussion and change will be a lengthy process. When the Conservative Government promised a five-year moratorium on curriculum change following the Dearing review, the sense of relief seemed to be universal, although in practice a change of Government was to render this pledge invalid. The focus upon standards and testing, particularly in literacy and numeracy, continues and the needs of music educators are again in danger of being obscured. To the question 'Has the National Curriculum for music achieved anything?', commentators have found multiple answers.

6.5 Debating the curriculum: the academic aftermath

For all the political attempts to silence the controversy that surrounded the National Curriculum, the decade that followed its implementation has seen commentaries on curriculum policies and practicalities develop into a new academic genre. In some respects, this is a dangerous state of affairs, promoting the belief that all curriculum debate must now be defined by the Government directives. However, even the onetime Chairman of the NCC admits that the 'shock therapy' of the National Curriculum implementation 'can galvanize but not convert' (Graham, 1993: 5), and the urge to make sense of the unprecedented changes to education seen under the Conservative Government is understandable.

Shepherd and Vulliamy (1994) tackle the over-riding conflict between educational and political goals which clouded the drafting of the music curriculum, attributing this to a Thatcherite struggle to define 'Englishness':

The Working Party ... had devised a curriculum which in their judgement would support in a positive and constructive manner the terrain of musical culture as it presently existed in England: not comprised solely of 'classical' music, but significantly multicultural, and characterised to a very considerable extent by 'popular' and 'folk' musics. This, clearly, did not represent the image of England that Thatcher's conservatives had in mind. If the thesis that music is significantly social is to be accepted, then the conservative image comes across as being exclusively white, upper-middle class and male.

(Shepherd & Vulliamy, 1994: 37)

If this argument was indeed in the minds of ministers during the consultation process, it was kept well hidden amongst the economic and practical concerns of the Working Group's proposals. Whatever the truth of this politically aggressive stance, it is apparent that an unspoken conflict of intention was the cause of disputes over terminology. Writing a curriculum by consensus is difficult enough, but to have that consensus overruled at the last moment must have been frustrating in the extreme. As Shepherd and Vulliamy point out (ibid.: 29), the curriculum developments of the 1970s and 1980s were threatened by the political definitions of music education, which apparently owed more to the post-war 'music appreciation' model than to the expansion into composition and popular music that had followed. The gradual evolution of music education was in danger of being halted, and the National Curriculum controversy made public the voices of dissent that had always been present to slow down the dissemination of ideas. What the politicians cannot have anticipated, however, was the strength of feeling in favour of practical music making amongst musicians and teachers. This opposition to Clarke's perceptions, and those of the National Curriculum Council, was a clear reflection that the developments of the 1970s and onwards had widespread support:

The orchestrated nature of the condemnation of the NCC's Consultation Report, with its widespread coverage not only in the educational and national press but on national radio and TV, had a considerable impact.

(Shepherd & Vulliamy, 1994: 33)

Shepherd and Vulliamy applaud the fact that the Working Group were 'still infused with the spirit of the 1960s' (ibid.: 34), and indeed the Group themselves recorded their debt to Paynter, Swanwick, Self and other innovators of earlier years:

> We want to acknowledge the wisdom and inspiration of musicians and
> music educators over the last three decades – those who responded to
> the Music Working Group, those who have continued the process of
> evolution from our initial proposal, and those who have influenced our
> thinking in less direct ways. Music education has undergone nothing
> short of a revolution since the 1960s.
>
> (Pratt & Stephens, 1995: xiii)

The Music Working Group were apparently eager to foster the development of
that revolution, but this does not seem to have been the Government's
motivation for the National Curriculum. Standardisation and development are
not easily compatible, and provide another example of the different visions of
the curriculum that were held by its creators.

Whilst the National Curriculum was marketed by the Government as a step
forward for British – or more specifically, English and Welsh – education,
some commentators have criticised the lack of vision shown in the documents.
Focusing excessively on measurement and standardisation, the curriculum
threatened to stifle professional initiative, and actively sought to halt the
'progressive' developments that were blamed for the apparent fall in standards:

> The National Curriculum, presented by Kenneth Baker as a radical
> reform, was in terms of control, extent, content and form, firmly
> rooted in the English past. It was essentially backward- rather than
> forward-looking, an attempt to preserve under the guise of change.
>
> (Aldrich, 1996: 38)

This view supports Shepherd and Vulliamy's (1994) perception of the music
curriculum controversy, and has been further investigated by Cox, who refers
to 'the perennial concerns which confront music educationists' (Cox, 1993b:
360). Such concerns have multiplied as access to different musical repertoire
and ideas has grown in recent decades, and the attempt to stifle this through
defining a curriculum was potentially damaging. The evolution and expansion
of music education is mirrored in the history of other curriculum subjects, and
the idea of preserving a 'Golden Age' of education through legislation seems
abhorrent in this context.

Those who criticise the National Curriculum, as it now exists in England,
are often careful to distance themselves from the argument that any form of
common curriculum is inherently wrong. Plummeridge (1996a: 31) reviews
the historical reluctance to adopt national schemes of work for music, but
points to the 'extremely competent and imaginative manner' in which the
Music Working Group approached their task:

> [The Working Group] produced reports which were in sympathy with what was becoming accepted theory and practice, namely, that children should engage in music through the three interrelated modes of performing, composing and listening. Although the present Order might not be without imperfections, it would seem slightly odd, if not perverse, to maintain that its content and structure were not desirable.
>
> (Plummeridge, 1996a: 32)

As Plummeridge implies, the manner of the National Curriculum's introduction has done more lasting harm than any of its details. The Government's increased intervention in educational matters was, after all, prompted by a belief that standards were falling due to professional incompetence, and this line of argument has been sustained by politicians and the media for well over a decade. From Callaghan's attack on the 'secret garden of education' in the now infamous Ruskin College speech of 1976 (Brooks, 1991: 4), to Major's espousal of the 'old-fashioned' educational values of 'high standards, sound learning, diversity and choice' in 1992 (Chitty & Simon, 1993: 144), Prime Ministers and their Education Secretaries have risked hostility from the profession in their willingness to denounce 'progressive' ideas and enforce their own view of schooling:

> Right from the start the National Curriculum was dogged by a persistent, blind and – perhaps worst of all – an extra-ordinarily arrogant belief on the part of civil servants and ministers of state that they knew more about the nuts and bolts of curriculum development, and about the management of change in schools, than teachers, local education authorities, academics and researchers, all of whom (particularly the latter two) soon came to be regarded with a degree of hostility, if not downright contempt.
>
> (Dainton, 1993: 96)

The initially vitriolic responses of the outcast academics and of teachers themselves have now taken on a certain weariness, after a further decade of legislation has replaced professional autonomy with external systems of pupil testing and teacher inspection. The Inspectorate, in their new incarnation as the Office for Standards in Education (Ofsted), no longer focus upon the role of disseminating innovation and good practice, but are concerned with measuring schools against national standards, with public condemnation for those who fail to meet the targets. The National Curriculum has been revised, although not fundamentally reconsidered, and its status in primary schools reduced by the introduction of national 'literacy hours' and 'numeracy hours' from September 1998. Whether the drive to raise standards has had a beneficial impact upon pupils is difficult to determine, but the effects upon the profession are self-evident:

> Given the low morale of some teachers in England, the constant assaults on them by governments and the press (and increasingly by pupils), the poor salary scales and career prospects for those who wish to remain in the classroom as opposed to taking on administrative duties, the increasing amount of extra-teaching duties, which can now take up more than half a working week of between fifty and fifty-five hours, and the poor self-image of teachers themselves, there are in the 1990s almost as many qualified schoolteachers in England, at least 300, 000, who are not currently teaching in schools, as those who are.
>
> (Aldrich, 1996: 59)

As classroom teachers engage with the immediate concerns of teaching the pupils in their care, the general picture of education presented to the public through Government propaganda and media reporting, is rarely supportive of the profession. As the political pressure grows, so the importance of sustaining an independent philosophical debate also increases, as research and innovation must not be stifled by league tables and standardised inspection targets.

Swanwick (1997) is amongst those who have challenged the fundamental notions of musical development that are present in the curriculum documents. The assessment of musical achievement, Swanwick argues (ibid.: 206), was not sufficiently considered in the drafting of the curriculum, resulting in a confused system that is of little use in informing educational practice:

> Any valid and reliable assessment model has to take account of both dimensions, what pupils are *doing* and what they are *learning*: curriculum activities on the one hand and educational outcomes on the other. ... This simple truth was obscured very early on as the machinery of the National Curriculum ground into motion.
>
> (Swanwick, 1997: 207)

Swanwick's objections were prompted by publication of the *Exemplification of Standards* (1996a), issued by the Schools Curriculum and Assessment Authority (SCAA) to encourage national moderation at the end of Key Stage 3, the end of compulsory music education. These documents, which included sample lessons for Year 9 students, were intended to complement the Standard Assessment Tests (SATs) in the core subjects, allowing schools to make a complete assessment of their 14-year-old pupils. SCAA's belief in the power of paperwork was perhaps misplaced, and little support was made available to teachers to facilitate local moderation or professional discussion. The tone of the document is surprisingly diffident, assuring teachers that 'there is no expectation or requirement that the records of individual teachers should follow any of the formats or represent the kind of commentaries included in this booklet' (SCAA, 1996a: 19). Swanwick remains unconvinced by the whole process, asserting that the cumulative nature of musical learning has not been recognised in the unduly simplistic assessment descriptions (Swanwick, 1997: 210). He proposes a series of 'layered criteria', where awareness of expressive and structural features is built up, before being employed in critical reflections on music (ibid.: 211). Summative assessment should not be allowed to obscure the usefulness of formative pupil-teacher dialogue:

> The important thing is to have a keen sense of the particularity of a pupil's music-making and critical ability at any specific time. ... [The] actual business of assessment need not be onerous or time consuming.
>
> (Swanwick, 1997: 214)

Assessment, record keeping, and comparisons between pupils seem to have encroached upon music education, and hardly generate the inspiring discussion of a few decades earlier. It must not be forgotten, however, that many practising teachers with commitment and imagination have brought individual vision to the National Curriculum Orders, and have shown willingness to respond to the challenges contained there. As in previous decades, the development of music education lies, not with those who publish ideas, but with those who take them up in the classroom and use them to provide musical experiences and opportunities for their pupils.

The picture of music education presented in the National Curriculum documents makes less inspiring reading than the texts of earlier music educators, but can be usefully considered as an amalgamation of developments in the preceding decades. Whereas innovators throughout the century have usually been committed to a single idea, such as Yorke Trotter's 'sound before the sign' focus (1914) or Paynter and Aston's promotion of composing in the classroom (1970), the Music Working Group took a co-ordinating role, bringing together ideas in the same way as Winn (1954) or Rainbow (1956/71). Summative texts, that offer an overview of contemporary concerns, have had a significant function throughout the development of music education, but must contribute something new if they are to generate more effective practice and discussion. The National Curriculum, in its final version (DfE, 1995), reveals little of the thinking and observation behind it, providing reassurance for those teachers with confidence in their own practice, but failing to give guidance where it might be necessary. Whilst, for the first decade at least, the presence of music in schools has been guaranteed by the curriculum document, in the longer term the text offers neither practical nor philosophical support to teachers. Politics, philosophy and educational practice cannot, it seems, be reconciled merely through legislation.

The 1988 Education Reform Act was possibly the most far-reaching educational legislation of the twentieth century, redefining the role of politicians in education in a way that would be difficult to reverse. Whilst the National Curriculum can be seen as part of the Conservative agenda, its implementation changed the nature of schooling to the extent that all political debate on education is now shaped by the effects of these reforms. As the brevity of the music document demonstrates, there is more to education at the close of the twentieth century than can be encapsulated in a Government directive. The National Curriculum may have been conceived as a solution to all Britain's apparent educational problems, but it must not be allowed to constrain the thinking that has contributed to the development of music education thus far. The final chapters of this book will therefore consider the ongoing debates that will take music education into the new millennium, before drawing conclusions about the impact of the past century of innovation in music teaching and learning. With the increase in music technology, greater access to the music of other cultures, and the assimilation of the many ideas that have contributed to the development of music education, the last decades of the twentieth century offer much scope for discussion.

Chapter 7

New directions, new perspectives: late 1980s–1990s

7.1 Connecting theory and practice

The level of political influence upon education has notably increased in the last decades of the twentieth century, placing the discussion of music education in a new context. Published writings of the late 1980s and 1990s reflect the plethora of ideas that had begun to emerge in the preceding decades, with the debates about popular and world musics taken up with renewed vigour by Farrell (1990) and Sorrell (1990), and new theories of musical perception and meaning given an educational slant by Green (1988; 1997) and Odam (1995). Other texts build more overtly on the ideas of earlier decades, with Paynter (1992) rationalising the ideas of *Sound and Silence* in the light of interim developments, and Swanwick (1988; 1994; 1999) continuing the theoretical arguments of *A Basis for Music Education*. Plummeridge, too, looks back at trends in music education (1991; 1996a/b), considering their impact on current practice. Educational thinking in general has come to reflect the preoccupations of an increasingly multi-cultural society, making equality of access and opportunity important concerns for practising teachers. Kwami (1996) offers a perceptive evaluation of early attempts to encompass other cultures and musics in the curriculum, and proposes an integrated approach that is sensitive to the experiences of all pupils. Green (1997) contributes a study of gender, raising awareness of the traditionally male-dominated model of musical experience that has formed the basis of the curriculum. Music teaching and learning jostle for attention amongst a wide range of social, political and educational priorities in schools, a fact that enlivens the curriculum debate, and makes the search for a coherent rationale for music education ever more important.

In selecting key texts from amongst current publications one is denied the benefit of hindsight, but it is important to evaluate those ideas that seem to be influencing contemporary music education practice. What is highlighted in the consideration of more recent music education history is the potential divide between the academic discussion of ideas, and the practising teacher who has little time to read and digest often complex arguments. Resources with more immediate impact, such as text books and teachers' guides, may well have greater short-term influence on the majority of teachers, and this is unlikely to be a new phenomenon. The texts of earlier decades, such as Somervell's recommendations for effective rhythm and notation teaching (1931) and Scholes' assertions of the benefits of 'musical appreciation' (1935), seem to make a closer connection between theory and practice than many current publications, addressing as they did arguments that were limited by perceptions of the scope of music education. Teachers today are faced with more challenging texts, which may incorporate aspects of aesthetic theory, music psychology, and social and developmental theories, as well as demanding a broad spectrum of musical knowledge. The complexities of contemporary music and education prevent a return to the simplicity of earlier generations, and the ideas generated by recent research should certainly be allowed to flourish. Their connection with the classroom, however, needs to be continually reinforced if the study of music education is not to become a hybrid academic form. Swanwick (1988: 6) has denounced the 'anti-intellectual' stance that is sometimes used as an easy resolution of this dilemma, and as Plummeridge (1991) points out, all teachers work from a theoretical basis, influenced by their own reflections on perceived good practice:

> All teachers operate against a background of ideas, beliefs, attitudes and assumptions which may be said to constitute *their* theory or theories, and it is the ability to constantly reflect on this background that is at the heart, not only of curriculum innovation and development, but of all educational practice.
>
> (Plummeridge, 1991: 9)

Influences on the classroom have always been more complicated than the published literature would suggest, but at a time when more is expected of teachers and academics alike, it seems necessary to make this understanding explicit. The heart of the problem is expressed in Paynter's memorable phrase, 'teachers are asked to teach too much' (Paynter, 1982: 31). The pressure of classroom teaching offers little opportunity for research or reflection, sometimes generating a defensive resistance to those ideas perceived to come from 'outside' the educational context. The potential exists for a fruitful relationship between schools and universities, but this is discouraged by the constraints of the educational system, meaning that research and practice achieve coherence for only the most determined music educators. With that proviso in mind, the theories of the past decade will now be considered, with their authors' perception of the links between ideas and practice forming a significant part of the evaluation.

7.2 Expanding definitions of music in education

Quite apart from the ideas of music educators and theorists, music teaching in the late twentieth century has been influenced by the increased availability of many different styles of music, notably those of other cultures. In an influx of resources comparable only with the introduction of the gramophone and radio in the 1920s, teachers now have access to recordings, instruments and musicians that can bring a new realm of music to their pupils (cf. Pitts, 1998b). Musical concepts can be approached in ways that challenge conventional Western views of music learning, performing and notation, as popular and world musics become more familiar to teachers. The recent re-printing of Small's *Music•Society•Education* (1977/96) is symptomatic of this growing interest, with Walser's new introduction stating that 'this volume found a home in many classrooms, [and] anyone who cares about music can profit from reading it' (Walser, 1996: ix). Following in the tradition of Small's ethnomusicological research, writers such as Farrell (1990) and Sorrell (1990) have carried out extensive fieldwork in India and Java respectively, making more information and practical ideas available. Music education had been prepared for this wider definition of its remit by the innovations of the 1970s, with composing and improvising offering a practical route to understanding different musics:

> The practice of group composition, which assists enormously in the development of creative skills, self-confidence, and corporate sense, is very common in traditional gamelan music, especially in Bali. Usually the composer teaches the outline of the piece (orally) to the rest of the group, who make suggestions and try them out until a satisfactory finished product is reached.
>
> (Sorrell, 1990: 14)

Sorrell's description of a musical culture where the players are never 'the executants of a received repertoire' (ibid.: 15) could have had little relevance for music classrooms in the generations dominated by singing and aural training. Whilst he does not make the connection explicit, Sorrell shares the perception of more recent music education innovators that participating at a creative level is relevant for all musicians, an idea that is supported by the performance practice of other cultures. Sorrell's book is not directly addressed to teachers, and he refrains from developing his earlier practical suggestions (Vulliamy & Lee, 1982: 199–211), stating only that the use of Orff instruments and of the voice could help to transfer a knowledge of the gamelan to the classroom. Sorrell's reticence about proffering examples that are best left to the 'trained teacher' (1990: 15) shows that the potential divide between theory and practice works both ways, in this case inhibiting an experienced academic and musician from infringing on the field of classroom practice.

Farrell's research into Indian music in education has been presented in a variety of formats, ranging from an academic text (1990) to a classroom guide with taped examples, published as part of the WOMAD Foundation's *Exploring the Music of the World* series (1994). Farrell avoids simplification, aiming to give teachers 'a working knowledge of the Indian musical system' (1990: 14) and challenging the Anglocentric comparisons and translations that 'reduce all music to a Western standard' (ibid.: 3):

> Much of the structure of Indian music will, at first, seem strange and new, but it becomes familiar more quickly when Western preconceptions about music structure are dropped and the music is accepted on its own terms. Then the unique form and beauty of the music shine through, and Indian music becomes yet another exciting dimension to the teaching and enjoyment of music.
>
> (Farrell, 1990: 3)

It is clear that contemporary writers are replacing early naive attempts at introducing world musics to the classroom with more sophisticated approaches that reflect the increased concern with structure and composing. Massey (1996) charts the progress of changing attitudes in schools, from the post-war belief that immigrants should be expected to adapt to 'our' culture, through the well-meaning 'Saris, Samosas and Steel Bands' approach to presenting the cultural traditions of the world, to the realisation – still seen as radical by some – that 'multi-cultural education has to permeate all aspects of a school's work' if it is to be effective (Massey, 1996: 7–16). With all the racial tension that such a chequered history carries with it, debate in this area of the curriculum is politically charged and highly sensitive. Fear of doing or saying the wrong thing, and so reinforcing cultural stereotyping and prejudice, has led to a disparity of advice, practical suggestions and theories in music, rather than the coherent picture that is necessary. Floyd (1996) reports that teaching world musics is most likely to engender insecurity and lack of confidence amongst music teachers, and offers the simple and eminently sensible answer that teachers must be interested in the music themselves before they try to share it with their pupils:

We should be aware of; have experience of; know music from other cultures in the first instance because this will enrich, widen and transfer our own individual cultural make-up. It needs to affect us first; anything that does not may lead to disinterest at best, and create or reinforce negative attitudes which could spill out into the community beyond school at worst.

(Floyd, 1996: 30)

Floyd's advice suggests that to teach world musics out of a sense of political, social or moral responsibility is not good enough; this aspect of teaching and learning needs justifying musically, as any other. The literature of recent years does not fulfil this need for open discussion very well, however, with pockets of often misleading advice combining with practical but theoretically unsubstantiated guides to create a confusing array of material. The echoes of all that was regrettable in the music appreciation movement are felt in such publications as Károlyi's (1998) guide to 'African and Oriental music' and Rodbard's (1996) 'musical journey through fourteen countries': these books, and many like them, illustrate and describe the music and traditions of different cultures, but they do not elucidate a rationale for teaching, giving only surface information that is open to misuse in the classroom. As in all aspects of the music curriculum, it is teachers themselves who must formulate such a rationale, but where world music texts fail even to acknowledge that there are questions to be answered, they do music and education a disservice.

There have been some attempts to address the important challenge of how music from another cultural and social context should be presented in the classroom, given that it takes a sensitive teacher to judge the balance between knowledge and activity, avoiding the danger of world music teaching becoming 'no better than the life of Beethoven' (Wiggins, 1996: 28). Learning by doing must be balanced with a respect for the cultural origins of the music, so that children can understand the music from the inside, both in terms of its musical structure and logic, and of its place in the society from which it originates. Roese (1998) is amongst those who cautions against 'stereotyping and tokenism' (ibid.: 19), emphasising the importance of giving accurate and considered information to children, rather than reinforcing vague Westernised perceptions of the music of other cultures. The broader view, that 'studying musical activity from the perspective of concepts of employed, in varying fashions, all over the world assists the western music teacher to teach music, rather than western music alone' (Stock, 1996: 152), emphasises the importance of retaining a musical and educational perspective, rather than being sidetracked by cultural bias or political crusades.

Some recent resources commonly found in secondary schools, such as Stock's *World Sound Matters* (1996b) and Metcalfe and Hiscock's *Music Matters* (1992), attempt to address the pitfalls of over-simplification, with the latter stating that pupils should gain understanding of 'the spirit rather than the letter' of world musics by 'investigating a few of the elements ... and handling them in a very simple fashion to create short pieces of their own' (Metcalfe & Hiscock, 1992: 94). As in all aspects of music teaching, however, there remains the potential for teachers to lose sight of the musical experience, focusing on information rather than experience, and so stifling the rich opportunities afforded by world musics. Boyce-Tillman (1996) recalls 'Cook's Tour' listening lessons in world musics, where comparisons with more familiar music meant 'returning to our own culture (here defined as Western European classical traditions) with a sense of relief, feeling that the "foreign" culture is strange, exotic and little able to be grasped' (ibid.: 50). Balancing musical, social and cultural understanding is a challenging task, and Swanwick's statement that 'music expands our universe of thought and feeling' (1992c: 138) suggests that it is the authenticity of the musical encounter that is ultimately important, with geographical and cultural knowledge forming only the context. Kwami (1996), on the other hand, highlights the importance of 'intercultural' understanding (ibid.: 61), seeing music education as an area in which the skills and background of all children can be valued equally:

> A comprehensive education programme needs to recognize that deviations do not equate with inferiority and that diversity can contribute to a rich and more meaningful tapestry of life and experiences.
>
> (Kwami, 1996: 61)

Despite the acknowledgement of world musics within GCSE and the National Curriculum, Kwami warns against the dangers of retaining a 'Eurocentric' perspective (ibid.: 62) that creates a musical élite from those children who have notational and instrumental skills. If 'music for all' is to be a genuine goal, it must not be dependent on the private financing of instrumental tuition, which as well as being socially divisive reinforces the Western assumption that musical literacy is paramount. A process of 'enculturation', incorporating the music learning processes and performing activities of other cultures, is Kwami's preferred way forward (ibid.: 72). As the remainder of this chapter will demonstrate, however, the claims for world music take their place amongst a multiplicity of perspectives, which together demonstrate the many roles and ideologies that music education in the 1990s is expected to fulfil.

7.3 The impact of new technology

With so many new ideas entering music education in the last twenty years, the introduction of music technology to the classroom has been a slow process. Electronic keyboards are now a familiar sight in secondary schools, but the level of debate over their use has been minimal, compared to their impact:

> While many authors have argued passionately on behalf of singing, the percussion band, musical appreciation and much else in the past, there is an eerie silence about electronic keyboards. There is no philosophy, and no Vaughan Williams or Orff has come forward to support their presence.
>
> (Salaman, 1997: 143)

The application of music technology in the classroom has developed at a local level (ibid.: 144), with teachers and advisers working to introduce new resources and find a relevant use for them. Their introduction has not always been thoroughly considered, with 'comparatively anonymous individuals based in ... commercial firms' (ibid.: 144) doing excellent work in offering practical support to teachers, but inevitably failing to engage in critical discussion. Like the radio and gramophone, the new technology had considerable novelty value, and many teachers have welcomed the chance to give all pupils access to a readily available instrument. The comparison continues, however, in that none of these electronic additions to the classroom can compensate for unfocused activities, and the need for a secure rationale becomes increasingly important. As Odam (1995), points out, in their haste to begin composing on the keyboard, many children are allowed to circumvent the necessary technical skills that will enable future musical development:

> Electronic keyboards on their own, used as instruments in their own right, have a good deal to offer in the classroom, but have certain inherent dangers of which teachers need to be well aware. ... Keyboards need to be learnt as instruments like any others. Children can use the 'one-finger' approach, as many of us do when typing, but what they can do will be very limited, as many of us find as typists.
>
> (Odam, 1995: 125)

The depressing sight of a room full of Year 7 pupils playing 'cabbage' and 'baggage' on keyboards with one finger is not so unusual (cf. Mills, 1994: 195), and illustrates the negative effects of these potentially valuable resources. Children are generally enthusiastic about working on keyboards, perhaps seeing a connection with the popular music they listen to and play at home. If this enthusiasm is to be harnessed productively, however, the use of keyboards as performing and composing tools needs careful thought.

Music technology, of course, goes beyond the simple electronic keyboard, with synthesizers, computer notation programmes and advanced recording equipment increasingly to be found in secondary schools:

> The electronic sound production technology of synthesizers has liberated the performer, who no longer needs to rely on the sound creating abilities of his or her own performance. The composer, too, has benefited from technological advances with the development of the music workstation as a compositional tool. ... Technology provides pupils with access to a musical environment that is not dependent on their own performance skills.
>
> (Hodges, 1996: 77)

Comber et al. (1993) share the belief that 'the widespread availability and relatively low cost of highly sophisticated music technology is revolutionising the scope and potential of music teaching' (1993: 124). However, they also draw attention to the 'profound influence upon gender related patterns of musical behaviour' that the new focus could have (ibid.: 124), seeing information technology as a masculine domain that could be threatening to girls, traditionally dominant in the field of music learning (ibid.: 125). Research carried out by the authors suggested that boys displayed greater confidence with computers at school and at home, a fact that may have changed even within the few years since the report, given the increased use of e-mail and the Internet in many homes and workplaces. Nevertheless, Comber's female subjects agreed that boys 'know what they are doing' in music technology (ibid.: 128), a perception which affected the girls' negative self-images, leading to a more reticent approach to experimentation with the new resources. Despite this potentially disturbing effect, teachers interviewed by Comber et al. reported an increase in the number of boys studying GCSE music, notably amongst those coming through the non-traditional routes of self-taught rock and pop groups (ibid.: 131). Clearly, there will be exceptions to any generalisations about gendered behaviour, particularly in the small GCSE music classes that many schools have. What Comber's research highlights, however, is the importance of considering the long-term effects on all aspects of music learning and teaching, given that music technology is reshaping the potential and focus of many music classrooms.

To reject the possibilities of music technology resources is to be accused of 'technophobia' (Kassner, 1996: 193), but if music learning is no longer to rely on performance skills then educational outcomes need to be reconsidered.

Whilst synthesizers and workstations may indeed liberate pupils to explore new worlds of sound, the danger is that this could become the high-tech version of the 'tearing-up paper to make different sound-effects' criticised some twenty years earlier (Swanwick, 1979: 10). A recent edition of the *British Journal of Music Education* devoted to articles on music technology began with the reminder that 'IT [Information Technology] is a *means* not an end' (Paynter, 1997b: 108), although several of the articles that followed still confined themselves to giving advice on purchasing equipment. Advice has also been forthcoming from the National Council for Educational Technology, who issued guidance to primary and secondary schools (NCET, 1996; 1997) on the implications of technology for music teaching. Intended to be of practical help, most of the information provided relates to 'choosing and using' equipment (1997), and there is little critical discussion. As a government funded research project, the aim was to help implement the technology elements of the music National Curriculum orders and, although the guides are clear and informative, they do little to promote professional debate. Where insightful comments do emerge, they only serve to emphasise the need for further discussion, as the authors acknowledge that, for example, 'it is the musical issues ... that surround a recording, or subsequent use of it, that make the recording exercise valid in the context of musical learning' (ibid.: 1). As in all aspects of music education, a clear sense of purpose is essential, and to engage with technology simply because it is new and expensive is not sufficient, a fact acknowledged even by enthusiasts:

> Technology can provide control over a musical environment which is rich in educational possibilities, although the danger is to become preoccupied with the technology for its own sake and not engage with music.

> (Hodges, 1996: 93)

Kassner (1996) attempts to reassure teachers about this and other potential difficulties, stating that teachers' fear of their own failure and educational redundancy are often contributing factors in a resistance to technological innovation (ibid.: 194). As at so many previous turning points in music education, a clinging to established pedagogy and knowledge is more comforting than an acceptance of change. In this case, Kassner argues, such conservatism denies pupils the opportunity 'to be musical ... in a future where technology will play an increasingly important role' (ibid.: 194). The innovations that bring with them a mass of new equipment are the hardest to resist, as once the money has been spent, schools expect a substantial educational return on their investment.

A fear of 'wasted time' and 'limited learning' are amongst the objections that Kassner anticipates (ibid.: 196), and indeed the addition to the music curriculum that technology apparently represents could seem like the overloading of an already full programme. Like any other resource in the music classroom, technology cannot be a substitute for effective teaching and learning, but must be made to support it. Research is currently underway to see how that can best be achieved, with Odam working in association with the Music Research Institute on a project funded by Yamaha (Odam & Walters, 1998). The investigation aims to 'identify good practice and ... generate materials and resources' (ibid.: 15), having acknowledged that the prominence of the keyboard in the classroom demands careful consideration of its use and development. Like the Schools Council Project of the 1970s (Paynter, 1982), the 'Creative Dream' project is working with schools, drawing ideas in from practising teachers, rather than aiming for a definitive and externally imposed 'method'. This combination of research and practical experience seems an appropriate direction for music education to be taking. Teachers now have access to a wealth of ideas and resources that can contribute to practical development in the classroom. Those texts that have attempted to construct a rationale for this diversity in contemporary music education will be considered in the following section.

7.4 Reinterpreting the past: evaluating developments

Swanwick, as one of the first to offer a coherent model of musical development (1979; Swanwick & Tillman, 1986), contributed further to these discussions (1988; 1994; 1999), taking a psychological perspective on the acquisition of musical knowledge within the curriculum. In the same year that the Education Reform Act was moving the debate into the political realm, Swanwick (1988) was considering the need for philosophical foundations in music education: 'Theories are not the opposite of practice but its basis' (Swanwick, 1988: 7). He returns to his earlier consideration of emotion in music (1979: 28), presenting a more explicit view that incorporates the debate on 'creativity' in the classroom that had flourished in the intervening years:

> The ultimately distinguishing feature of musical individuality, originality and quality is not found at the level of inventing new sound materials or even in making expressive gestures, but in unique relationships brought about by musical speculation – the transformation of sound and gesture into musical structure.
>
> (Swanwick, 1988: 30)

Swanwick sees music education as 'facilitating psychological access to music' (ibid.: 33), a modern stance on the belief that listening, or even 'appreciation', can be effectively taught in the classroom. His arguments illustrate that the changing language and assertions of music educators are often a thin disguise for ideas that are broadly similar, with the following extract, for example, having clear resonance with the work of Scholes (1935) and his contemporaries:

> The role of the educator is to familiarize students with different structural conventions through active engagement – exploring and observing how musical ideas can become established and transformed through various ways of repeating and contrasting.
>
> (Swanwick, 1988: 100)

The context makes it clear that Swanwick is advocating more practical involvement than his predecessors, demonstrating the evolving assumptions that have given music education its impetus for change throughout the twentieth century. Like Farrell (1990) and Kwami (1996), Swanwick recognises the increasingly broad definition of music that teachers are expected to bring to the classroom, suggesting that a focus on musical elements and structures can help to provide coherence and allow music teaching to be 'culturally transcendental' (ibid.: 105):

> Teachers cannot expect to be *skilled* in all the musics of the world, but they must be *sensitive* to many and skilled in at least one.
>
> (Swanwick, 1988: 116)

The role of the music teacher, it seems, is ever-expanding, and Swanwick envisages schools as a 'clearing house' of ideas (ibid.: 118), enabling children to have access to a wide variety of musical knowledge and experiences. With the music curriculum increasing all the time, the belief that a complete education can be contained within it is outdated: 'There is more to life than schools and colleges, and there is more to education than the curriculum' (ibid.: 155).

Returning to the concept of musical elements and structure in a later book (1994), Swanwick qualifies his earlier belief that learning about music by observing 'structural conventions' (1988: 100) is necessarily the most effective route to musical understanding:

> There is a risk of real and worthwhile musical knowledge eluding us if we choose to promote, rehearse or present music simply because it

demonstrates some concept, perhaps that of minor tonality, or mixed
metres, or opera, or folksong, or a modulation to the dominant.

(Swanwick, 1994: 33)

Musical analysis, Swanwick argues, must be pursued through 'engagement
with the interactive elements of materials, expressive character and structure'
(ibid.: 38), an approach which represents a synthesis of the views of previous
decades. The experimentation of the 1970s remains, tempered with the
structured approach to acquiring musical knowledge that was more typical of
the first half of the twentieth century. Swanwick's views are apparently rooted
in a lingering mistrust of the teaching practices of the 1970s, which he asserts
were sometimes too much occupied with 'sound' and not sufficiently with
'music':

> The educational principles and activities then being advocated often
> went beyond exploring sound and it was usually recognised that
> something important has to happen *with* sound – at least in our
> imagination – before we are actually engaged with music. However,
> the idea was sown that sound might be synonymous with music and
> some teaching was influenced to the extent that making lists of sounds,
> inventing new sounds, recording sounds and identifying different
> categories of sound became supremely important.
>
> (Swanwick, 1994: 127)

This distaste for a focus on sound instead of music recurs in Swanwick's
most recent book (1999) in which he considers the nature and educational
implications of 'understanding within musical discourse' (ibid.: 2). Here
Swanwick reacts to interim developments in music education, acknowledging
the importance of cultural variation and stating that the task of music teachers
is to 'bring musical conversation from the background of our awareness to the
foreground' (ibid.: 35). Drawing attention to the wealth of community music
resources currently underused in schools (ibid.: 100), Swanwick urges teachers
to retain a sense of 'musical intention linked to educational purposes' (ibid.:
45), whilst recognising that pupils bring with them a range of musical
experiences and perceptions that must be accommodated in the classroom:

> Discourse – musical conversation – by definition can never be a
> monologue. Each student brings a realm of musical understanding
> into our educational institutions. We do not introduce them to music,
> they are already well acquainted with it, though they may not have
> subjected it to the various forms of analysis that we may feel are
> important for their further development.
>
> (Swanwick, 1999: 53)

There is a new realism in Swanwick's writing, as he describes music as 'challenging, complex and taxing' (ibid.: 100), having watched the 'enthusiastic and energetic approach' of teacher training students suffer after two or three years in schools, 'when the shine has rubbed off and the system has ground their energy away' (ibid.: 102). These are timely reminders that to talk of ideas and ideals is not sufficient; practical ways must be found to make these work in the classroom to the benefit of pupils and teachers of music. The twentieth century has seen a vast growth in thinking about music and its place in education, but the challenges of the classroom are perennial and still need to remain at the heart of the debate.

Swanwick is not alone in his reinterpretation of the ideals of the 1970s, with Paynter's decision to 're-present the case for creativity as a basis for the music curriculum' (Paynter, 1992: 23) in *Sound and Structure* offering another opportunity to evaluate the contemporary debate from a historical perspective. Paynter and Aston may have regretted the misinterpretations of their original ideas, which occurred when teachers adopted the practical suggestions contained in *Sound and Silence* (1970) without fully considering their musical and educational implications. However, the impetus for change, of which they were a part, was vital to move music education forward and challenge the assumptions of previous decades. Having established composition in the classroom, further thought was needed to sustain its relevance and value:

> Our first concern was to demonstrate that children could work imaginatively with sounds to create their own music in much the same way as they had been seen to work and produce using other arts materials. In *Sound and structure* my object is to build upon that principle, following the project format of *Sound and silence* but examining more closely the structuring processes: the techniques we evolve in musical composition to help us make something of our first thoughts and to hone and refine ideas in order to obtain the utmost clarity and coherence in the finished piece of music.
>
> (Paynter, 1992: 7)

Sound and Structure (1992) is a more explicitly theoretical book, with a substantial introductory chapter that incorporates philosophical approaches to understanding music and education. The projects themselves include 'teaching points' that are widely referenced, indicating the kind of discussion and extension work that could evolve from the central tasks. The simplistic interpretation that *Sound and Silence* (1970) had sometimes suffered from is guarded against here:

Even when an activity is brief, or mainly experimental, the aim should
be to make pieces of music, not merely to explore possibilities. At the
heart of all this is the creation of musical structures, and as often as
possible students should be able to feel that they have made something
which is complete in itself.

(Paynter, 1992: 28)

The projects of *Sound and Structure* tend to focus on different ways of
thinking about music, integrating technique and intuition to develop
compositional skills and a 'view of the musical world' (ibid.: 25):

We can, of course, benefit from examining closely other composers'
ways of dealing with certain kinds of problem, or other performers'
interpretations of particular works, but we must also learn to use and
to trust our own aural imagination, and to approach every composing
and performing opportunity afresh.

(Paynter, 1992: 38)

The excitement of creating music with children remains, but Paynter's later
writing demands more of its readers, encouraging teachers to engage fully with
the ideas and opportunities of learning music, and to respond to the discoveries
that are made in their own classrooms. After the struggle to bring composing
into the secondary curriculum, the new challenge is to build upon initial ideas
to ensure a rich and varied programme.

Another writer to bring the ideas of the 1970s into a modern context is
Schafer (1995), the Canadian composer who had been a significant influence
upon the British innovators of that time. Apparently rejecting Swanwick's
(1988) notion that concern with sound is insufficient basis for music education,
Schafer retains a commitment to the 'sonic experience' and to the 'ear
cleaning' activities of his earlier years (1995: 95). His enthusiasm for learning
by participation remains, with his ironic comment, 'Of course one learns
nothing while laughing' (ibid.: 93), typifying his style:

That is the Schafer method: to keep doing one exercise after another in
no particular order except to maintain a balance between the
physically active and the mentally stimulating, so that the whole takes
on the form of a mosaic or cluster rather than a linear progression.

(Schafer, 1995: 94)

Schafer's insistence that 'just *doing*' (ibid.: 94) should be at the heart of music
education is refreshingly naive, preserving the idealism of previous decades
without feeling any need for justification. Like Paynter, he demands an

intellectual and musical commitment from his readers, but makes less attempt to clarify this through discussion and examples. His tenacity is impressive, for all it circumvents the criticisms of the intervening years, demonstrating that the contemporary music education debate has room for many voices.

7.5 Moving forward: new theories of music in education

Paynter (1997a) also occupies a place alongside those more recent writers who have offered new theories of music education, interpreting the developments of the past twenty years in a way that allows for future growth. Together with Odam's (1995) ideas on approaching music through the different brain hemispheres, and Green's (1988; 1997) theories of musical ideology and gendered musical meaning, Paynter's discussion of musical perception in education has moved the debate into new areas:

> The Performing-Composing-Appraising curriculum makes sense only if its elements are seen to be diversifying an essential unity of creative musical thought. Composing is not an optional extra; in effect it underpins the whole curriculum, and it is the surest way for pupils to develop musical judgement and to come to understand the notion of 'thinking' in music.
>
> (Paynter, 1997a: 18)

Extending the views implicit in *Sound and Structure* (1992), Paynter argues that music is an essential part of education, achieving its greatest impact 'when presentation and reception are matched' (1997a: 16), that is to say, when the 'musical significance' is understood. Paynter sets his categories of increasing musical perception alongside the 'hierarchy of needs' defined by Maslow in 1970, paralleling the growth in musical sophistication with the awareness of self that Maslow describes as passing from physiological needs, through love and belonging, to self-actualisation (cited in Paynter, 1997a: 14). Paynter's application of this development to the musical context demonstrates the progression from the awareness of sound to the apprehension of a musical 'idea':

Music as Idea: whole – complete – "It speaks of perfection"
Technical understanding: knowing about the details understanding structural devices
Points of special relevance to the listener: social and cultural reference
Preference: knowing what we like and what is popular among those with whom we associate
Awareness of music: sensuous features which immediately capture our interest

(Paynter, 1997a: 9)

This development, from the enjoyment of sound to the understanding of the way music works is an 'intellectual adventure' (ibid.: 9) that provides a framework for practical music making in the classroom. Paynter warns teachers against the temptation to simplify, stating that there should always be the potential for complex perceptions to emerge (ibid.: 17). From a philosophical distance, Paynter is clarifying his 'project' approach to music education, which allows pupils to work at differentiated levels of understanding within an authentic musical experience. The challenge for education is to cultivate 'mastery of musical thinking and making' in teachers and pupils, with the practical developments that have affected the vast majority of secondary classrooms needing a secure intellectual and musical foundation in order to thrive. As Paynter asserts; 'Believing in what we teach is what it is all about' (ibid.: 18).

Another music educator who welcomes practical innovation whilst seeking to provide a rational context for its development is Odam, who in *The Sounding Symbol* (1995) addresses the apparent conflict between the aural and written presentation of music in the classroom. In phrases reminiscent of Yorke Trotter's (1914: 76) belief in teaching the sound before the sign, which was reiterated by Mainwaring (1951: 12), Odam suggests that undue reliance on a notational system can be a hindrance to the development of aural skills:

> Thinking in sound, imagining sound, constructing possible sounds in
> the head and improvising music all have to be established as skills
> before the symbols for these things are learnt. When we eventually
> use the symbols we have already to know how they will sound.
>
> (Odam, 1995: 4)

Drawing on recent research into left- and right-brain hemisphere responses to music, Odam suggests that the logical/left and intuitive/right hemispheres both need to be activated for a full response to music (ibid.: 16). In order that the 'sound (right brain) may proceed the symbol (left brain)' (ibid.: 18), Odam urges a move away from the general focus of education on logical processes, suggesting that music lessons involving metaphor as well as analysis will achieve a more balanced response:

> A rule of thumb to allow us to provide the right brain with advantage
> and also stimulate the left brain emerges as
> • first engage the ear through action (right brain)
> • next move to analysis through action (left brain)
> • finally achieve synthesis through action (both).
>
> (Odam, 1995: 26)

At the simplest level, such an approach demands that music is always heard or made rather than merely discussed, a fault that becomes more prevalent in the 'upper reaches of education' (ibid.: 26). When Odam asserts that 'each lesson must contain heard music of the best quality' (ibid.: 32), echoes of the music appreciation approach are heard, but his essential concern is that concepts should be explained through music rather than words, a point that the best of his predecessors would indeed have supported.

In considering the role of the teacher in music education, Odam draws up a list of desirable qualities more specific than the now familiar 'facilitator' or 'enabler' categories. Successful practice depends, he argues, on the sharing and demonstration of musical behaviour by the teacher, the opportunity for children to compose and improvise, and the development of scan-reading notation skills and aural awareness (ibid.: 127). The activities of music lessons must be planned to 'advantage the ear' (ibid.: 23), developing all elements of musical awareness through a variety of tasks and approaches:

> Ultimately, musical meaning can be expressed, approached and
> understood only through its medium of sound. ... Music is a sounding
> symbol. The bottom line is that the successful study of music depends
> on developing the ear. Nothing is more important than this.
>
> (Odam, 1995: 129)

Odam's work illustrates the wider areas encompassed by the more recent debate on music education, drawing upon scientific and psychological theory to bring new insight upon music in the curriculum. By focusing on the neurological and developmental aspects of music learning, rather than on the assertion of its value in the curriculum, he allows the discussion to develop in its own terms instead of being restricted by self-justification. The greater strength of the music education debate is evident in the diverse examples of classroom practice to which Odam refers and in his confidence that the finer details of learning and teaching music will find a receptive audience. The practical developments of the preceding decades have not only changed the scope of secondary music teaching, but have also provided a foundation for insightful discussion of musical development and understanding.

Green (1988; 1997) also absorbs the wider context of musical and educational theory in her writings, incorporating aesthetic and sociological viewpoints in her discussions or musical meaning and ideology. Making a distinction between cultural 'delineated' meanings and inherent 'musical' value (1988: 66), she argues against the connections between white culture and classical music that have persisted despite the good intentions of the GCSE music syllabuses:

> In fact, anyone of any nationality or race is a perfectly suitable listener to the inherent meanings of any music, so long as they have learnt how to listen, so long as they are familiar with the style: schools are supposedly there to generate such learning.
>
> (Green, 1988: 67)

Green's argument, that musical meaning must be freed from its cultural connotations and considered for its inherent values, is part of a drive to ensure 'genuine access' to music in the curriculum (ibid.: 114). Reviving the debates of the 1970s over the relevance of popular and classical music to young people, Green warns of the dangers of reinforcing socially stereotyped perceptions of music:

> Teaching people only about what is relevant and understandable merely affirms their social situation, locks them into blind acquiescence of all that they do not understand, and still perpetuates the universal appearance of a classical music which derives its cultural hegemony precisely from the fact that it is neither relevant to, nor understood by, the majority of the populace.
>
> (Green, 1988: 119)

191

The focus on musical concepts and structures advocated by Paynter (1992) and Odam (1995) does not seem to have rendered the debate over musical genres obsolete, as the heated response to the initial drafts of the National Curriculum demonstrated. Green makes clear the responsibility of the teacher to ensure that the delineated meanings of music, generated by its social and cultural associations, are not unthinkingly reinforced in the classroom. In a more recent book (1997) she extends this argument to encompass the area of gendered musical meaning, stressing the importance of presenting valid role models and equality of access in the music curriculum:

> The school has a hand in the perpetuation of the gender politics of music, not only through gendered musical practices but also in the discourse surrounding music and, most fundamentally, in the very meanings and experience of music itself.
>
> (Green, 1997: 229)

Green's interviews with teachers and pupils link the discussion of musical meaning with the challenges of providing an accessible and valuable education. Her observations of the problems facing music teachers who conscientiously try to include a variety of music and activities are perceptive, with the expectations of teachers and pupils shown to constrain the boundaries of music in the classroom:

> The mere fact that music is in the curriculum affects pupils' judgements of its style, such that any music which the teacher requires them to study is taken to be classical. Popular music, contrastingly, is *by definition* music which the teacher does not require them to study, and, in the minds of many pupils, as soon as the teacher does make this requirement, the music will cease to be popular.
>
> (Green, 1997: 146)

The teaching of music, it seems, is far more complicated than the educators of previous generations had suspected. Whilst the concerns with selecting and presenting appropriate musical opportunities are timeless, today's teachers are faced with complex questions concerning the purpose of music in the broader curriculum, and with the analysis of their teaching according to sociological and psychological criteria. Music education must take its place in the broader discussions of schooling, with the development of children's attitudes and awareness set alongside more traditional concerns with their intellectual and emotional growth.

7.6 The place of music in the curriculum

Another debate to survive the intervening years of curriculum and examination reform is the complex question of music's place within the broader arts curriculum (cf. Section 4.4). The investigations that culminated in *The Arts in Schools* report (Calouste Gulbenkian Foundation, 1982/89), had been led by Robinson, who continued his research by leading *The Arts 5–16* project. This work spanned the introduction of the National Curriculum, beginning in 1985 as part of the School Curriculum Development Committee's work, and completed under the auspices of the National Curriculum Council in 1989 (NCC Arts in Schools Project, 1990a/b). The aim of the project was to find a coherent framework for arts teaching throughout compulsory schooling, through research involving a partnership with over two hundred primary and secondary schools.

Considering the potential for collaboration between arts teachers, the Arts in Schools Project looked first at the historical development of the individual disciplines, and suggested that the absence of a common theoretical language had been 'an obstacle to coherent planning' (ibid.: 2). Music, the report asserts, has traditionally been strongest outside the curriculum, and is in particular need of consideration alongside the other arts:

> Interestingly, the visual arts are currently moving towards an increased emphasis on 'critical studies', just when music education is emphasising the importance of pupils making their own music. It may be that these disciplines are moving to converge on common ground. The danger is that without common reference points to signal this opportunity, they will simply pass each other going in opposite directions.
>
> (NCC Arts in Schools Project, 1990a: 15)

Eager to avoid the misconceptions that result from comparing the *activities* of the arts, the Project team focus upon the shared *processes* that connect the key areas of 'making and appraising' (ibid.: 49) across the curriculum:

> Although the pianist trying the first few notes of a new composition is engaged in a different activity from the sculptor making the first marks on a piece of clay, they are engaged in similar processes of exploration which are common to art-making in all media. It is these underlying processes which substantiate the place of the arts in education and which teachers, in planning the specific activities of arts lessons, should promote.
>
> (NCC Arts in Schools Project, 1990a: 47)

This sensitivity to the fundamental connections between the arts is a refreshing move away from the 'themed' approach to combined arts teaching, where music inevitably takes a subservient position as background to a content-based dance or drama event. The logical conclusion to this argument is that studying all the arts is superfluous, providing only a repetition of opportunities to 'explore' or 'create' in different media. The Project report recommends that pupils should be allowed to specialise 'in areas where their interests are sharpest' (ibid.: 41), spending their final years of compulsory schooling (Key Stage 4) pursuing one or two arts in depth, with the support of combined arts courses. Proposing this on educational grounds, the report acknowledges the danger that economic considerations will begin to drive such a policy, observing that collaborative arts teaching can often result in 'a net reduction in the time and resources that were previously available to the separate specialist courses' (ibid.: 42). Elsewhere, the Project team point to the enormous commitment required from arts teachers if 'a flexible and responsive pedagogy' is to result (NCC Arts in Schools Project, 1990b: 35). Far from offering a cheap or easy solution to arts provision, collaborative and integrated teaching makes greater demands upon teachers and pupils. At secondary school level, the successful practice endorsed by the Project ranges from the appointment of an arts co-ordinator, or the sharing of resources such as school visits, through to more elaborate work involving team teaching. Persuading staff that collaborative teaching 'may enrich rather than inhibit the teaching of their own discipline' (ibid.: 78) is an important consideration. The threat to teachers' professional status is also significant, with successful heads of music perhaps feeling nervous about 'losing [their] identity in a larger arts consortium' (Plummeridge, 1991: 60). Music, as a late entrant to the 'expressive arts' curriculum, is in particular danger of being swamped by cross-curricular work, deriving less obvious benefit from the 'themed' approaches that, despite the NCC Project's theories, still seem to dominate the concept of integrated teaching.

In the wider literature of arts education, music has also suffered from its delayed entry to the 'creative' movement and consequent marginalisation within theories of expressive arts teaching (cf. Ross, 1978; Witkin, 1974). Music features little in the writings of Abbs (1989; 1991; 1994), who tends to discuss creativity with reference to the content-led arts of literature and drama, whilst making generalisations about 'the arts' that implicitly include music:

> What we are describing is a process which has a fair chance of culminating in knowledge, in the cognition of human nature and an evaluation of that nature. Art is, thus, an epistemological activity, one

of the most subtle agents we have for the realization of the perennial injunction: 'Know thyself and be thyself'.

(Abbs, 1989: 199)

The abstract nature of music is not well served by such theories of self-realisation, although Abbs' discussion of the 'babble and rhapsody' (1991: 300) of the creative process has clear parallels with the considerations of sound and form that occupy composers (cf. Paynter, 1992). Where Abbs is merely insensitive to the needs of music, Ross remains openly confrontational, continuing his earlier portrayal (1978: 235) of music as a poor relation in the arts curriculum:

> Old dogs have found it hard to learn new tricks, and what should have been fun becomes another exercise in notation or music criticism; what should have been creativity becomes an exercise in formulaic variation on an eight-bar blues motif. So we are back to boring old music – only worse, since some pupils will see the new curriculum as the academic invasion of a highly personal musical space.
>
> (Ross, 1995: 189)

There is an element of truth in Ross's assertion that the enthusiasm and energy demanded by new music teaching techniques is not to be found in every secondary school classroom. However, to accept the accusation that most music teachers are 'disillusioned classical musicians' (ibid.: 189) seems unduly defeatist, and it is a testimony to the increased strength of music in the curriculum that Ross's comments provoked some debate. His statement that 'music can't be taught' (ibid.: 192), generated the defence that the limitations of some classrooms do not render curriculum innovation invalid (Plummeridge, 1997: 23). Counteracting Ross's claim that music teachers 'behave like people with a subject to teach' (Ross, 1995: 192), Plummeridge supports the idea of a 'musical dialogue' between teachers and pupils, comparable to the activities of successful drama lessons:

> We come to understand what it is to behave musically by being with people who display musicality in their own actions. ... People catch the flavour of music and learn to think musically by being involved in a variety of pursuits over a period of time.
>
> (Plummeridge, 1997: 26)

Gammon (1996) adopts a similar tactic, agreeing with Ross that the 'prescriptive and overloaded' National Curriculum has led to some unfocused and unsuccessful music teaching (ibid.: 107). He offers an alternative model that integrates performing, composing and appraising to give a coherent music curriculum:

> The creative aspect (composing) has the dominant role but is fed by, and feeds into, the performative and responsive aspects (performing and listening). The functional aspect, though central, is a function of the three major areas of activity. The whole is surrounded by the amorphous realm of fact and context.
>
> (Gammon, 1996: 108)

Gammon also acknowledges the disparity between 'home' and 'school' music that Ross (1995: 186) blames for much pupil disaffection with music in the curriculum. The fine balance between taking children 'as presented' whilst extending their 'cultural horizons' is difficult to achieve, and Gammon offers no easy solutions (ibid.: 111). Having accepted some of the practical constraints from which Ross has generalised, Gammon rejects the stereotypical view of the frustrated music teacher, saying that valuable but diminishing in-service training is encouraging professional development: 'Progress in educational practice comes through the clarification of aims, the creation of a broad consensus of purpose, and by the sharing of good practice' (ibid.: 118).

Gammon's eloquent response cannot entirely refute Ross's criticisms, supported as they are by some reliable and recent sources. Swanwick's survey (1989) of primary and secondary music teaching, carried out between 1986 and 1987, offers a small-scale picture of pre-National Curriculum practice, investigating the multiple roles of the music teacher and the status of music within the curriculum (ibid.: 156). An analysis of 108 music lessons in 23 secondary schools generated information regarding the percentage of time spent on different activities, which can be summarised as follows:

% of lesson	Activity
2.5%	Transmitting information
18%	Group, individual or whole class composition
9.5%	Music listening
22%	Skill acquisition
6.7%	Performance
10%	Time lost due to late starts

(Swanwick, 1989: 161)

The variation in the activities observed is proof of the expanding music curriculum, with teachers attempting to accommodate the perceived aims of the GCSE in providing a broad and balanced musical education. Swanwick reports 'a strong professionalism' amongst the teachers, which would seem to challenge Ross's later criticisms (Ross, 1995), although Swanwick admits to the limited scope of his study and warns against generalising. Swanwick's evidence is relevant to Ross's argument to the extent that the laudable aims of music educators were not always being realised:

> Firstly, the children were being challenged to extend themselves musically: secondly, the behaviour of the teacher was musically sensitive at all times. Apart from the rare realisation of these very high expectations, the detailed evidence and the general impression indicates that music education, though conscientiously prepared and effectively carried out, is not often very demanding.
>
> (Swanwick, 1989: 166)

Swanwick's research reflects an apparent conflict in the music education practice of the late 1980s, with teachers endeavouring to implement the reforms of the preceding years, but not always connecting their ideals with their classroom teaching. Swanwick urges a greater connection between research and teaching, calling for more support for teachers in the classroom, and more opportunity for them to develop away from it:

> It is vital for the future of music education, for what the Secretary of State calls 'tomorrow's world', that teachers are given opportunities to expand their horizons beyond the circuits of their schools or LEA's, to engage in discussion with other colleagues, to participate in discussion, reading, reflection, music making, curriculum development and research.
>
> (Swanwick, 1989: 170)

With the introduction of the National Curriculum serving only to increase the pressures upon music teachers, such advice does not seem to have been heeded. The opportunity for reflection is a rare thing in education, and it requires a particular determination and energy to seek opportunities to question classroom practice and implement significant change.

More recent surveys have offered similar evidence of variety in the quality, opportunity and priorities of music teachers across the country. The evidence of Ofsted (Office for Standards in Education), the school inspectorate, is of course politically charged, measuring school effectiveness against the criteria of the National Curriculum. However, the findings of the inspectors (Ofsted, 1995) present a familiar picture, suggesting that whilst pupils 'respond with enthusiasm to lessons which are taught well and resourced properly', there is discontinuity between primary and secondary music teaching, and an inconsistency between schools (ibid.: 3). A sensitivity to the 'significant ...

pressures' (ibid.: 4) of the music teacher's role precedes demands for greater 'recording, reporting and assessment' and for lessons that 'take account of, and develop, pupils' previous achievement' (ibid.: 5). It is tempting to be cynical about this external evaluation of music teaching, given that it does little to develop the practice and perceptions of individual teachers, but the descriptions of more and less successful lessons give a useful overview of current practice:

> Lessons in which the teaching is good or very good usually have composing and appraising as their dominant activities, and employ performing as a supporting skill.

> Learning suffers when the activities set lack challenge, are not resourced with instruments of suitable quality, or take place in an environment so noisy that pupils cannot hear their work well enough to be able to make judgements about how to improve it, or assess the effects of any changes that they make.

> (Ofsted, 1995: 12)

These observations reinforce Paynter's (1992) approach to composing in the classroom, emphasising that activities must be purposeful and progressive if they are to be musically and educationally worthwhile. The message does not seem to have reached a certain proportion of music teachers, and the inspectors' role, as evaluators rather than advisers, can play little part in changing this. The problem of dissemination is significant, with the need to share effective teaching and ideas remaining a concern. The culture of grading and even failing lessons is not particularly helpful in this context, given that the impetus for genuine change must come from the teacher rather than from the perceived threat of external agents. The opportunities for professional dialogue have been damaged by the confrontational nature of recent education reform, making the task of writers and researchers in music education more difficult.

Inspection evidence is also used as an 'Ofsted guide to good teaching' (1998), indicating that the culture of external evaluation, rather than the development of a personal rationale, is increasing its power in education. Mills (1998) summarises the findings of the latest music inspections, suggesting that 'the quality of teaching in Key Stage 3 is improving, and ... is already very high from Key Stage 4 onwards' (ibid.: 59). Inspectors have, however, reported 'specific and persistent problems', including 'continuity and progression', 'developing ... musical imagination' and 'participation in music at school' (ibid.: 60). Specific examples are given of good practice, where teachers have successfully avoided these problems, with support for singing coming across strongly (ibid.: 69). The Ofsted team conclude that there is 'an encouraging picture of arts education in schools in England' (Ofsted, 1998: 85), and inevitably see inspection as playing an important role in sustaining that development. Of itself, this view is nothing new, but the increased public accountability of schools, coupled with the publication of league tables and inspection reports, could mean that these external evaluations are allowed to dominate the development of the curriculum. Whilst there are useful lessons to be drawn from such national regulation, it is no substitute for the intellectual rigour and practical commitment to developing education that has generated change in previous decades.

Mills (1996), in the course of her work as an Ofsted inspector, has paid particular attention to the problem of transition between primary and secondary schooling, suggesting that the expectations of secondary music teachers often disregard the progress pupils have already made (Mills, 1996: 5). Asserting that teaching needs to be 'diagnostic, differentiated and demanding' (ibid.: 13), she summarises five attitudes that allegedly pervade teaching in the first year of the secondary school:

1 *Sheep and goats* [children separated by musical ability testing, with the less able given less tuition]
2 *They do nothing at primary school* [no practical recognition of earlier achievements]
3 *Back to basics* ['empty vessels' approach, with low teacher expectations]
4 *Praise them regardless* [low pupil expectations generated by praising of lacklustre work]
5 *No keyboards before Christmas* [specialist resources withheld, reducing pupils' interest]

(Mills, 1996: 7–11)

Comparing these ideas with those of a group of thirty Year 7 pupils in a Sheffield school suggests that children's own reactions to the change between primary and secondary music teaching can be much more mundane (Interviews: 16 October 1997) Concerns such as 'we had to sit boy, girl, boy, girl, which I hated – now we can sit with our friends' frequently take priority over subject content. The children's rejection of 'boring singing' as being associated with primary school supports the inspectors' view that insufficient progression in this activity can lead to pupil disaffection: 'The singing heard in Y6 class lessons is often no more accurate or expressive, or in no more parts, than that heard in Y3 or Y4 in the same school' (Ofsted, 1995: 7). The Sheffield pupils interviewed saw 'playing instruments' as a significant change in their musical experience at secondary school, with one child summarising his first term: 'We write a lot of musical signs and use lots of instruments and listen to music'.

The varied perceptions of the children are a warning to secondary school teachers that their educational aims are not always made explicit. For every child who concludes 'Music is fun', there is one who can only make the observation, 'We sit on chairs and not on benches'. Mills (1996) does not offer an 'ideal' category for secondary teachers to aspire to, but suggests that closer co-operation between primary and secondary schools, including joint appointments and in-service training, could alleviate the problems (ibid.: 13). Her tone is jocular, but the criticisms are harsh, pointing to a significant fault in current music education provision. There is some way to go, it seems, before the developing ideas of the late twentieth century are realised in effective and consistent practice.

Everitt's (1997) review of musical opportunities for young people gives a wider picture, evaluating the impact of community music projects in a manner comparable with the report of the Cambridgeshire Council of Musical Education, published over sixty years earlier (1933). Everitt's account of music in schools highlights the divide that exists between composing in the classroom and performance in individual instrumental lessons. Everitt calls for an exchange of good practice between classroom teachers, who are typically more successful in encouraging experimentation and imaginative musical responses in large group work, and instrumental teachers, who are experienced in teaching specific skills to small numbers of children (ibid.: 77). As communities in their own right, and in connection with the wider local population, opportunities exist within schools for collaborative teaching and learning in music. Everitt's focus on 'participatory music' draws attention to the fact that musicians and educators working in and around schools often share similar goals, without ever considering a sharing of practice and expertise. He reminds us, too, that the effects of music teaching go beyond the classroom, having an impact on the cultural life of future generations, as well as immediate effects on the pupils who engage with music or, as Everitt describes it, 'the very language of the brain, the seat of intellect, emotion and the control of physical behaviour' (ibid.: 31).

The concern with cultural life that Everitt addresses is also present in the report of the National Advisory Committee on Creative and Cultural Education (NACCCE), which states that 'creating the right synergy and achieving the right balance in education is an urgent task' (1999: 9). Throughout the report, the committee emphasise the need to promote creative thinking and cultural understanding across the curriculum, with the arts forming only one aspect of that task. Music receives most detailed coverage in the chapter entitled 'Funding and Resources' (ibid.: 140), where the committee calls for greater funding and equality of access to instrumental tuition across the country. For arts teachers, the report might seem to offer few new ideas, and often seems to shift the emphasis away from arts subjects in its discussions and recommendations. However, in broadening the perspective on creative and cultural education in this way, the mundane goals of recent educational legislation are replaced by more ambitious aims, in which music has a significant role to play. Further research and discussion is necessary for these aims to be articulated and implemented, in order that energy should be channelled into the arts, and their place as one of the most direct routes towards creative and cultural development asserted.

The Campaign for Music in the Curriculum (1998) followed the same tendency to approach the discussion of arts education from a politically influenced angle, this time by exploring recent research linking music with brain development. Describing music as the 'Fourth R', the campaign cites research and case studies from different countries to support the view that music facilitates learning across the curriculum, in a presentation that is undoubtedly well-meaning but, because of its methodological weaknesses and obvious bias, can make little contribution to reasoned debate. Pseudo-scientific reports of this nature have attracted popular interest in recent years, but are in danger of diverting attention from the unique nature of music, treating it as a means to an end rather than a worthwhile subject in itself. Thanks to research in music psychology we now know much more about musical perception, development and intelligence (cf. Sloboda, 1985; Hargreaves, 1986; Deliège & Sloboda, 1995), but such evidence cannot of itself resolve educational dilemmas, and the questions of why and how best to teach music in schools remain.

With so many diverse claims being made for music in the curriculum, teachers are faced with the task of ensuring that a coherent curriculum is constructed from the formidable range of activities, resources and ideas available. The closing decades of the twentieth century have seen a reappraisal of the 1970s innovations that changed the course of music teaching, with Paynter (1992) and Swanwick (1988; 1994; 1999) evaluating the impact of composing in the classroom and offering a new rationale for today's teachers. The trinity of performing, composing, and listening/appraising, established in the GCSE criteria and reinforced through the National Curriculum now forms the foundation for music education, and must be used to support the diverse demands of popular music, world musics, and technology. This wealth of opportunity has to be considered alongside reductions in the instrumental music service to give a complete picture of 1990s education, but there is, nevertheless, cause for optimism, as discussion expands to include broader educational and musical concerns, and practice develops to encompass the new opportunities available to children as musicians.

Historical research in music education has much to offer the debate on potential directions and developments in contemporary practice. The closing chapter of this book will evaluate the challenges facing today's music educators within this historical framework, demonstrating that the innovation and idealism that characterise the best writing of earlier decades can help to shed new light on present educational theory and practice. Learning from the past does not necessitate imitation, but rather acknowledges that the processes of discovery, interpretation and application of ideas that all teachers go through is part of an inheritance that must be understood in order to be fully evaluated.

Chapter 8

Ideals and opportunities:
a century of music education

8.1 Learning from the past: a summary of research findings

The literature of music education in the twentieth century testifies to the ongoing commitment to afford music a secure place in the curriculum, and to ensure that children are allowed to develop their musical skills and understanding according to the priorities of the time. The huge expansion in the scope of music education in the latter half of the century has generated increasingly complex questions about the place and purpose of music in teaching and learning, and about the type of encounters with music that secondary education should include.

Recurring themes across the century show that the balance between performing, composing and appraising that today's curriculum strives for has taken decades to reach stability, with the evolution of ideas slowed down by the strong influence of existing pedagogy. Attitudes have overlapped across the generations, with the timeless ideals of Yorke Trotter (1914), for example, enduring well beyond the practical, even mundane, focus of Winn (1954) or Rainbow (1956/71). Green (1997) confirms that teachers' backgrounds are still a significant factor in their own work, with the intention to embrace new ideas often undermined by existing beliefs and expectations:

> Most secondary school music teachers, although they have willingly and enthusiastically embraced new values and skills, remain classically trained themselves, and their backgrounds inevitably influence what is at the centre of their educational projects. In this sense, it is not so much the *content* of what they teach as the pedagogy itself which is affected by their training.
>
> (Green, 1997: 145)

The limitations of published sources as an agency for change has to be acknowledged, yet their significance as representatives of the innovations and priorities of past decades is considerable. Swanwick has spoken of the pleasure of making connections with practising teachers, either in an innovatory role, or as with this reaction to *A Basis for Music Education* (1979), as a reinforcement for ideas that were already evolving in schools:

> One compliment was from a teacher in Hampstead who said, 'When I read the book, I realised why what I was doing was okay, or wasn't okay', which I think is also nice, because it's confirmatory of professional practice, so it's not an island of ideas, it's actually a mainland of activity.
>
> (Swanwick: Interview, 24 November 1997)

Writers on music education cannot expect to change the world overnight, indeed many would deplore any such unquestioning approach to their ideas. Publications can, however, act as encouragement or guidance where the willingness to respond to innovation already exists. Combined with the influence of practising teachers, advisers and musicians, they contribute to the gradual evolution that allows the best ideas of a previous decade to be retained, whilst a rationale for the future develops.

No history of music education can ever be complete, because the gradual change that occurs in individual classrooms, for specific teachers and their pupils, goes largely undocumented. It is this slow questioning and development of practice, influenced by colleagues, educational and musical role models, and by the pupils themselves, that is the essence of music education, with the ideas that reach publication offering only a partial picture. Music education history is absorbed more than it is studied, with teachers making connections with the past through their own education and training, before going on to redefine these received attitudes and ideas in their classroom practice. The published texts studied here reveal a gradual shift in the views and methods of music educators in the twentieth century, broadly demonstrating an increasing acceptance of a wider musical repertoire, and a similar recognition of the variety of musical opportunities that can be made available to children.

To take an evolutionary approach to music education history is only one possible interpretation of events, and invites the charge of over-simplification or excessive tidiness of narrative. It is clear, however, that in tracing changes in practice, the views of particular writers and educators speak more clearly than others to contemporary teachers and researchers. These writers appear to focus the fluctuating ideals and problems of their time, bringing them forward for consideration by the next generation. At any point, a multitude of possibilities exist in education, which are gradually settled and prioritised by the teachers, politicians and wider society of the time. The history we are left with is not the only one, but is one that identifies the moments of chaos and continuity, of excitement and fear, that have driven change within music classrooms and universities. The following summary of research findings highlights the enduring commitment to music and education that prominent writers of the twentieth century have demonstrated, and allows us to take stock before considering the relevance of these ideas to music education today:

1900–1935

The beginning of the century, represented by the writings of Mills (1905) and Yorke Trotter (1914), offers an immediate insight upon the challenges facing music educators at any time. The ideas of both these writers are inspirational, demanding a music education for all children that goes beyond the confines of the rote learning approaches of the day, to develop children's 'inner nature' (Yorke Trotter, 1914: 136) and raise their awareness of the potential of musical expression. These aims were to be reiterated in the different contexts of subsequent decades, but for the moment were largely obscured by the practical dictates of MacPherson (1922; 1923), Somervell (1931) and Scholes (1935), all highly influential figures with decided views on musical appreciation, singing and aural training. From the accounts of contemporary teachers, including Wood (1925) and Donington (1932), it can be inferred that the task of reconciling ideals with practical objectives was resolved differently at a local level according to teachers' interests and circumstances. Inevitably, practical suggestions that could be acted upon, or even delivered directly to the classroom through radio broadcasts, had more immediate impact than abstract discussions which, whilst offering new perspectives on music education, could not offer instant solutions to the challenges of the classroom. Yorke Trotter's decision to record his 'principles of musicianship' (Yorke Trotter & Chapple, 1933) is perhaps an indication of the frustration felt by an idealist whose vision remained a minority stance. The development of music education in the decades to follow was to be a continual reconciling of far-reaching aims with pressing practical concerns, with the pace of change, at least until the 1970s, generally hastened by new resources, rather than by new perceptions.

1935–1955

Music education reached the outbreak of World War II in a state of flux, with the ambitions of significant innovators tempered by the confines of amateur music making at the time, and the perception that listening and singing should be the principal activities of the secondary music curriculum. The intervention of wartime evacuation and devastating loss of life generated reform in the education system as a whole, leading to compulsory secondary schooling for all and the raising of the school leaving age. With the expansion in secondary education offering scope for the development of the curriculum, other arts subjects flourished, with music remaining caught between attempts to achieve 'academic' status, and unfavourable comparisons with creative developments in art and English. Music in schools was heavily dependent on the enthusiasm and availability of specialist staff, with the teaching of Smith (1947) and Barnes (1983) typical of a performance-based curriculum that was greatly influenced by the teacher's own musical background. The new interest in music psychology pointed the way forward for a curriculum subject struggling to find an identity, with Mainwaring (1941; 1951) arguing for a 'progressive, purposive' curriculum (1951: 1) based on practical involvement with a wide range of music. A willingness to experiment and learn with the children was seen as essential to the music teacher's role (ibid.: 5), with an emphasis on musical, rather than verbal, explanations (ibid.: 11). Although Mainwaring's refreshing emphasis on the enjoyment and experience of music was a timely challenge to the most dreary renderings of the 'music appreciation' approach, the development of music psychology was also to have a potentially damaging effect, with a new focus on musical ability testing undermining the belief that music should be equally accessible to all children. Once again, a period of change in music education had generated a diversity of practice, greatly influenced by teachers' own musical experiences, and only becoming coherent and progressive where a secure place in the curriculum had been established by the still scarce specialist music teachers of the time.

1955–1975

The diversity that was emerging at the end of the 1950s grew in the following decades as new ideas developed from a growing interest in popular, world and contemporary musics. Education committee reports, notably *Half Our Future* (Ministry of Education, 1963), reflected a changing educational climate, with the differing needs of adolescents given more careful consideration than in the years of public and grammar school domination. Music, however, continued to lag behind, with lack of facilities (DES, 1956/69: v) and a restricted curriculum (Ministry of Education, 1963: 140) hampering the development of effective and imaginative teaching. A new generation of composer-teachers was on the verge of changing entrenched attitudes, with Self (1967), Schafer (1965; 1967; 1969) and Paynter and Aston (1970) offering models of music teaching and learning that were influenced by their own composition approaches and those of their contemporaries. The reaction to change was mixed, with Walker

(1983) and Salaman (1983) amongst those who would later recall the difficulties of reflecting on established practice and moving towards the creative, project-based approaches of these prominent innovators. Deliberate efforts to assimilate the new ideas were made through local projects (North West Regional Curriculum Development Project, 1974), and in some published texts (Brocklehurst, 1971), but a cautious response was typified by the Schools Council Working Paper, *Music and the Young School Leaver: Problems and Opportunities* (1971). With the introduction of composing and improvising to the secondary classroom, the purpose of music teaching was under scrutiny, and a perceived conflict between 'traditional' and 'progressive' methods was emerging. The task of resolving the aims and activities of composing, performing and listening to form a coherent curriculum faced all music teachers, with those who hoped to circumvent it soon to be challenged afresh by the introduction of the GCSE.

1975–1985

An additional reaction to the developments of the 1960s and 1970s was an increased tendency to theorise, with Swanwick (1979) making one of the first attempts to provide a model of the music curriculum within which classroom practice could be evaluated. His search for a 'conceptual framework' (ibid.: 6) resulted in the 'CLASP' mnemonic, with composition, 'audition' and performance forming the basis of the curriculum, supported by literature studies and skill acquisition (ibid.: 45). Research some years later (Swanwick, 1989) would show that this balance of activities was not always achieved in practice, but the ambition to find a curriculum that matched practical involvement with structured learning was clearly stated. The absorption of new ideas into mainstream classroom practice was further complicated by the expansion of the popular music culture, which presented another challenge to teachers who were keen to make music education interesting and relevant to their pupils. Vulliamy and Lee (1976/80) tackled the question of 'relevance' in their early texts, and also provided one of the first introductions to world music in the classroom (1982), acknowledging the increased demands upon teachers and calling for more in-service training (1982: 3). Not only were the activities of the music classroom becoming more varied and challenging, but the traditional repertoire was also being expanded, at least in those schools where the willingness to embrace new ideas existed. The Schools Council Project, *Music in the Secondary School Curriculum* (Paynter, 1982), provided teachers with an opportunity to share the ideas and difficulties that were developing in the classroom, with Paynter co-ordinating a rationale that went some way to clarifying the misinterpretations of 1970s ideas that were in danger of undermining new approaches to music learning. As the arts debate broadened, notably through the research of Witkin (1974) and Ross (1978), music teachers continued to grapple with the practical and intellectual challenges that faced them and, once again, seemed to be in danger of becoming disconnected from the rest of the arts curriculum.

1985–2000

The arrival of the General Certificate of Secondary Education (GCSE) in the mid-1980s was an unexpected source of resolution for some of the difficulties facing music teachers. The decision to make performing, composing and listening the foundations of the music syllabuses gave official credence to ideas that had been only partially understood and accepted, and provided all teachers with a framework for their teaching. After the separation of 'O' Level and CSE approaches to teaching music, the arrival of a coherent programme for all pupils was welcomed by many, even if the inevitable concern over standards was also voiced (North, 1987). What was lacking in the introduction of the new examination was sufficient support for teachers, who were left to reconcile their new role as examiners of composition and performance, with their principal function as facilitators of learning. Like the National Curriculum, which was introduced less than a decade later, the outline of the GCSE syllabus left room for interpretation, and the fundamental questions of purpose and priorities in music teaching could still be avoided. After its brief flirtation with theoretical models (Swanwick, 1979), music education was once again dominated by practical influences, this time implemented at a national, statutory level. Political interest in education as a whole was expanding, and the need for music to assert its place in the curriculum, and define its intentions within the classroom, became increasingly urgent.

The external influences of GCSE and the National Curriculum have been in danger of defining the music education debate in subsequent years, but the texts of the late 1980s and 1990s have in fact continued the lines of thought that were emerging before these compulsory changes. The awareness of world musics has increased (Farrell, 1990; Sorrell, 1990), along with a greater use of music technology in the secondary classroom (Hodges, 1996; Salaman, 1997). There remains the possibility that developments in music education will be driven entirely by practical opportunities, rather than by an underlying rationale, although Swanwick (1988; 1994; 1999) and Paynter (1992) have both contributed to a reappraisal of recent innovations, considered in the light of interim developments. Odam (1995) and Green (1988; 1997) have broadened discussion of the music classroom through their interests in learning theories and sociology respectively, offering hope that the future of music in schools will not be entirely determined by governments and examination boards. As throughout the century, however, the sense that practical suggestions have the greatest immediate impact remains, but is made all the more disturbing by the fact that such measures are now imposed and inspected (Ofsted, 1995; 1998). The wide variety of musical experiences that are made accessible to the present generation of pupils is impressive, but needs to be evaluated according to a well-developed rationale.

This summary of the changing perspectives on music education demonstrates that a determination to afford music a stable and valued place in the curriculum has been present throughout the century. Change has been brought about not only through the ideas of prominent innovators, but also as a result of new musical resources and educational perspectives, which teachers have had to engage with for themselves in order to develop a coherent teaching programme. With dissemination a key problem in moving educational practice forward, change has often been slow, and developments not always connected. Nevertheless, the diversity of practice and opportunity that has emerged has been beneficial in defining the scope of music education, with new ideas generally representing an expansion, rather than a replacement, of existing approaches. In the classrooms of the 1990s, elements of historical practice are evident: the use of schools broadcasting continues in a significant number of primary schools, aural training and notation skills are maintained by many teachers, and the strong performing tradition in most secondary schools builds on the musical focus of the post-war years. The purpose and practice of music education have been reconsidered by each generation, as opportunities and resources have become available, and the search for a curriculum that lays the foundation for independent musical learning and enjoyment continues. With two-thirds of current and former pupils in a recent survey (Harland et al., 1995: 272) stating that they would have welcomed more arts involvement at school, there is clearly potential for continued curriculum development. The teacher at the end of the twentieth century is faced with the challenge of resolving the historical and contemporary aims of music education, both of which are present in the National Curriculum, to ensure that music teaching and learning retain vibrancy and momentum.

8.2 Looking to the future: implications of the research

Some of the practical concerns that will take music education into the next century are those that have occupied educators in the last hundred years. Whether and how to teach staff notation; how to involve all children in lively musical performance; which musical genres should form the focus of the listening curriculum; fundamentally, what to include and what to leave out? This last question, far from diminishing as discussion of the music curriculum has flourished, has become ever more consuming as access to musical activities and repertoire has increased. The National Curriculum, as the official attempt to consolidate the place of music in schools, is little more than a starting point for teachers, who must define schemes of work according their own interests and resources. The evolution of practice goes on, with the questions multiplying as more opportunities and possibilities are discovered.

The ideas of the past have an immediate relevance for contemporary music educators, allowing the questioning of current practice in a historical context. Teachers struggling to find a place for today's new technology in their classroom, could find helpful parallels with the introduction of the gramophone, when 'novelty value' also threatened to supersede musical purpose (Scholes, 1935: 173). The search for a coherent curriculum, within the confines of each generation's definitions of music and of education, yields many arguments which have pertinence to today's teachers, either as beliefs to oppose or as models to build upon. The texts studied here encompass the inspiring ideals of the early twentieth century (Mills, 1905; Yorke Trotter, 1914), the determination of the post-war years (Mainwaring, 1941; Hale, 1947), and the innovation of the 1960s and 1970s (Schafer, 1965; Paynter & Aston, 1970). Elements of all these are found in the writings and teaching of the late twentieth century, with the abundance of ideas and resources making it increasingly important for teachers to engage with current publications and research, in order to support or challenge their own developing rationale. Plummeridge's reminder that 'all teachers operate against a background of ideas, beliefs, attitudes and assumptions which may be said to constitute *their* theory or theories' (1991: 9), is of the greatest relevance as music education enters the new century. Indeed, his own summary would not be out of place in the texts of much earlier music educators, suggesting that although ideas and methods may change, the principal goals of music teaching remain very closely related:

> If as a result of their experiences in schools pupils can eventually see some point in music and musical activity then their progress will be very real indeed. They may never be technically 'advanced' but this

will not prevent them from valuing music as a realm of meaning and
form of understanding.

(Plummeridge, 1991: 82)

For research to have relevance for practising teachers, it needs to be directly
applicable to their work, affecting either their pupils' development or their own
professional or musical identity. The challenging question of disseminating
ideas in the teaching profession remains, and the search for more effective
ways to link research and practice in a mutually beneficial way is of immediate
concern. The models of shared practice developed through the century have
included the writing of books by teachers and academics, the broadcasting of
lessons through radio and television, and the establishment of research projects,
notably *Music in the Secondary School Curriculum* (Paynter, 1982) and the
more recent *The Arts in Schools* (NCC Arts in Schools Project, 1990a). The
co-operation between teachers and researchers fostered in these latter projects
is an area that needs further development, particularly in the age of the National
Curriculum and school accountability. The traditional image of the isolated
music teacher delivering the whole music curriculum to the majority of the
school, without opportunity for professional or musical development away
from the classroom, is one that should be questioned as a matter of urgency. A
healthy suspicion appears to exist in schools of research that is imported from
universities and government advisory committees, but this should not be taken
as a decision to isolate teachers from developments outside their educational
community. It remains the case that 'teachers are asked to teach too much'
(Paynter, 1982: 31), and ways must be found to remedy this, with scope for
joint research projects between schools and universities to work for the benefit
of education at all levels.

To suggest that solutions to contemporary music education practice lie
entirely in the past would be a regressive step, but the fashionable tendency to
deny the significance of previous approaches is equally damaging. Educational
progress, as depicted in the public arena of politics and journalism, is too often
seen as a journey between one 'bandwagon' and the next, with new ideas
drawing some of their strength from ridiculing their predecessors. The course
of change in music education has demonstrated that such an approach is
unhelpful, as each generation has carried forward the best practice of earlier
years, building on established work to gradually move ideas into new territory.
Even in the 1970s, when the introduction of composing to the classroom
seemed to refute previous beliefs, a balanced approach was sought, which
retained the valuable performing and listening work of the post-war years
whilst absorbing the influences of the avant-garde. Far from being a series of
disparate activities, music education has undergone a slow evolution, drawing

its enduring values into the next decade, but setting aside those practices that have become obsolete. The process implies the need for reflection by practising teachers, for it is those at the heart of education who can best perceive the effectiveness of what they are doing and identify those areas where there is potential for development. Teachers need to be supported in this self-reflection by their professional colleagues, and by academics and researchers, who can construct between them a picture of the changing state of music education (cf. Pitts, 1998c). The texts of the past offer one context for discussion, in that they highlight universal challenges to the music teacher, as well as providing models of teaching and learning that can be considered in an unthreatening way. To read Yorke Trotter (1914) today is not merely historically interesting, but can also illuminate concerns that have endured the curriculum changes of this century to remain at the heart of music education. Similarly, to look at Mainwaring's ideas (1941; 1951), or Schafer's (1965; 1967; 1969), or the early Paynter's (Paynter & Aston, 1970) does not imply that their suggestions should be adopted, but rather that some of their enthusiasm for engaging in music with young people might be absorbed. Likewise, a comparison of changing ideas between the 1970s and 1990s, through the work of Paynter (Paynter & Aston, 1970; Paynter, 1982; 1992; 1997a) or Swanwick (1979; 1988; 1994; 1999), can be helpful in finding a context for contemporary practice, and perceiving the changing perspectives that have emerged over time.

What comes across strongly from the texts of the past is that the integration of practical and intellectual perspectives on music education is essential to coherent argument and practice. The array of 'teachers' guides' that have followed the introduction of the GCSE and the National Curriculum are no substitute for independent thought, and the acceptance of imposed systems of teaching can ultimately stifle progress. Whilst the legislation of the past twenty years has undoubtedly changed the course of music education, it does not of itself constitute a rationale for music in the curriculum (cf. Pitts, 2000). Music may be enshrined in law, and the activities of the classroom regulated by inspectors, yet the daily transactions of teaching and learning must still have a rational foundation. Music educators deal with a vast area of knowledge and experience, and the construction of a coherent programme of learning is vital for teachers and pupils alike, if the time allocated to music in the curriculum is to be used effectively. So much educational development at the end of the twentieth century seems to be dependent on politics and economics, and it is of the greatest importance that legislation is not allowed to stifle curriculum debate. Once again, there is potential for a mutually beneficial and overlapping relationship between teachers and researchers in ensuring that the necessary reflection and discussion can take place. For that to happen, however, the links between theory and practice that have been unquestioningly asserted by the writers of the past need to be re-established in educational discussion. Developing new ideas and evaluating existing practice is part of what it means to be a good teacher, and if there is at present insufficient time for teachers to do these things, that does not make them any less desirable.

The relevance of this research, then, is in the foundation that it lays for discussion and evaluation, providing an overview of the developments that have led to music education practice at the close of the twentieth century. Connections with present ideals and past ambitions offer a fertile ground for self-development, and whilst this can be no substitute for time to reflect and research for oneself, the opportunity to link contemporary ideas with the work of others can be a source of energy and inspiration. Music education has not reached a point of completion now, or at any other time in the century, and an understanding of the continual progression from existing practice to new ideas can help to put the concerns of everyday teaching into perspective. In evaluating the ideas of the past, teachers will necessarily be considering their own methods and ideals, in a manner that is free from the competitive focus of today's educational debate. The past has shown that there are few right answers in education, only the continual striving for more valuable and enjoyable ways to allow children to grow in musical understanding and experience.

8.3 Potential for future research

The opportunity for future research in the history of music education is vast, with each period of change in the twentieth century giving scope for detailed archive research at a local and national level. This book has principally considered the published texts of the century, in order to gain an overview of changing attitudes and ideas, with the limitations of this approach readily acknowledged. School textbooks, archive radio and television broadcasts, and interviews with teachers and pupils would all yield further information more appropriate to a closely-focused study of a particular era (cf. Cox, 1996). The changing nature of the resources available to music teachers is a particularly important part of the historical development of classroom practice, and could illuminate new aspects of the experiences available to children of different generations. Immediate comparisons can be seen, for example, between publications written specifically for children, which reflect the classroom approaches and musical priorities of the age. Children reading *The Young Musician* in 1936 were encouraged to complete musical quizzes and competitions, play and sing the short pieces printed in the magazine, and read ongoing stories about 'The adventures of the Solfa family' (Gwen Dodds, 1936: 264). A modern equivalent is hard to find, but the latest edition of *Music Scholar* shows changes that go beyond the inevitable stylistic alterations, including articles on music technology and the cost of studying a musical instrument, as well as featuring a timeline of twentieth century music and interviews with musical role models (Jenkins, 1997). Publishers have evidently recognised the changing needs of music students across the generations, and a detailed comparison of the textbooks and teachers' guides of different eras would offer a new perspective on the predominant values of the time.

Other contemporary challenges that could be given a historical context include the connection between instrumental teaching, with its separate system of examinations and individual tuition, and the classroom, where pupils are rarely called upon to use the skills they have developed in their instrumental lessons. Metcalfe (1987) has cited the separate development of performing examinations as a factor in music's low status in the School Certificate, and to a certain extent the disparity between the technical skills of instrumental tuition and general musical development in the classroom remains. Recent reports from music teaching organisations (MANA, 1995; FMS/NAME, 1998) on developing a coherent curriculum for instrumental teaching have demonstrated that an awareness of the need for new teaching styles and integrated approaches is emerging, but a more sustained investigation is needed to build upon this realisation:

> For too long instrumental tuition has been regarded as a 'bolt-on' to the music curriculum, undertaken by a few, taught in isolation from mainstream music and delivered in a style which often bore no relation to the teaching and learning taking place in the broader music education programme adopted within the class or, for that matter, in other curriculum areas. Of course attitudes are changing and it is now possible to identify similarities rather than differences in the approach and styles of some instrumental and class music teachers, but this is by no means universal.
>
> (MANA, 1995: 3)

The duality of music learning has a long tradition in schools, and its questioning would be timely as county instrumental services are put under increasing financial pressure. Peripatetic music lessons in schools have suffered in recent years from a reduction in funding, meaning that many schools have had to charge pupils for tuition, thus restricting access to those who are able to support the cost of providing an instrument, lessons and sheet music. With instrumental teaching removed further from the majority of pupils by this barrier, it is easy to argue that any changes in approach should come from the peripatetic teachers, who can more easily adapt to the focus of classroom music, rather than from class teachers who are attempting to meet a wide range of pupil needs. The traditional apprenticeship model of instrumental tuition can be difficult to reconcile with the more exploratory environment that often characterises the music classroom, and the resultant tension may cause pupils to reject one or other as being an inferior view of music learning. Instrumental pupils need to be able to use and share their skills in the classroom, if these separate strands of learning are to generate a coherent whole. The MANA report sees professional development for instrumental teachers as a potential way forward, including shared planning with class teachers, increased use of improvisation and composition, and more effective forms of assessment (MANA, 1995: 12). The dangers of separate systems appear to have been recognised, with the scope for more inventive use of available resources forming an important area for historical research and practical development.

The role of extra-curricular activities, too, is open to historical investigation, with a consideration of the effects that these aspects of school music have had upon pupils, schools and teachers as classroom approaches have developed. Hargreaves' (1982) discussion of the value of arts performances for all pupils retains its relevance as education becomes ever more focused upon results and qualifications:

> Individual performers may be outstanding and get credit for it. But the success of a few does not, as happens in classrooms, automatically generate a sense of failure in the rest. ... Each makes a contribution, the competent execution of which brings a sense of being valued. Solidarity and dignity are conferred simultaneously.
>
> (Hargreaves, 1982: 152)

The impact of musical performances upon children's musical and emotional development, although difficult to quantify, is widely acknowledged, but such performances are given little recognition as part of the music teacher's workload. The different skills required to motivate a class and to organise a performance, are assumed to be part of the average music teacher's professional equipment, with extra-curricular activities generally carried out in addition to a full teaching timetable (Plummeridge, 1991: 112). Whilst few music teachers would deny that the public profile of their job is important and fulfilling, the increasing demands of the curriculum necessitate a reappraisal of the extent to which one or two individuals can be extended to sustain such multifarious roles. Historical research can help to account for the present expectations of music in schools, but an investigation of the ways in which these can be most effectively sustained or developed would also be potentially beneficial.

Teachers themselves are in the ideal position to research and reflect upon these ideas, bringing as they do the insiders' knowledge of the practicalities of teaching music today, together with their own perspectives on change in the classroom. The relationship between academic research and the practical implementation of ideas needs to be made stronger, if the political agendas of the late twentieth century are to be challenged as we enter the new millennium. Combining the roles of researcher and teacher is not easy, as I know from experience, but this twofold perspective on school life and learning is an enriching one. My intention here has been to highlight some of the concerns of previous generations of music teachers, and to bring their ideas and innovations to light, allowing today's music educators to see their own practice in its historical context. The potential for development of these ideas is immense, and is the province of anyone involved in music education. Cage's words on sound apply equally to history: 'we are in it and like it, making it' (1968/78: 190). If inspiration from the past is allowed to inform the developments of the future, the debate can continue with similar energy and high regard for the place of active musical experience in the education of all children.

Appendix: National Curriculum terminology and personalities

Music Working Group membership

Sir John Manduell CBE *Chairman*	Composer. Principal, Royal Northern College of Music.
John Stephens *Vice-Chairman*	Former LEA Senior Staff Inspector for Music, and former HMI. Director of Music Education, Trinity College of Music.
David Adams	Head of Music, Sawston Village College, Cambridge.
Dr Kevin Adams	Head of Music, Maestag Comprehensive School, Mid Glamorgan.
Michael Batt	Freelance musician and composer.
Michael Brewer	Director of Music, Chetham's School, Manchester.
Philip Jones CBE	Principal, Trinity College of Music.
Colin Johnson	Artist manager – popular music (resigned Oct. 1990).
Gillian Moore	Education Organiser, London Sinfonietta.
Professor George Pratt	Head of Music, Huddersfield Polytechnic.
Linda Read	Head of Infant Department and whole-school music co-ordinator, Elburton Primary School, Plymouth.
Julian Smith	Chairman, Music for Youth and consultant, W H Smith Ltd.
Christine Wood	Former junior school music teacher. Partner, Lovely Music, Tadcaster, North Yorkshire (specialist suppliers of music to schools).
Assessors	
Barnie Baker	Department of Education and Science.
Leon Crickmore	Her Majesty's Inspectorate.

Secretaries of State for Education 1979–2000

1979–81: **Mark Carlisle**, with right-wing Rhodes Boyson as his Junior Minister. Carlisle introduced the Assisted Places Scheme, but did little towards the idea of a national curriculum.

1981–86: **Keith Joseph**, published a White Paper, *Better Schools* (DES, 1985b) rejecting the idea of a national curriculum.

1986–89: **Kenneth Baker** 'was the enthusiast for and the driving force behind the national curriculum' (Lawton, 1993). He hastened the legislative process, but left the education department to become Conservative party Chairman before the Education Reform Act (1988) had taken full effect.

1989–90: **John MacGregor** is remembered as a mild and conciliatory figure, welcomed by teachers, but criticised by political colleagues for not promoting educational ideas sufficiently strongly in the 1990 general election campaign.

1990–92: **Kenneth Clarke** pursued the 'anti-expert policy' (Lawton, 1994) that characterised Tory thinking on education, seeking a reform of teacher education and announcing a review of HMI in 1991. Serving under both Thatcher and Major, Clarke intervened in specific curriculum matters to an unprecedented level, including his infamous criticisms of the Music Working Group documents.

1992–95: **John Patten** published the White Paper *Choice and Diversity* (DfE, 1992), and was responsible for implementing the national system of testing in schools. During Patten's time in office, Sir Ron Dearing conducted a review of the National Curriculum that considerably reduced the original requirements.

1995–1997: **Gillian Shephard** continued the focus on standards and testing, and in 1996, proposed a national curriculum for teacher training colleges. Often publicly critical of the teaching profession, Shephard sought to defend increasingly discredited Conservative policies from opposition attack.

1998–1999+: **David Blunkett** became the first Labour Secretary of State to have an influence upon the educational reforms of the Conservative Party. In his first year in office, he set national targets for literacy and numeracy and announced the 'slimming down' of the primary curriculum, reviving the debate about the place of music in a balanced education.

National Curriculum terminology

Pupils are organised in key stages, according to age:

Reception	First year in school (age 4+).
	Not included in the National Curriculum.
KEY STAGE 1	Year 1 (age 5–6)
	Year 2 (age 6–7)
	Standard Assessment Tests (SATs)
KEY STAGE 2	Year 3 (age 7–8)
	Year 4 (age 8–9)
	Year 5 (age 9–10)
	Year 6 (age 10–11)
	Standard Assessment Tests (SATs)
KEY STAGE 3	Year 7 (age 11–12)
	Year 8 (age 12–13)
	Year 9 (age 13–14)
	Standard Assessment Tests (SATs)
KEY STAGE 4	Year 10 (age 14–15)
	Year 11 (age 15–16)
	16+ Examinations e.g. GCSEs

Over the four **key stages**, the curriculum of 1992 was structured in ten **levels of attainment**, each of which was described through a series of **statements of attainment**, with a number of suggested activities offered. Following a review chaired by Sir Ron Dearing in 1993, these ten levels were reduced to eight **level descriptions** with an additional description for exceptional performance. Levels of attainment are grouped in **attainment targets (ATs)**. The curriculum for a specific key stage is also referred to as the **programme of study**.

The Music Working Group's *Interim Report* (DES, 1991a) also contained two **profile components**, 'Making Music' and 'Understanding Music', within which their four attainment targets were grouped, but these were later abandoned and the attainment targets reduced to three, subsequently to two.

In music, art and physical education, levels of attainment were originally offered only as guidance for teachers, and in the revised National Curriculum it is the **End of Key Stage Descriptions** that indicate expected standards of achievement. There are no **Standard Assessment Tests (SATs)** in music, but for the **core** subjects (English, Maths and Science), national tests are administered by teachers at the end of Key Stages 1, 2 and 3, with the results published in league tables.

The changing shape of the music curriculum

December 1990: *Interim Report* of the Music Working Group published.
Curriculum structure: Profile component 1: Making Music
(AT 1 – Performing; AT 2 – Composing)
Profile component 2: Understanding Music
(AT 3 – Listening; AT 4 – Knowing)

June 1991: *Final Report* submitted to the National Curriculum Council.
Curriculum structure: AT 1 – Performing
AT 2 – Composing
AT 3 – Appraising

January 1992: *Consultation Report* of the National Curriculum Council.
Curriculum structure: AT 1 – Performing and Composing
AT 2 – Knowledge and Understanding

April 1992: *Music in the National Curriculum* orders implemented in schools.
Curriculum structure: AT 1 – Performing and Composing
AT 2 – Listening and Appraising

May 1994: *Draft Proposals* of the School Curriculum and Assessment Authority (SCAA). ATs of April 1992 retained, following revision of National Curriculum as recommended by Sir Ron Dearing.

January 1995: *Music in the National Curriculum* revised orders implemented in schools. 'Slimmed down' curriculum has little effect on music, which was already published in a simpler form than earlier subject documents.

1999–2000: Curriculum review underway, with the promised five-year moratorium overshadowed by the introduction of literacy and numeracy hours outside the National Curriculum. The declaration that music should be optional in primary schools provokes another public debate, and the government promises that no such instructions will be included in the new National Curriculum orders.

Bibliography

Abbs, P. (ed.) (1987) *Living Powers: The Arts in Education*. London: Falmer Press.

Abbs, P. (ed.) (1989) *The Symbolic Order: A Contemporary Reader on the Arts Debate*. London: Falmer Press.

Abbs, P. (1991) 'From Babble to Rhapsody: On the Nature of Creativity', in *British Journal of Aesthetics*, **31 (4)**: 291–300.

Abbs, P. (1994) *The Educational Imperative: A Defence of Socratic and Aesthetic Learning*. London: Falmer Press.

Addison, R. (1975) 'Children (even musical ones) Make Music', in *Music in Education*, **39 (372)**: 60–63.

Aldrich, R. (1996) *Education for the Nation*. London: Cassell.

Aston, P. (1968) 'Music in a Liberal Education: (2) A Creative Approach to Harmony in the Classroom', in *Music in Education*, **32 (329)**: 17–20.

Barber, M. & Graham, D. (eds) (1993) *Sense, Nonsense and the National Curriculum*. London: Falmer Press.

Barnard, H. C. (1947/61) *A History of English Education From 1760*. London: University of London Press.

Barnes, N. J. (1983) 'Music at King Edward VII School, Sheffield from 1947–1976: Archive Material'. Unpublished.

Bentley, A. (1966) *Musical Ability in Children and its Measurement*. London: Harrap.

Bentley, A. (1975) *Music in Education: A point of view*. London: National Foundation for Educational Research.

Bentley, E. (1989) 'Music in Schools in England during the twentieth century'. PhD thesis: University of Manchester.

Blacking, J. (1973) *How Musical is Man?* London: Faber & Faber.

Blishen, E. (ed.) (1969) *The school that I'd like*. Harmondsworth: Penguin.

Blunkett, D. (1998) 'Facing the music', in *Times Educational Supplement*, 22 May: p. 13.

Board of Education (1926) *Report of the Consultative Committee on The Education of the Adolescent* [*The Hadow Report*]. London: HMSO.

Board of Education (1927) *Handbook of Suggestions for Teachers*. London: HMSO.

Board of Education (1933) *Recent Developments in School Music*. London: HMSO.

Board of Education (1938) *Secondary Education with Special Reference to Grammar Schools and Technical High Schools* [*The Spens Report*]. London: HMSO.

Board of Education (1943) *Curriculum and Examinations in Secondary Schools* [*The Norwood Report*]. London: HMSO.

Borland, J. E. (1927) *Musical Foundations: A Record of Musical Work in Schools and Training Colleges, and a Comprehensive Guide for Teachers of School Music*. London: Oxford University Press.

Boyce-Tillman, J. (1996) 'A framework for intercultural dialogue in music', in Floyd, M. (ed.) (1996) *World Musics in Education*. Aldershot: Scolar Press.

Britton, J. (ed.) (1963) *The Arts and Current Tendencies in Education*. London: Evans.

Brocklehurst, B. (1962) *Music in Schools*. London: Routledge & Kegan Paul.

Brocklehurst, B. (1971) *Response to Music: Principles of Music Education*. London: Routledge & Kegan Paul.

Brooks, R. (1991) *Contemporary Debates in Education: An Historical Perspective*. London: Longman.

Buck, P. C. (1944) *Psychology for Musicians*. London: Oxford University Press.

Burnett, M. (1977) 'In Defence of Pop', in Burnett, M. (ed.) (1977) *Music Education Review: Volume 1*. London: Chappell.

Burnett, M. (ed.) (1977) *Music Education Review: Volume 1*. London: Chappell.

Cage, J. (1968/78) *Silence*. London: Marion Boyars.

Cain, T. (1985) 'Teacher as Guide: The Teacher's Role in the Secondary School Music Lesson', in *British Journal of Music Education*, **2** (1): 5–18.

Calouste Gulbenkian Foundation (1965) *Making Musicians*. London: Calouste Gulbenkian Foundation.

Calouste Gulbenkian Foundation (1978) *Training Musicians*. London: Calouste Gulbenkian Foundation.

Calouste Gulbenkian Foundation (1982/89) *The Arts in Schools: Principles, Practice and Provision*. London: Calouste Gulbenkian Foundation.

Cambridgeshire Council of Musical Education (1933) *Music and the Community: The Cambridgeshire Report on the Teaching of Music*. Cambridge: Cambridge University Press.

Campaign for Music in the Curriculum (1998) *The Fourth 'R': The case for music in the school curriculum*. West Horsley: Campaign for Music in the Curriculum.

Chitty, C. & Simon, B. (1993) *Education Answers Back: Critical Responses to Government Policy*. London: Lawrence & Wishart.

Claxton, G. (1978) *The Little Ed Book*. London: Routledge & Kegan Paul.

Clegg, A. (1971) *Revolution in the British Primary Schools*. Washington, D C: National Education Association.

Colles, H. C. (1942) *Walford Davies: A Biography*. London: Oxford University Press.

Comber, C., Hargreaves, D. J. & Colley, A. (1993) 'Girls, Boys and Technology in Music Education', in *British Journal of Music Education*, **10**: 123–34.

Cook, H. C. (1917) *The Play Way: An Essay in Educational Method*. London: Heinemann.

County Council of the West Riding of Yorkshire (1931) *Report of the Consultative Committee on the Curriculum of the Senior School.* Wakefield: West Riding Education.

Cox, G. (1991a) '"The Right Place of Music in Education': a history of musical education in England 1872–1928 with special reference to the role of HMI'. PhD thesis: University of Reading.

Cox, G. (1991b) '"Sensitiveness to the Higher Rhythms": Arthur Somervell and his vision of music education', in *Westminster Studies in Education,* **14**: 69–82.

Cox, G. (1993a) *A History of Music Education in England 1872–1928.* Aldershot: Scolar Press.

Cox, G. (1993b) 'Music in the National Curriculum: some historical perspectives', in *The Curriculum Journal,* **4 (3)**: 351–62.

Cox, G. (1996) 'School music broadcasts and the BBC 1924–57', in *History of Education,* **25 (4)**: 363–71.

Cox, G. (1997) '"Changing the face of school music": Walford Davies, the gramophone and the radio', in *British Journal of Music Education,* **14**: 45–53.

Curtis, S. J. (1948/67) *A History of Education in Great Britain.* London: University Tutorial Press.

Dainton, S. (1993) 'The National Curriculum and the Policy Process', in Barber, M. & Graham, D. (eds) (1993), *Sense, Nonsense and the National Curriculum.* London: Falmer Press.

Davies, C. (1992) 'Listen to my song: a study of songs invented by children aged 5 to 7 years', in *British Journal of Music Education,* **9**: 19–48.

Deliège, I. & Sloboda, J. A. (1995) *Musical Beginnings: Origins and Development of Musical Competence.* Oxford: Oxford University Press.

Dennis, B. (1970) *Experimental Music in Schools: Towards a New World of Sound.* London: Oxford University Press.

Department for Education (1992) *Choice and Diversity: A New Framework for Schools.* London: HMSO.

Department for Education (1995) *Music in the National Curriculum: England.* London: HMSO.

Department for Education and Employment (1996) *Press Release: Shake up of teacher training and new focus on leadership skills for headteachers,* 18 September: 302/96.

Department of Education and Science (1956/69) *Music in Schools* [*Pamphlet No. 27*]. London: HMSO.

Department of Education and Science (1967) *Children and their Primary Schools: A Report of the Central Advisory Council for Education (England)* [*The Plowden Report*]. London: HMSO.

Department of Education and Science (1985a) *Music from 5 to 16: Curriculum Matters 4 (An HMI Series).* London: HMSO.

Department of Education and Science (1985b) *Better Schools.* London: HMSO.

Department of Education and Science (1991a) *National Curriculum Music Working Group: Interim Report*. London: DES.

Department of Education and Science (1991b) *Music for ages 5 to 14* [*Final Report*]. London: DES.

Department of Education and Science (1992) *Music in the National Curriculum: England*. London: HMSO.

Devlin, T. & Warnock, M. (1977) *What Must We Teach?* London: Temple Smith.

Donington, M. (1932) *Music throughout the Secondary School*. London: Oxford University Press.

Driver, A. (1936) *Music and Movement*. London: Oxford University Press.

Everitt, A. (1997) *Joining In: An Investigation into Participatory Music*. London: Calouste Gulbenkian Foundation.

Farmer, P. (1979) *Music in the Comprehensive School*. London: Oxford University Press.

Farrell, G. (1990) *Indian Music in Education*. Cambridge: Cambridge University Press.

Farrell, G. (1994) *Exploring the Music of the World: Music of India*. London: Heinemann/WOMAD Foundation.

Federation of Music Services/National Association of Music Educators (1998) *A Common Approach*. London: Faber.

Fisher, G. (1982) 'Teaching steel band music', in Vulliamy, G. & Lee, E. (eds.) (1982), *Pop, Rock and Ethnic Music in School*. Cambridge: Cambridge University Press.

Fletcher, P. (1987/89) *Education and Music*. Oxford: Oxford University Press.

Floyd, M. (1996) 'Approaching the Musics of the World', in Floyd, M. (ed.) (1996) *World Musics in Education*. Aldershot: Scolar Press.

Flynn, P. & Pratt, G. (1995) 'Developing an understanding of appraising music with practising primary teachers', in *British Journal of Music Education*, **12 (2)**: 127–58.

Gamble, T. (1984) 'Imagination and Understanding in the Music Curriculum', in *British Journal of Music Education*, **1 (1)**: 7–25.

Gammon, V. (1996) 'What is wrong with school music? – a response to Malcolm Ross', in *British Journal of Music Education*, **13 (2)**: 101–22.

Gilbey, C. L. V. (1964/68) 'Music in the Grammar School', in Rainbow, B. (ed.) (1964/68) *Handbook for Music Teachers*. London: Novello.

Gipps, C. V. (1993) 'The Profession of Educational Research', in *British Educational Research Journal*, **19 (1)**: 3–16.

Graham, D. (1993) 'Reflections on the first four years', in Barber, M. & Graham, D. (eds.) (1993) *Sense, Nonsense and the National Curriculum*. London: Falmer Press.

Graham, D. & Tytler, D. (1993) *A Lesson for Us All: The making of the national curriculum*. London: Routledge.

Grant, W. (ed.) (1963) *Music in Education: Colston Papers No. 14*. London: Butterworths.

Green, L. (1988) *Music on Deaf Ears: Musical meaning, ideology, education*. Manchester: Manchester University Press.

Bibliography

Green, L. (1997) *Music, Gender, Education*. Cambridge: Cambridge University Press.

Griffiths, P. (1977) 'The York Project', in *Music in Education*, **41 (384)**: 74–7.

Gwen Dodds, M. E. (ed.) (1936) *The Young Musician*, **2 (11)**.

Hadow, W. H. (1924) *Music [Home University Library: Vol. 112]*. London: Thornton Butterworth.

Hale, N. V. (1947) *Education for Music*. London: Oxford University Press.

Hancox, G. (1988) 'The Dissemination of Innovation, with special reference to the Schools Council Project, "Music in the Secondary School Curriculum"'. MEd thesis, University College Cardiff, University of Wales.

Hargreaves, D. (1982) *The Challenge for the Comprehensive School: Curriculum, Culture and Community*. London: Routledge & Kegan Paul.

Hargreaves, D. J. (1986) *The Developmental Psychology of Music*. Cambridge: Cambridge University Press.

Harland, J. (1988) 'Running up the Down Escalator: crisis management as curriculum management', in Lawton, D. & Chitty, C. (eds) (1988), *The National Curriculum*. London: Institute of Education/Kogan Page.

Harland, J., Kinder, K. & Hartley, K. (1995) *Arts in Their View: A study of youth participation in the arts*. Slough: National Foundation for Educational Research.

Harvey, J. (1982/94) *These Music Exams*. London: Associated Board of the Royal Schools of Music.

Hodges, R. (1996) 'The new technology', in Plummeridge, C. (ed.) (1996b) *Music Education: Trends and Issues*. London: Institute of Education.

Holbrook, D. (1961) *English for Maturity*. Cambridge: Cambridge University Press.

Holbrook, D. (1964) *English for the Rejected*. Cambridge: Cambridge University Press.

Holbrook, D. (1967) *Children's Writing: A Sampler for Student Teachers*. Cambridge: Cambridge University Press.

Horton, J. (1972) *British Primary Schools Today: Music*. London: Macmillan.

Illich, I. (1970) *Deschooling Society*. London: Pelican.

Jenkins, L. (1997) *Music Scholar: An education guide for young musicians*. London: Rhinegold.

Johnson, W. W. (1936) *The Gramophone in Education*. London: Pitman.

Jones, T. (1986) 'Education for Creativity', in *British Journal of Music Education*, **3 (1)**: 63–78.

Károlyi, O. (1998) *Traditional African and Oriental Music*. London: Penguin.

Kassner, K, (1996) 'RX for technophobia', in Spruce, G. (ed.) (1996) *Teaching Music*. London: Routledge/Open University.

Kemp, A. E. (1996) *The Musical Temperament: Psychology and Personality of Musicians*. Oxford: Oxford University Press.

Kendall, S. E. (1989) 'The Significance of Innovatory Ideas and Enduring Values in Music Education'. DPhil thesis: University of York.

Kwami, R. (1996) 'Music education in and for a multi-cultural society', in Plummeridge, C. (ed.) (1996b) *Music Education: Trends and Issues*. London: Institute of Education.

Langer, S. K. (1957) *Problems of Art*. London: Routledge & Kegan Paul.

Lawrence, I. (1978) *Composers and the Nature of Music Education*. London: Scolar Press.

Lawson, J. & Silver, H. (1973) *A Social History of Education in England*. London: Methuen.

Lawton, D & Chitty, C. (eds) (1988) *The National Curriculum*. London: Institute of Education/Kogan Page.

Lawton, D. (1993) 'Is There Coherence and Purpose in the National Curriculum?', in Chitty, C. & Simon, B. (eds) (1993), *Education Answers Back*. London: Lawrence & Wishart.

Lawton, D. (1994) *The Tory Mind on Education 1979–94*. London: Falmer Press.

Lawton, P., Wilkes, R., Smith, A., Lewis, M., Bloor, J. & Eyes, J. (eds) (1995) *'Tha'll never gerr in theer...': A living history of King Edward VII School, 1905–1995*. Sheffield: King Edward VII School.

Long, N. (1959) *Music in English Education*. London: Faber & Faber.

Lowe, R. (1988) *Education in the Post-War Years*. London: Routledge.

Mackerness, E. D. (1964) *A Social History of English Music*. London: Routledge & Kegan Paul.

Mackerness, E. D. (1974) *Somewhere Further North: A History of Music in Sheffield*. Sheffield: J. W. Northend.

MacPherson, S. (1922) *The Musical Education of the Child*. London: Joseph Williams.

MacPherson, S. (1923) *The Appreciation Class: A Guide for the Music Teacher and the Student*. London: Joseph Williams.

Mainwaring, J. (1941) 'The Meaning of Musicianship: A Problem in the Teaching of Music', in *British Journal of Educational Psychology*, 11 (3): 205–14.

Mainwaring, J. (1951) *Teaching Music in Schools*. London: Paxton.

Marshall, S. (1963) *An Experiment in Education*. London: Cambridge University Press.

Marshall, S. (1968) *Adventure in Creative Education*. Oxford: Pergamon Press.

Massey, I. (1996) 'Getting in Tune: Education, Diversity and Music', in Floyd, M. (ed.) (1996) *World Musics in Education*. Aldershot: Scolar Press.

Mellers, W. (1968) 'Music in a Liberal Education: (4) The Scope of School Music: Notes on a University Course', in *Music in Education*, 32 (331): 130–33.

Metcalfe, M. (1987) 'Towards the Condition of Music: The Emergent Aesthetic of Music Education' in Abbs, P. (ed.) (1987) *Living Powers: The Arts in Education*. London: Falmer Press.

Metcalfe, M. & Hiscock, C. (1992) *Music Matters*. Oxford: Heinemann.

Mills, E. (1905) *Music and Education*. Oxford: Blackwell.

Mills, J. (1991/93) *Music in the Primary School*. Cambridge: Cambridge University Press.

Mills, J. (1994) 'Music in the National Curriculum: The First Year', in *British Journal of Music Education*, 11: 191–6.

Mills, J. (1996) 'Starting at secondary school', in *British Journal of Music Education*, **13** (1): 5–14.

Mills, J. (1998) 'Music', in Office for Standards in Education (1998) *The Arts Inspected*. Oxford: Heinemann.

Ministry of Education (1949) *Story of a School: A Headmaster's experience with children aged seven to eleven* [*Pamphlet No. 14: Author – A. L. Stone*]. London: HMSO.

Ministry of Education (1960) *Secondary School Examinations other than the G.C.E.* London: HMSO.

Ministry of Education (1963) *Half Our Future* [*The Newsom Report*]. London: HMSO.

Montgomery, R. (1978) *A new examination of examinations*. London: Routledge & Kegan Paul.

Music Advisers' National Association (1995) *Instrumental Teaching and Learning in Context: Sharing a Curriculum for Music Education*. Melton Mowbray: MANA.

Music Curriculum Association (1991) 'Recommendations and comments on National Curriculum Music Working Group, Interim Report'. Unpublished.

National Advisory Committee on Creative and Cultural Education (1999) *All Our Futures: Creativity, Culture and Education*. London: DfEE.

National Council for Educational Technology (1996) *Primary Music – a pupil's entitlement to IT*. Coventry: NCET.

National Council for Educational Technology (1997) *The Music IT Pack*. Coventry: NCET.

National Curriculum Council (1992a) *National Curriculum Council Consultation Report: Music*. York: NCC.

National Curriculum Council (1992b) *Music: Non-Statutory Guidance*. York: NCC.

National Curriculum Council Arts in Schools Project (1990a) *The Arts 5–16: A Curriculum Framework*. London: Oliver & Boyd.

National Curriculum Council Arts in Schools Project (1990b) *The Arts 5–16: Practice and Innovation*. London: Oliver & Boyd.

Neill, A. S. (1962) *Summerhill*. Harmondsworth: Penguin.

Neill, H. (1998) 'Comedian dell'arte' [Interview with Professor Ken Robinson], in *Times Educational Supplement*, 5 June: p. 26.

Niblett, E. (1955) *School Music: An Instructional Handbook*. London: Blandford Press.

North, J. (ed.) (1987) *The GCSE: An examination*. London: Claridge Press.

North West Regional Curriculum Development Project (1974) *Creative Music Making and the Young School Leaver*. London: Blackie.

Odam, G. (1995) *The Sounding Symbol: Music Education in Action*. Cheltenham: Stanley Thornes.

Odam, G. & Walters, D. (1998) 'Dreaming or Awake: Composition in the Classroom', in *Yamaha Education Supplement*, Issue 28: 13–15.

Office for Standards in Education (1995) *Music: A review of inspection findings 1993/94*. London: HMSO.

Office for Standards in Education (1998) *The Arts Inspected*. Oxford: Heinemann.

O'Hear, A. (1991) 'Out of sync with Bach', in *Times Educational Supplement*, 22 February: p. 28.

Pape, M. (1970) *Growing up with Music*. London: Oxford University Press.

Payne, V. (1970) 'Review of *Sound and Silence*' in *Music in Education*, **34 (343)**: 160.

Paynter, J. (1967) 'Music in a Liberal Education: (1) Learning from the Present', in *Music in Education*, **31 (328)**: 622–6.

Paynter, J. (1982) *Music in the Secondary School Curriculum*. Cambridge: Cambridge University Press.

Paynter, J. (1992) *Sound and Structure*. Cambridge: Cambridge University Press.

Paynter, J. (1996) 'Editorial', in *British Journal of Music Education*, **13 (3)**: 181.

Paynter, J. (1997a) 'The form of finality: a context for musical education', in *British Journal of Music Education*, **14 (1)**: 5–21.

Paynter, J. (1997b) 'Editorial', in *British Journal of Music Education*, **14 (2)**: 107–108.

Paynter, J. & Aston, P. (1970) *Sound and Silence: Classroom Projects in Creative Music*. London: Cambridge University Press.

Petch, J. (1953) *Fifty Years of Examining: The Joint Matriculation Board 1903–1953*. London: Harrap.

Pitts, S. E. (1998) 'Looking for Inspiration: Recapturing an Enthusiasm for Music Education from Innovatory Writings', in *British Journal of Music Education*, **15 (1)**: 25–36.

Pitts, S. E. (1998b) 'Popular and world musics in the secondary classroom: a historical perspective', in *Ensemble: The Journal of the Music Masters' and Mistresses' Association*, **48**: 14–17.

Pitts, S. E. (1998c) 'The Implications of Historical Research for Contemporary Music Education Practice in England', in *Arts Education Policy Review*, **100 (2)**: 26–31.

Pitts, S. E. (2000) 'Reasons to Teach Music: Establishing a place in the contemporary curriculum', in *British Journal of Music Education*, **17 (1)**: forthcoming issue.

Plaskow, M. (ed.) (1985) *The Life and Death of the Schools Council*. London: Falmer Press.

Plummeridge, C. (1980) 'Creativity and Music Education – The Need for Further Clarification', in *Psychology of Music*, **8 (1)**: 34–40.

Plummeridge, C. (1991) *Music Education in Theory and Practice*. London: Falmer Press.

Plummeridge, C. (1996a) 'Curriculum development and the problem of control', in Plummeridge, C. (ed.) (1996b) *Music Education: Trends and Issues*. London: Institute of Education.

Plummeridge, C. (ed.) (1996b) *Music Education: Trends and Issues*. London: Institute of Education.

Plummeridge, C. (1997) 'The rights and wrongs of school music: a brief comment on Malcolm Ross's paper', in *British Journal of Music Education*, **14 (1)**: 23–7.

Postman, N. & Weingartner, C. (1969) *Teaching as a Subversive Activity*. Harmondsworth: Penguin.

228

Pratt, G. & Stephens, J. (1995) *Teaching Music in the National Curriculum*. Oxford: Heinemann.

Rainbow, B. (1956/71) *Music in the Classroom*. London: Heinemann.

Rainbow, B. (ed.) (1964/68) *Handbook for Music Teachers*. London: Novello.

Rainbow, B. (1985) *Onward from Butler: School Music 1945–1985*. Coventry: Curwen Publications.

Rainbow, B. (1989) *Music in Educational Thought and Practice: A Survey from 800 BC*. Aberystwyth: Boethius Press.

Read, H. (1943/56) *Education Through Art*. London: Faber & Faber.

Read, H. (1966) *The Redemption of the Robot: My Encounter with Education Through Art*. London: Faber & Faber.

Redfern, H. B. (1986) *Questions in Aesthetic Education*. London: Allen & Unwin.

Richardson, M. (1935) *Writing and Writing Patterns Books I–V*. London: University of London Press.

Richardson, M. (1948) *Art and the Child*. London: University of London Press.

Rodbard, T. (1996) *World Music: A musical journey through fourteen countries*. London: Mews Music.

Roese, C. (1998) 'World Music: Why bother?', in *Ensemble: The Journal of the Music Masters' and Mistresses' Association*, **48**: 18–20.

Ross, M. (1978) *The Creative Arts*. London: Heinemann.

Ross, M. (ed.) (1981) *The Aesthetic Imperative: Relevance and Responsibility in Arts Education*. Oxford: Pergamon Press.

Ross, M. (ed.) (1986) *Assessment in Arts Education: A Necessary Discipline or a Loss of Happiness?* Oxford: Pergamon Press.

Ross, M. (1995) 'What's Wrong With School Music?', in *British Journal of Music Education*, **12 (3)**: 185–201.

Ross, M., Radnor, H., Mitchell, S. & Bierton, C. (1993) *Assessing Achievement in the Arts*. Buckingham: Open University Press.

Salaman, W. (1983) *Living School Music*. Cambridge: Cambridge University Press.

Salaman, W. (1997) 'Keyboards in schools', in *British Journal of Music Education*, **14 (2)**: 143–9.

Schafer, R. M. (1965) *The Composer in the Classroom*. Toronto: BMI Canada.

Schafer, R. M. (1967) *Ear Cleaning: Notes on an Experimental Music Course*. Toronto: BMI Canada/Universal Edition.

Schafer, R. M. (1969) *The New Soundscape*. London: Universal Edition.

Schafer, R. M. (1975) *The Rhinoceros in the Classroom*. London: Universal Edition.

Schafer, R. M. (1995) 'Argentinian Soundscapes', in *British Journal of Music Education*, **12 (2)**: 91–101.

Scholes, P. (1925) *Everybody's Guide to Broadcast Music*. London: Oxford University Press/Hodder & Stoughton.

Scholes, P. A. (1935) *Music, The Child and The Masterpiece*. London: Oxford University Press.

Scholes, P. A. (1938) *The Oxford Companion to Music*. (10th edn, 1970: ed. Ward, J. O.) Oxford: Oxford University Press.

Schools Council (1966) *The Certificate of Secondary Education: Experimental Examinations: Music*. London: HMSO.

Schools Council (1971) *Music and the Young School Leaver: Problems and Opportunities*. [*Schools Council Working Paper 35*]. London: Evans/Methuen.

School Curriculum and Assessment Authority (1994) *Music in the National Curriculum: Draft Proposals*. London: HMSO.

Schools Curriculum and Assessment Authority (1996a) *Consistency in Teacher Assessment: Exemplification of Standards in Music: Key Stage 3*. London: SCAA Publications.

Schools Curriculum and Assessment Authority (1996b) *Music Key Stage 3: Optional Tests and Tasks*. London: SCAA Publications.

Scott-Clark, C. & Hymas, C. (1996) 'Quarter of pupils have bad teachers', in *Sunday Times*, 28 January: p. 5.

Seabrook, M. (1994) *Max: The Life and Music of Peter Maxwell Davies*. London: Victor Gollancz.

Seashore, C. E. (1938) *Psychology of Music*. New York: Dover.

Secondary Schools Examinations Council (1932) *The School Certificate Examination*. London: HMSO.

Secondary Schools Examinations Council (1963) *The Certificate of Secondary Education: Some suggestions for teachers and examiners*. London: HMSO.

Self, G. (1965) 'Revolution', in *Music in Education*, **29 (313)**: 126–7.

Self, G. (1967) *New Sounds in Class*. London: Universal Edition.

Sheffield City Archives (1919–22) 'School Management Sub-Committee Minutes September 1919 to February 1922' [Document CA 522/23]. Unpublished.

Sheffield City Archives (1922) 'Governors of the Pupil Teacher Centre Minute Book' [Document CA 622/11]. Unpublished.

Sheffield City Archives (1930–31) 'School Management Sectional Sub-Committee Minute Book No.11, May 1930 to May 1931' [Document CA 522/36]. Unpublished.

Shepherd, J. & Vulliamy, G. (1994) 'The Struggle for Culture: a sociological case study of the development of a national music curriculum', in *British Journal of Sociology of Education*, **15 (1)**: 27–40.

Simpson, K. (1964/68) 'The Teacher's Task: Aims', in Rainbow, B. (ed.) (1964/68) *Handbook for Music Teachers*. London: Novello.

Slade, P. (1954) *Child Drama*. London: University of London Press.

Sloboda, J. A. (1985) *The Musical Mind: The Cognitive Psychology of Music*. Oxford: Oxford University Press.

Small, C. (1977/80) *Music•Society•Education*. London: Calder.

Bibliography

Small, C. (1977/96) *Music•Society•Education* [new edition with foreword by Robert Walser]. London: University Press of New England.

Smith, W. J. (1947) *Music in Education*. London: Faber & Faber.

Somervell, A. (1931) *The Three R's in Music (Reading, Writing, Rhythm)*. London: Boosey & Co.

Sorrell, N. (1982) 'Balinese Music', in Vulliamy, G. & Lee, E. (eds) (1982), *Pop, Rock and Ethnic Music in School*. Cambridge: Cambridge University Press.

Sorrell, N. (1990) *A Guide to the Gamelan*. London: Faber & Faber.

Southern Examining Group (1987a) *GCSE Music: A Teachers' Guide*. Oxford: SEG.

Southern Examining Group (1987b) *Music: Coursework Memorandum*. Oxford: SEG.

Southern Examining Group (1996) *Music GCSE Syllabus*. Oxford: SEG.

Spencer, P. (1993) 'GCSE Music: A Survey of Undergraduate Opinion', in *British Journal of Music Education*, **10 (2)**: 73–84.

Spruce, G. (ed.) (1996) *Teaching Music*. London: Routledge/Open University.

Stock, J. P. J. (1996a) 'Concepts of world music and their integration within western secondary music education', in Spruce, G. (ed.) (1996), *Teaching Music*. London: Routledge/Open University.

Stock, J. P. J. (1996b) *World Sound Matters*. London: Schott.

Swanwick, K. (1968) *Popular Music and the Teacher*. Oxford: Pergamon Press.

Swanwick, K. (1979) *A Basis for Music Education*. Slough: NFER-Nelson.

Swanwick, K. (1988) *Music, Mind and Education*. London: Routledge.

Swanwick, K. (1989) 'Music in Schools: A Study of Context and Curriculum Practice', in *British Journal of Music Education*, **6 (2)**: 155–71.

Swanwick, K. (1992a) *Music Education and the National Curriculum*. London: Tufnell Press.

Swanwick, K. (1992b) 'Open Peer Commentary: Musical Knowledge: The Saga of Music in the National Curriculum', in *Psychology of Music*, **20 (2)**: 162–79.

Swanwick, K. (1992c) 'Music education and ethnomusicology', in *British Journal of Ethnomusicology*, **1**: 137–144.

Swanwick, K. (1994) *Musical Knowledge: Intuition, analysis and music education*. London: Routledge.

Swanwick, K. (1997) 'Assessing Musical Quality in the National Curriculum', in *British Journal of Music Education*, **14 (3)**: 205–15.

Swanwick, K. (1999) *Teaching Music Musically*. London: Routledge.

Swanwick, K. & Tillman, J. (1986) 'The Sequence of Musical Development: A Study of Children's Compositions', in *British Journal of Music Education*, **3 (3)**: 305–39.

Taylor, D. A. (1977) 'Trends and Factors in the Teaching of School Music in Britain with particular reference to the 1965–1975 decade'. MA thesis: University of Sheffield.

Taylor, D. A. (1979) *Music Now: A guide to recent developments and current opportunities in music education*. Milton Keynes: Open University Press.

Terry, P. (1994) 'Musical Notation in Secondary Education: Some Aspects of Theory and Practice', in *British Journal of Music Education*, **11 (2)**: 99–111.

United Nations Educational, Scientific and Cultural Organization [UNESCO] (1955) *Music in Education: Proceedings of the International Conference on the Role and Place of Music in the Education of Youth and Adults*. Switzerland: Unesco.

Vickerman, C. (1986) 'The Arts in Public Examinations', in Ross, M. (ed.) (1986), *Assessment in Arts Education: A Necessary Discipline or a Loss of Happiness?* Oxford: Pergamon Press.

Viola, W. (1942) *Child Art*. London: University of London Press.

Vulliamy, G. (1975) 'Music Education: Some Critical Comments', in *The Journal of Curriculum Studies*, **7 (1)**: 18–25.

Vulliamy, G. & Lee, E. (eds) (1976/80) *Pop Music in School*. Cambridge: Cambridge University Press.

Vulliamy, G. & Lee, E. (eds) (1982) *Pop, Rock and Ethnic Music in School*. Cambridge: Cambridge University Press.

Walker, R. (1983) 'Innovation in the Music Curriculum', in *Psychology of Music*, **11 (2)**: 86–96.

Walser, R. (1996) 'Foreword to the 1996 edition', in Small, C. (1977/96), *Music•Society•Education*. Hanover: Wesleyan University Press .

Wardle, D. (1976) *English Popular Education 1780–1975*. Cambridge: Cambridge University Press.

West Riding Education Committee (1953) *Ten Years of Change*. Wakefield: West Riding Education.

West Riding Education Committee (1965) *Education 1954–64*. Wakefield: West Riding Education.

Wiggins, T. (1996) 'The world of music in education', in *British Journal of Music Education*, **13**: 21–9.

Winn, C. (1954) *Teaching Music*. London: Oxford University Press.

Witkin, R. W. (1974) *The Intelligence of Feeling*. London: Heinemann.

Wood, T. (1925) *Music and Boyhood: Some Suggestions on the possibilities of Music in Public, Preparatory and other Schools*. London: Oxford University Press.

Woodhead, C. (1996) 'Judgment day for the educators', in *The Times*, 6 February: p. 18.

Wyatt, S. (1987) 'Music', in North, J. (ed.) (1987) *The GCSE: An examination*. London: Claridge Press.

Yorke Trotter, T. H. (1914) *The Making of Musicians*. London: Herbert Jenkins.

Yorke Trotter, T. H. (1924) *Music and Mind*. London: Methuen.

Yorke Trotter, T. H. & Chapple, S. (1933) *Principles of Musicianship for Teachers and Students*. London: Bosworth.

Index